Goldmann Texte ANGLISTIK–AMERIKANISTIK

Herausgegeben von Herbert Mainusch und Edgar Mertner

Band 5

British Government Today

Das Regierungssystem Großbritanniens zur Zeit des Eintritts in die Europäische Gemeinschaft

Texte ausgewählt

von Dieter Grosser und Gerhard A. Ritter

Bei der Zusammenstellung der folgenden Texte haben sich die Herausgeber dieses Bandes von dem Gesichtspunkt leiten lassen, daß es sich um eine Einführung für alle diejenigen handeln soll, die das gegenwärtige britische Regierungssystem näher kennenlernen wollen, ohne selbst Fachleute auf den Gebieten der Politikwissenschaft, der modernen Geschichte oder der Sozialwissenschaften zu sein. Das Buch wendet sich daher besonders an die Lehrer und Studierenden des Englischen und legt ihnen eine Auswahl von Dokumenten und Analysen englischer Sozialwissenschaftler vor, die dem Stand der wissenschaftlichen Diskussion entsprechen und zugleich die wichtigen Probleme in einer für Laien verständlichen Form erläutern. Alle Autoren, die in diesem Band zu Worte kommen, erfreuen sich hoher wissenschaftlicher Anerkennung.

Prof. Dr. DIETER GROSSER ist Direktor des Seminars für Politikwissenschaft an der Universität Münster.

Prof. Dr. GERHARD RITTER ist Direktor des Historischen Seminars, Ordinarius für Neuere Geschichte an der Universität Münster.

Die Herausgeber, Prof. Dr. HERBERT MAINUSCH und Prof. Dr. EDGAR MERTNER, sind Direktoren des Englischen Seminars der Universität Münster.

British Government Today

Das Regierungssystem Großbritanniens zur Zeit des Eintritts in die Europäische Gemeinschaft

Texte ausgewählt von Dieter Grosser
und Gerhard A. Ritter

Goldmann Texte ANGLISTIK-AMERIKANISTIK
Band 5

WILHELM GOLDMANN VERLAG MÜNCHEN

70310 · Made in Germany · I · 115 · © by Wilhelm Goldmann Verlag GmbH, München. Fotosatz: IBV-Lichtsatz KG, Berlin. Druck: Presse-Druck, Augsburg.
Verlagsnummer 11905 · P/Pay
ISBN 3-442-11905-7

Contents/Inhalt

Einleitung

Ziel der Herausgeber dieses Bandes ist es, Studenten der Anglistik eine Auswahl von Analysen britischer Politiker und Sozialwissenschaftler sowie von Dokumenten vorzulegen, die als Einführung in das britische Regierungssystem und das spezielle Vokabular britischer Politik geeignet sind, und die auch im Englischunterricht der Abschlußklassen von höheren Schulen verwendet werden können. Es wurden lediglich Autoren von anerkannter Bedeutung aufgenommen; andererseits mußte darauf geachtet werden, daß die Texte wichtige Probleme in einer auch für Laien verständlichen Form erläutern. Der Band erhebt daher weder den Anspruch, für den gegenwärtigen Stand der britischen Politikwissenschaft repräsentativ zu sein, noch alle Aspekte der Verfassungswirklichkeit des Vereinigten Königreichs zu zeigen.*

Das britische Regierungssystem gilt nach wie vor als Modell repräsentativer Demokratie, obwohl sich immer wieder gezeigt hat, daß britische Institutionen nicht oder nur mit erheblichen Veränderungen in andere Gesellschaften übertragen werden können. Großbritannien ist ein eindrucksvolles Beispiel dafür, daß Institutionen im Zusammenhang mit der Gesellschaft gesehen werden müssen, in der sie sich entwickelt haben, der sie dienen sollen und die sie selbst wiederum beeinflussen.

Die britische Gesellschaft ist weitaus stärker von historischer Kontinuität gekennzeichnet als die Gesellschaft der Bundesrepublik. Trotz der 1832 begonnenen, erst 1948 mit der Abschaffung der letzten Formen doppelter Stimmabgabe abgeschlossenen »Demokratisierung« des Wahlrechts, trotz des Aufstiegs der Labour Party zur Regierungsfähigkeit nach dem Ersten Weltkrieg, trotz der Verstaatlichung des Gesundheitswesens, des Transports und der Kohle- und Stahlindustrie nach dem zweiten Weltkriege haben soziale Normen, die sich in der aristokratisch-großbürgerlichen Gesellschaft des 18. Jahrhunderts entwickelten, erhebliche Bedeutung. Die mangelnde

* Einen Gesamtüberblick über das britische Regierungssystem und dessen Diskussion in Quellen vor allem des letzten Jahrzehnts bietet: Sir W. Ivor Jennings und Gerhard A. Ritter: *Das britische Regierungssystem. Leitfaden und Quellenbuch*, 2. Aufl. Köln und Opladen 1970

Dynamik großer Teile der britischen Industrie kann zum Teil auf eine fehlerhafte staatliche Wirtschaftspolitik und auf Besonderheiten des Gewerkschaftswesens zurückgeführt werden. Sie ist aber auch dadurch bedingt, daß Unternehmer und leitende Angestellte der Leistungssteigerung und Expansion nicht in gleichem Maße höchste Priorität zubilligen, wie es in den USA und der Bundesrepublik die Regel ist, sondern eher dazu neigen, Erreichtes zu konsolidieren und ihren Lebensstandard in traditioneller Weise zu genießen. Der Civil Service geht immer noch, trotz der im Fulton Bericht geforderten und teilweise realisierten Reform (vgl. S. 218ff.), davon aus, daß hohe Allgemeinbildung vor allem in den Geisteswissenschaften den Beamten in die Lage versetze, sich in die Probleme der öffentlichen Verwaltung einzuarbeiten – eine Vorstellung, die in der Mitte des 19. Jahrhunderts entwickelt wurde und damals auch ihre Berechtigung gehabt haben mag. Großbritannien leistet sich ein Bildungssystem, das trotz der Gründung einer Reihe von gut ausgestatteten neuen Universitäten die traditionelle Führungsposition von Oxford und Cambridge unangetastet läßt und zwar wissenschaftliche Spitzenleistungen erbringt, aber trotz aller Stipendien die Kinder der Wohlhabenden begünstigt, die in guten, aber teuren Privatschulen auf die schwierigen Aufnahmeprüfungen dieser Eliteuniversitäten besser vorbereitet werden als die Besucher staatlicher Schulen.
Das Land leistet sich eine Gewerkschaftsbewegung, die in über 600 Einzelgewerkschaften zersplittert ist. Die Folge ist, daß in jedem größeren Betrieb mehrere Gewerkschaften um Mitglieder konkurrieren, und zwar vor allem dadurch, daß sie versuchen, möglichst hohe Löhne für ihre Mitglieder durchzusetzen. Dagegen wäre wenig einzuwenden, wenn nicht gleichzeitig die Zersplitterung und die damit verbundene mangelnde Autorität bei den Arbeitern wilde Streiks und die Anwendung »restriktiver Praktiken« begünstigte, mit denen kleine Gruppen Rationalisierungsmaßnahmen verhindern können, die sie aus traditionellen, aber von der technischen Entwicklung überholten Tätigkeiten und Positionen zu verdrängen drohen. Der Produktivitätsfortschritt wird behindert, hohe Nominallohnsteigerungen bringen Inflation, aber keinen entsprechenden Reallohngewinn. Trotz aller Kritik auch innerhalb der Labour Party sind die Versuche, das Gewerkschaftswesen zu reformieren, bisher stets und auch unter der Regierung Wilson gescheitert, und zwar nicht zuletzt, weil die Arbeiter das Prinzip, erworbene Rechte zu respektieren, auch wenn sie funktionslos geworden sind, übernommen haben.

Auch die zu scharfen inneren Auseinandersetzungen führende Industrial Relations Bill der Regierung Heath ändert daran nicht viel, sondern sucht die Streikhäufigkeit vor allem dadurch zu verringern, daß Arbeitern Einspruchs- und Kompensationsmöglichkeiten bei ungerechtfertigter Entlassung gegeben werden und der »National Industrial Relations Court« einen angekündigten Streik in Industrien von besonderer Bedeutung aussetzen kann, bis eine Urabstimmung der Arbeiter über den Streikbeschluß stattgefunden hat. Für Arbeiter in der Bundesrepublik bilden die Bestimmungen des Betriebsverfassungsgesetzes einen weitaus wirksameren Schutz gegen Entlassung und Verschlechterung der Arbeitsbedingungen, die Beziehungen zwischen den Tarifparteien sind durch Gesetz genauer geregelt, die Arbeiter eines Betriebes in der Bundesrepublik werden nur durch eine einzige straff organisierte Gewerkschaft vertreten. Die Mehrzahl der britischen Arbeiter hat eine bessere Organisation der Arbeitsmarktbeziehungen und des Gewerkschaftswesens immer als Vorstufe für staatliche Reglementierungen betrachtet und ebenso abgelehnt wie die Mitbestimmung nach deutschem Modell; man glaubt, in scharfem, wenn auch begrenzten Konflikt mit den Unternehmern mehr erreichen zu können als durch den Zwang zur Gemeinsamkeit, den man von Mitbestimmung erwartet, und nimmt eher ein gewisses Maß an Chaos und Ineffektivität in Kauf, als Individualismus und Spontaneität in straffen Großorganisationen zu ersticken.
Im britischen Parteiensystem dominiert seit dem Ende des vorigen Jahrhunderts die Konservative Partei. Seit durch die Reformen 1884/85 annähernd das allgemeine und gleiche Männerwahlrecht geschaffen und die liberale Partei durch die Abspaltung ihres rechten Flügels (Whigs) und der Gegner der Gewährung der Selbstverwaltung an Irland 1886 geschwächt worden war, kam 17mal ein Wahlergebnis zustande, das einer Partei eine absolute Mehrheit im Unterhaus gab. (Das schließt nicht aus, daß diese etwa im Krieg oder zur Bewältigung besonderer Probleme – wie der Weltwirtschaftskrise – andere Parteien an der Regierung beteiligte und ihnen unter Umständen, wie das die Konservativen 1918–1922 und 1931–1935 taten, sogar den Posten des Premierministers überließen.) Zwölfmal waren das die Konservativen, viermal die Labour Party (davon je einmal mit Mehrheiten von nur 5 bzw. 4 Sitzen) und einmal die Liberalen. Minderheitsregierungen wurden dreimal (nach den Wahlen von 1892, vom Januar 1910 und vom Dezember 1910) von den Liberalen und zweimal (nach den Wahlen von 1923 und 1929) von

der Labour Party gebildet. Die Konservativen sind zwar mit den Interessen der City verflochten, werden aber auch heute noch rund von einem Drittel der Arbeiter gewählt (vgl. S. 92). Sie sind niemals eine Partei des reinen Wirtschaftsliberalismus gewesen, und haben in ihrer Mehrheit seit dem ersten Weltkrieg zunehmend die Notwendigkeit erkannt, den Wohlstand breiter Schichten der Bevölkerung durch staatliche Eingriffe in Einkommensverteilung und Wirtschaftsprozeß zu sichern. Labour hatte stets einen aktiven und lautstarken linken Flügel; auf die praktische Politik der Partei und vor allem der von ihr gestellten Regierungen gewannen aber radikale Forderungen selten Einfluß. Um Wahlen zu gewinnen, müssen sich beide Parteien um die Schichten mit mittlerem Einkommen bemühen, was zwangsläufig zu einer gewissen Annäherung der konkreten Zielsetzungen führt. Allerdings gibt es Schwankungen des Polarisierungsgrades der Wählerschaft. Zwischen 1945 und 1951 war die Polarisierung ausgeprägt: Labour machte den Versuch, durch Verstaatlichung von Kohle, Stahl und Transport sowie des Gesundheitswesens die Weichen in Richtung auf Sozialismus zu stellen, die Konservativen fühlten sich in ihrer Existenz bedroht und antworteten mit scharfen Angriffen gegen den »Kollektivismus« und die drohende Diktatur von Funktionären. In den 50er Jahren verbreitete sich auch unter den Arbeitern die Ansicht, daß Sozialisierung wenig an der Situation des einzelnen Arbeiters ändert; der Ost-West-Konflikt trug dazu bei, daß die große Mehrheit der Bevölkerung das gemeinsame Interesse an Wohlstand und Sicherheit in den Vordergrund stellte. Die Polarisierung ging zurück. Trotz des Suez-Debakels 1956 und trotz relativ geringer wirtschaftspolitischer Erfolge blieben die Konservativen 1951–1964 im Amt. Wilson versuchte vor allem nach der Konsolidierung seiner Unterhausmehrheit 1966, wirtschaftliche Strukturveränderungen und eine Reform des Gewerkschaftswesens zu erzwingen, um Stabilität und wirtschaftliches Wachstum zu erreichen. Gleichzeitig griff er die seit Jahrzehnten diskutierte Parlamentsreform auf. Der umfangreiche Apparat staatlicher Rahmenplanung in der Wirtschaft und der Preis- und Lohnstopp erwiesen sich jedoch als von geringer Wirkung, die Gewerkschaftsreform scheiterte am Widerstand des linken Flügels der eigenen Partei und der scharfen Gegnerschaft der Gewerkschaften, die Parlamentsreform kam über eine begrenzte Verbesserung des Ausschußwesens des Unterhauses und die Einrichtung eines parlamentarischen Ombudsmanns für die Verwaltung mit relativ geringen Kompetenzen nicht hinaus. Die Wahlniederlage Wilsons

1970 kann nicht zuletzt als Folge einer verbreiteten Enttäuschung darüber angesehen werden, daß Labour dem Lande weder Stabilität und Wachstum noch leistungssteigernde Reformen bringen konnte. Die erneute Übernahme der Regierung durch die Konservativen nach nur 6jähriger Amtszeit Labours hat allerdings die Kluft zwischen Labour und den Konservativen vertieft; die Labour Party vertritt heute wieder eine »linkere« Position, die Polarisierung hat zugenommen.

Seit Mitte der 60er Jahre zeigen sich Grenzen der Integrationsfähigkeit des Zweiparteiensystems. Schottische und Waliser Nationalisten konnten die Unzufriedenheit mit der wirtschaftlichen Benachteiligung der Randgebiete nutzen und errangen örtliche Erfolge; die Liberalen, die 1964 immerhin über 11% der Wähler gewannen und auch 1966 und 1970 ca. 8% der Stimmen erhielten, werden durch das relative Mehrheitswahlrecht allerdings daran gehindert, im Parlament eine Rolle zu spielen.

Die Einführung des Verhältniswahlsystems wird aber nach wie vor nur von einer kleinen Minderheit befürwortet. Die meisten Wähler wünschen eine starke Regierung, als deren Voraussetzung eine einheitliche und straff organisierte Parlamentsmehrheit gilt, zugleich aber eine Regierung, die der beständigen Kritik einer kräftigen und potentiell regierungsfähigen Opposition ausgesetzt ist und durch ein Votum der Wähler abgesetzt werden kann, wenn die Opposition mit ihrer Kritik überzeugt. Dafür ist das Zweiparteiensystem vorteilhaft, und dafür wird die Benachteiligung von politischen Minderheiten durch das Wahlsystem in Kauf genommen. Die in der Bundesrepublik verbreitete These, innerparteiliche Demokratie sei Voraussetzung für Demokratie im Staat, wird in England nur mit Einschränkung vertreten. Das Unterhaus gilt als das von den Wählern bestellte Forum der Nation. Die Anhängerschaft der Parteien in den Wahlen ist daher erheblich größer und in der Regel weniger radikal als deren Mitglieder oder gar die aktiven Kader in den Wahlen, so daß eine völlige Ausrichtung der Politik der Regierung oder der Fraktion nach den politischen Vorstellungen der kleinen militanten Basis die Gefahr des Verlusts an Anhängern und damit an politischer Macht mit sich bringen würde.

In der Fraktion dominiert die sogenannte *Frontbench*, d.h. die Mitglieder des vom Parteiführer in seiner Funktion als Premierminister oder als Führer der Opposition eingesetzten Kabinetts bzw. Schattenkabinetts, die je eine der sich gegenüberliegenden Vorderbänke im Unterhaus einnehmen.

Die Parteien haben nicht nur, aber doch in erster Linie die Aufgabe, Hilfsorganisationen für die politischen Führungsgruppen im Unterhaus zu sein. In der 2,8 Millionen Mitglieder starken Konservativen Partei ist die ausschlaggebende Rolle der »Parliamentary Party«, also der Fraktion, in der Gesamtpartei unbestritten. Fraktionen und außerparlamentarische Partei, die »National Union«, sind organisatorisch getrennt. Beschlüsse des obersten außerparlamentarischen Parteiorgans, der Parteikonferenz, gelten als Empfehlungen, sind aber für die Parteiführung nicht verbindlich.
Der Labour Party gehören neben 800 000 Einzelmitgliedern über 6 Millionen Gewerkschaftsmitglieder korporativ an; die Gewerkschaften bringen nicht nur den größten Teil der Parteifinanzen auf, sondern sie haben auch rund 80% der Stimmen auf der jährlichen Parteikonferenz. Im Selbstverständnis der Partei hat die Parteikonferenz größeres Gewicht als bei den Konservativen; dennoch werden Beschlüsse der Parteikonferenz, die den Absichten einer Labour-Regierung zuwiderlaufen, lediglich als unangenehme Schönheitsfehler, nicht aber als verbindliche Auflagen betrachtet (vgl. S. 169ff.). Eine Bindung der Regierung an Beschlüsse außerparlamentarischer Gremien würde nicht nur als unerträgliche Beeinträchtigung ihres politischen Handlungsspielraums angesehen werden; sie stünde nach britischer Auffassung auch im Widerspruch zu dem Prinzip, daß eine Regierung ebenso wie jeder Abgeordnete der ganzen Nation verantwortlich ist.
In den »Parliamentary Parties« des Unterhauses wird die Abstimmungsdisziplin mindestens ebenso straff eingehalten wie in den Fraktionen des Deutschen Bundestages, und die Vormachtstellung der Führungsgruppen ist eher noch ausgeprägter. Etwa ein Drittel der Mitglieder der Regierungsfraktion sind mit der Regierung verbunden – vom Kabinettsminister bis zu parlamentarischen Privatsekretären. Schon dieses »Patronagepotential« sichert jeder Regierung einen festen Rückhalt in der eigenen Fraktion. Die für die Erhaltung der Fraktionsdisziplin vor allem verantwortlichen »Whips« organisieren den »two-way-traffic« zwischen Vorderbank und Hinterbank; sie geben den Abgeordneten nicht nur Informationen und Anweisungen, wie abzustimmen ist, sondern tragen die Wünsche, Anregungen und Kritik der Hinterbänkler an die Fraktionsführung bzw. Regierung weiter. Wer sich in einer wichtigen Frage der Fraktionsdisziplin entzieht, riskiert Strafmaßnahmen, die bis zum Entzug des »Whip«, d.h. des Einladungsschreibens zu den Fraktionssitzungen und damit zum Ausschluß aus der Fraktion ge-

hen können. Wer allerdings einen festen Rückhalt in seinem Wahlkreis hat, kann den Konflikt mit der Fraktionsführung durchstehen; er wird in der Regel vor dem Wahlkampf wieder in die Fraktion aufgenommen, wenn er Gewähr bietet, den Wahlkreis für die Partei zu gewinnen. Wichtiger als alle Disziplinarmittel der Fraktionsführung ist die Rücksicht auf den Zusammenhalt und die Wirkungsmöglichkeiten der Fraktion. Der Abgeordnete der Regierungspartei wird die Fraktionsdisziplin in der Regel nur dann verletzen, wenn er sicher ist, daß er dadurch keine Abstimmungsniederlage seiner Partei im Parlament und damit unter Umständen einen Regierungssturz herbeiführt. Neuwahlen nach einer inneren Krise der Regierungspartei würden dieser mit großer Wahrscheinlichkeit keinen Erfolg bringen und die politischen Chancen auch der Rebellen verringern. Auch die Opposition macht einen besseren Eindruck vor der Öffentlichkeit, wenn sie geschlossen auftritt. Krisen bleiben trotzdem nicht aus. Als ein Teil der Labour-Fraktion 1967 gegen die Lohnpolitik Wilsons rebellierte, interpretierte der Premier das Verhältnis von Regierungschef und Parlamentsmehrheit mit den Worten, erste Pflicht der Abgeordneten der Regierungspartei sei es, den Premier zu unterstützen (*The Times* vom 3. 3. 1967).

Die Schwäche des Parlaments gegenüber einer immer mächtiger werdenden Regierung wird oft behauptet, seltener eindeutig nachgewiesen (vgl. S. 129ff.). Bagehot, der vor über 100 Jahren seine brillante Analyse der britischen Verfassungswirklichkeit schrieb (vgl. S. 18ff.), sah in der Fusion von Legislative und Exekutive durch das Kabinett das Wesentliche der englischen Verfassung und bezeichnete das britische System als »Kabinettsregierung«. Er wußte, daß beim Kabinett in der Regel die politische Initiative und der Schwerpunkt politischer Macht lag; da zu seiner Zeit die straff organisierte moderne Partei noch nicht entstanden war, konnte er das volle Ausmaß der Kontrolle des mit der Führung der Regierungspartei weitgehend identischen Kabinetts über die Unterhausmehrheit noch nicht erfassen. Als Crossman 1963 seine Einführung zu einer Neuausgabe von Bagehot schrieb, ging er einen Schritt weiter; nicht mehr beim Kabinett, sondern beim Premier selbst liege die Macht, das Kabinett sei wie einst Krone und später Unterhaus zum »dignified part of the constitution« herabgesunken.

Thesen wie die vom Machtverlust des Unterhauses und des Kabinetts dürfen jedoch nicht überzogen werden.

Das Gewicht des Unterhauses im Regierungssystem hängt vor allem davon ab, wie solide die Mehrheit der Regierung ist. Eine in sich geschlossene Mehrheitspartei gibt der Regierung die Möglichkeit, die Unterhausmehrheit in erster Linie zur Verabschiedung der Regierungsvorlagen zu verwenden und die Opposition auf für die Öffentlichkeit bestimmte Kritik zu beschränken. Auch in dieser Situation ist die Macht der Regierung nicht Willkür. Die Geschlossenheit der Mehrheit ist eben nicht allein die Folge von Patronagepotential, Disziplinarmitteln und Furcht vor einem Sturz der Regierung, sondern ergibt sich auch aus einer Regierungspolitik, die die Wähler zu überzeugen scheint und dem Abgeordneten einen Sieg bei den nächsten Wahlen in Aussicht stellen kann. Ernste Zweifel an der Wählerwirksamkeit der Politik der Regierung bei den eigenen Hinterbänklern können die Stellung des Premiers schwächen und zu seiner Ablösung durch einen Rivalen innerhalb der eigenen Partei führen. Die Opposition kann einen Regierungschef nur dadurch stürzen, daß sie die Wahlen gewinnt und zur Mehrheit wird. Die eigene Partei kann und wird ihn auswechseln, wenn sie nicht mehr davon überzeugt ist, daß sie unter seiner Führung die Wahlen gewinnen kann. In beiden Parteien wird der Parteiführer und damit, wenn die Partei die Mehrheit hat, faktisch der Premier durch die Mitglieder der Unterhausfraktion gewählt. Der »innere Kreis«, der in der Konservativen Partei noch 1963 bei dem Wechsel Macmillan – Home die ausschlaggebende Rolle spielte und der Krone einen gewissen Einfluß auf die Selektion des Kandidaten in Situationen gab, in der die Konservativen nicht eindeutig auf eine bestimmte Person festgelegt waren, ist seit 1965 zumindest formell ausgeschaltet. Darin kann eine Stärkung der Stellung des Unterhauses allgemein gesehen werden. Auch die Stellung des Premiers im Kabinett läßt sich mit einer zugespitzten Kurzformel nicht beschreiben. Das Verhältnis zwischen Regierungschef und Kabinettsmitgliedern wechselt je nach der persönlichen Autorität und dem Temperament des Regierungschefs. Allerdings kann der Premierminister ernennen und vor allem auch entlassen, ohne jemanden fragen zu müssen, und er macht von diesem Recht – im Gegensatz zu den Kanzlern der Bundesrepublik – ausgiebig Gebrauch. Andererseits wird er sorgfältig darauf achten, Parteifreunde mit eigener Hausmacht möglichst ins Kabinett zu nehmen und bei Personal- und Sachentscheidungen nicht wichtige Interessengruppen innerhalb seiner Partei zu verprellen. Er entscheidet in einem Kräftefeld, dessen verschiedene Faktoren durchaus unterschiedliches Gewicht haben können. So war Macmillan 1962 in der Lage, 7 seiner 21 Kabinettsmitglieder auf einen Schlag zu entlassen; im gleichen Jahr wurde die Entscheidung für den Eintritt in die EWG aber erst nach einer Reihe von Kabinettsberatungen getroffen, bei denen das Kabinett den Vorschlag des Regierungschefs hätte zurückweisen können. Berühmte Beispiele für eigenmächtiges Handeln des Premiers sind Attlees Entscheidung, die Atombombe bauen zu lassen, und Edens Vorbereitung der Suez-Intervention. Allerdings kann eigenmächtiges Handeln, vor allem wenn es sich als falsch herausstellt, Gegenkräfte im Parlament und Kabinett aktivieren und den Sturz des Premiers herbeiführen.

Das Plenum des Kabinetts ist mit über 20 Mitgliedern zu groß, als daß es alle wichtigen Entscheidungen treffen könnte. Für Diskussionen, die auf sachliche Klärung von Problemen, die Abstimmung der Politik zwischen den betroffenen Ressorts und die Festlegung der Richtlinien der Politik zielen, sind die Kabinettsausschüsse und ein kleiner Kreis besonders wichtiger Kabinettsmitglieder, das sogenannte »inner cabinet«, geeigneter. Auch die immer größere Komplexität der Voraussetzungen und Folgen jeder wichtigen politischen Entscheidung führt dazu, daß nur noch die von Spezialisten beratenen zuständigen Minister, nicht aber die Mehrzahl der Kabinettsmitglieder sachkundig zu einem Problem Stellung nehmen können.

Solange es eine starke Opposition im Unterhaus gibt und die Wähler auch bereit sind, die Kritik dieser Opposition zu honorieren und der Regierung die Mehrheit zu entziehen, ist die Machtverteilung zwischen Parlament und Regierung bzw. Kabinett und Premier nicht das wichtigste Problem der britischen Verfassung. Ernster sind die Probleme, die sich aus der Überlastung des Regierungssystems mit schwierigen, in ihren Konsequenzen kaum übersehbaren und zunehmend kontroversen Entscheidungen ergeben. Auch in Großbritannien hat die Regierung die Verantwortung für Vollbeschäftigung und Wachstum, ausreichende Bildung und soziale Sicherheit übernehmen müssen, und auch dort reichen Regierungsorganisation und die überkommenen Institutionen kaum noch aus, die Fülle der Aufgaben effizient wahrzunehmen. Vor allem als Konsequenz der Übernahme wirtschaftlicher und sozialer Aufgaben ist die Ministerialbürokratie enorm ausgeweitet worden. Dem Kabinett fehlt es jedoch an Zeit, die verschiedenen Maßnahmen ausreichend zu koordinieren, und es kommt, wie auch in der Bundesrepublik, nicht selten zu Fehlleistungen, weil die Politik des eines Ministeriums von der des anderen blockiert wird. Die starke Stellung der Regierung gegenüber dem Parlament bei der Gesetzgebung hat den Vorteil, daß die Regierung im Consensus mit der Parlamentsmehrheit führen kann; sie hat den Nachteil, daß manche Gesetzentwürfe unzureichend vorbereitet und durchdacht im Parlament durchgeboxt werden und sich hinterher als schädlich herausstellen.

Zwar läßt sich die Regierung bei der Vorbereitung der Gesetzentwürfe durch die betroffenen Verbände beraten: nach verbreiteter Meinung nutzt sie den im Unterhaus vertretenen Sachverstand jedoch nur unzureichend. Die Mitglieder des Unterhauses haben nach wie vor weniger Hilfskräfte und Sachmittel für selbständige politische Arbeit, als die des Deutschen Bundestages; das Ausschußwesen ist im Vergleich zur Bundesrepublik oder gar zu den USA unterentwickelt; auch wirken die wenigen, mit geringen Kompetenzen ausgestatteten Sachausschüsse nicht an der parlamentarischen Beratung von Gesetzentwürfen mit. Der durchschnittliche Parlamentarier hat zu geringe Möglichkeiten, durch Spezialisierung die Kenntnisse zu erwerben, die er braucht, um den Spezialisten aus den Ministerien und Verbänden gewachsen zu sein; das Unterhaus kann daher kaum Korrektiv gegen einseitige oder übereilte Vorhaben der Regierung sein.

Im Oberhaus sitzen seit 1958 neben den erblichen Lords, von denen nur ein Teil an den Beratungen regelmäßig teilnimmt, die Pairs auf Lebenszeit, d.h. von der Krone auf Vorschlag der Regierung berufene ehemalige Unterhausabgeordnete oder Funktionäre der Parteien und Verbände, pensionierte hohe Beamte, Wissenschaftler und Unternehmer. Sie sind sachkundig auf den verschiedensten Gebieten und haben auch Zeit zur Diskussion; daher können sie manche wichtigen Probleme gründlicher und auch auf höherem Niveau erörtern als die Commons. Dem Oberhaus werden vom Unterhaus nicht kontroverse, aber technisch komplizierte Bills zur Verbesserung überlassen. Die Regierung übernimmt dann häufig bei der erneuten Beratung im Unterhaus die »amendments« der Lords. Eine Oberhausreform, die den Anteil der Pairs auf Lebenszeit erhöhte, würde auch das politische Gewicht des Oberhauses verstärken. Es ist daher verständlich, daß der Plan der Regierung Wilson, das Oberhaus ausschließlich aus Lebenszeitpairs zusammenzusetzen, auch in der Labour Party umstritten blieb, und es ist tatsächlich zu fragen, ob es nicht konsequenter wäre, das Oberhaus ganz abzuschaffen und dafür die Arbeitsmöglichkeiten des Unterhauses weiter zu verbessern.

Der Beitritt Großbritanniens zur Europäischen Gemeinschaft wird nicht nur die Wirtschaft zu schwierigen Anpassungen zwingen; er bedeutet auch eine Herausforderung der politischen Institutionen des Landes. Der Beitritt war notwendig geworden, als die wirtschaftliche Bedeutung der Commonwealth-Verflechtung für Großbritannien allmählich sank, die EFTA zu keinem überzeugenden Erfolg wurde, dafür sich aber die EWG zu einem Wirtschaftsfaktor von immer größerem Gewicht entwickelte. Die britische Industrie dürfte auf die Dauer von dem Beitritt beträchtliche Wachstumsimpulse erhalten. Ein gewichtiger ökonomischer Nachteil, vor allem für die unteren Einkommensschichten, wird das Ansteigen der Lebensmittelpreise durch die Übernahme der Agrarmarktordnung der Gemeinschaft sein (vgl. S. 231 ff.). Die erheblichen Umstellungsprobleme werden eine Erweiterung der staatlichen Planungs- und Lenkungsbefugnisse erfordern. Zugleich werden Kompetenzen von London nach Brüssel übertragen werden müssen; wie jedes Mitglied der Europäischen Gemeinschaft, so wird auch Großbritannien bereits Mitte der 70er Jahre vor der Alternative stehen, entweder die Zollunion und den gemeinsamen Agrarmarkt weiterzuentwickeln zu einer Wirtschafts- und Währungsunion – was die Aufgabe der einzelstaatlichen Souveränität im Kernbereich des modernen Staates bedeutet – oder aber das bisherige Maß an wirtschaftlicher Integration zu gefährden. Ob Großbritannien bereit sein wird, die politischen Konsequenzen der angestrebten wirtschaftlichen Integration zu ziehen, oder ob es ähnlich wie das gaullistische Frankreich es vorziehen wird, bei der Zollunion stehenzubleiben, läßt sich zur Zeit noch nicht übersehen.

Die Herausgeber haben nur in Ausnahmefällen einige zum Verständnis des Textes notwendige Anmerkungen gemacht, die im Unterschied zu den jeweils durchnumerierten Anmerkungen in den Texten mit einem Stern (*) versehen wurden.

1

WALTER BAGEHOT

The Cabinet

Aus: The English Constitution. Fontana Classics of History and Thought; 8. Auflage London 1971, S. 59–81.

Das Werk ist zuerst 1867 erschienen. BAGEHOT war Bankier, politischer Journalist, Literaturkritiker und Herausgeber der Zeitschrift *The Economist*. Das Buch *The English Constitution* gilt als bedeutendste Analyse der britischen Verfassungswirklichkeit vor dem Entstehen eines modernen Parteiensystems. Allerdings ist seine Darstellung nicht in allen Punkten zutreffend. Das amerikanische Regierungssystem hat er aus eigener Anschauung nicht gekannt und interpretiert es falsch. Dennoch sind seine Bemerkungen über das »Präsidentielle System« hier mit aufgenommen, weil durch sie BAGEHOTS Beurteilung der englischen Verhältnisse deutlicher wird.

'On all great subjects,' says Mr. Mill, 'much remains to be said,' and of none is this more true than of the English Constitution. The literature which has accumulated upon it is huge. But an observer who looks at the living reality will wonder at the contrast to the paper description. He will see in the life much which is not in the books; and he will not find in the rough practice many refinements of the literary theory.

It was natural – perhaps inevitable – that such an undergrowth of irrelevant ideas should gather round the British Constitution. Language is the tradition of nations; each generation describes what it sees, but it uses words transmitted from the past. When a great entity like the British Constitution has continued in connected outward sameness, but hidden inner change, for many ages, every generation inherits a series of inapt words – of maxims once true, but of which the truth is ceasing or has ceased. As a man's family go on muttering in his maturity incorrect phrases derived from a just observation of his early youth, so, in the full activity of an historical constitution, its subjects repeat phrases true in the time of their fathers, and inculcated by those fathers, but now true no longer. Or, if I may say so, an ancient and ever-altering constitution is like an old man who still wears with attached fondness clothes in the fashion of his youth: what you see of him is the same; what you do not see is wholly altered.

There are two descriptions of the English Constitution which have exercised immense influence, but which are erroneous. First, it is laid down as a principle of the English polity, that in it the legislative, the executive, and the judicial powers are quite divided – that each is entrusted to a separate person or set of persons – that no one of these can at all interfere with the work of the other. There has been much eloquence expended in explaining how the rough genius of the English people, even in the middle ages, when it was especially rude, carried into life and practice that elaborate division of functions which philosophers had suggested on paper, but which they had hardly hoped to see except on paper.

Secondly, it is insisted that the peculiar excellence of the British Constitution lies in a balanced union of three powers. It is said that the monarchical element, the aristocratic element, and the democratic element, have each a share in the supreme sovereignty, and that the assent of all three is necessary to the action of that sovereignty. Kings, lords, and commons, by this theory, are alleged to be not only the outward form, but the inner moving essence, the vitality of the Constitution. A great theory, called the theory of 'Checks and Balances', pervades an immense part of political literature, and much of it is collected from or supported by English experience. Monarchy, it is said, has some faults, some bad tendencies, aristocracy others, democracy, again, others; but England has shown that a Government can be constructed in which these evil tendencies exactly check, balance, and destroy one another – in which a good whole is constructed not simply in spite of, but by means of, the counteracting defects of the constituent parts.

Accordingly, it is believed that the principal characteristics of the English Constitution are inapplicable in countries where the materials for a monarchy or an aristocracy do not exist. That Constitution is conceived to be the best imaginable use of the political elements which the great majority of States in modern Europe inherited from the mediæval period. It is believed that out of these materials nothing better can be made than the English Constitution; but it is also believed that the essential parts of the English Constitution cannot be made except from these materials. Now these elements are the accidents of a period and a region; they belong only to one or two centuries in human history, and to a few countries. The United States could not have become monarchical, even if the Constitutional Convention had decreed it, even if the component States had ratified it. The mystic reverence, the religious allegiance, which are essential to a true monarchy, are imaginative sentiments that no legislature can manufacture in any people. These semi-filial feelings in Government are inherited just as the true filial feelings in common life. You might as well adopt a father as make a monarchy: the special sentiment belonging to the one is as incapable of voluntary creation as the peculiar affection belonging to the other. If the practical part of the English Constitution could only be made out of a curious accumulation of mediæval materials, its interest would be half historical, and its imitability very confined.

No one can approach to an understanding of the English institutions, or of others, which, being the growth of many centuries, exercise a wide sway over mixed populations, unless he divide them into two classes. In such constitutions there are two parts (not indeed separable with microscopic accuracy, for the genius of great affairs abhors nicety of division): first, those which excite and preserve the reverence of the population – the *dignified* parts, if I may so call them; and next, the *efficient* parts – those by which it, in fact, works and rules. There are two great objects which every constitution must attain to be successful, which every old and celebrated one must have wonderfully achieved: every constitution must first *gain* authority, and then *use* authority; it must first win the loyalty and confidence of mankind, and then employ that homage in the work of government.

There are indeed practical men who reject the dignified parts of Government. They say, we want only to attain results, to do business: a constitution is a collection of political means for political ends, and if you admit that any part of a constitution does no business, or that a simpler machine would do equally well what it does, you admit that this part of the constitution, however dignified or awful it may be, is nevertheless in truth useless. And other reasoners, who distrust this bare philosophy, have propounded subtle arguments to prove that these dignified parts of old Governments are cardinal components of the essential apparatus, great pivots of substantial utility; and so they manufactured fallacies which the plainer school have well exposed. But both schools are in error. The dignified parts of Government are those which bring it force – which attract its motive power. The efficient parts only employ that power. The comely parts of a Government *have* need, for they are those upon which its vital strength depends. They may not do anything definite that a simpler polity would not do better; but they are the preliminaries, the needful prerequisites of *all* work. They raise the army, though they do not win the battle.

Doubtless, if all subjects of the same Government only thought of what was useful to them, and if they all thought the same thing useful, and all thought that same thing could be attained in the same way, the efficient members of a constitution would suffice, and no impressive adjuncts would be needed. But the world in which we live is organised far otherwise.

The most strange fact, though the most certain in nature, is the unequal development of the human race. If we look back to the early ages of mankind, such as we seem in the faint distance to see them – if we call up the image of those dismal tribes in lake villages, or on wretched beaches – scarcely equal to the commonest material needs, cutting down trees slowly and painfully with stone tools, hardly resisting the attacks of huge, fierce animals – without culture, without leisure, without poetry, almost without thought – destitute of morality, with only a sort of magic for religion; and if we compare that imagined life with the actual life of Europe now, we are overwhelmed at the wide contrast – we can scarcely conceive ourselves to be of the same race as those in the far distance. There used to be a notion – not so much widely asserted as deeply implanted, rather pervadingly latent than commonly apparent in political philosophy – that in a little while, perhaps ten years or so, all human beings might, without extraordinary appliances, be brought to the same level. But now, when we see by the painful history of mankind at what point we began, by what slow toil, what favourable circumstances, what accumulated achievements, civilised man has become at all worthy in any degree so to call himself – when we realise the tedium of history and the painfulness of results – our perceptions are sharpened as to the relative steps of our long and gradual progress. We have in a great community like England crowds of people scarcely more civilised than the majority of two thousand years ago; we have others, even more numerous, such as the best people were a thousand years since. The lower orders, the middle orders, are still, when tried by what is the standard of the educated 'ten thousand', narrow-minded, unintelligent, incurious. It is useless to pile up abstract words. Those who doubt should go out into their kitchens. Let an accomplished man try what seems to him most obvious, most certain, most palpable in intellectual matters, upon the housemaid and the footman, and he will find that what he says seems unintelligible, confused, and erroneous – that his audience think him mad and wild when he is speaking what is in his own sphere of thought the dullest platitude of cautious soberness. Great communities are like great mountains – they have in them the primary, secondary, and tertiary strata of human progress; the characteristics of the lower regions resemble the life of old times rather than the present life of the higher regions. And a philosophy which does not ceaselessly remember, which does not continually obtrude, the palpable differences of the various parts, will be a theory radically false, because it has omitted a capital reality – will be a theory essentially misleading, because it will lead men to expect what does not exist, and not to anticipate that which they will find.

Every one knows these plain facts, but by no means every one has traced their political importance. When a State is constituted thus, it is not true that the lower classes will be wholly absorbed in the useful; on the contrary, they do not like anything so poor. No orator ever made an impression by appealing to men as to their plainest physical wants, except when he could allege that those wants were caused by some one's tyranny. But thousands have made the greatest impression by appealing to some vague dream of glory, or empire, or nationality. The ruder sort of men – that is, men at *one* stage of rudeness – will sacrifice all they hope for, all they have, *themselves*, for what is called an idea – for some attraction which seems so transcend reality, which aspires to elevate men by an interest higher, deeper, wider than that of ordinary life. But this order of men are uninterested in the plain, palpable ends of government; they do not prize them; they do not in the least comprehend how they should be attained. It is very natural, therefore, that the most useful parts of the structure of government should by no means be those which excite the most reverence. The elements which excite the most easy reverence will be the *theatrical* elements – those which appeal to the senses, which claim to be embodiments of the greatest human ideas, which boast in some cases of far more than human origin. That which is mystic in its claims; that which is occult in its mode of action; that which is brilliant to the eye; that which is seen vividly for a moment, and then is seen no more; that which is hidden and unhidden; that which is specious, and yet interesting, palpable in its seeming, and yet professing to be more than palpable in its results; this, howsoever its form may change, or however we may define it or describe it, is the sort of thing – the only sort – which yet comes home to the mass of men. So far from the dignified parts of a constitution being necessarily the most useful, they are likely, according to outside presumption, to be the least so; for they are likely to be adjusted to the lowest orders – those likely to care least and judge worst about what *is* useful.

There is another reason which, in an old constitution like that of England, is hardly less important. The most intellectual of men are moved quite as much by the circumstances which they are used to as by their own will. The active voluntary part of a man is very small, and if it were not economised by a sleepy kind of habit, its results would be null. We could not do every day out of our own heads all we have to do. We should accomplish nothing, for all our energies would be frittered away in minor attempts at petty improvement. One man, too, would go off from the known track in one direction, and one in another; so that when a crisis came requiring massed combination, no two men would be near enough to act together. It is the dull traditional habit of mankind that guides most men's actions, and is the steady frame in which each new artist must set the picture that he paints. And all this traditional part of human nature is, *ex vi termini*, most easily impressed and acted on by that which is handed down. Other things being equal, yesterday's institutions are by far the best for to-day; they are the most ready, the most influential, the most easy to get obeyed, the most likely to retain the reverence which they alone inherit, and which every other must win. The most imposing institutions of mankind are the oldest; and yet so changing is the world, so fluctuating are its needs, so apt to lose inward force, though retaining outward strength, are its best instruments, that we must not expect the oldest institutions to be now the most efficient. We must expect what is venerable to acquire influence because of its inherent dignity; but we must not expect it to use that influence so well as new creations apt for the modern world, instinct with its spirit, and fitting closely to its life.

The brief description of the characteristic merit of the English Constitution is, that its dignified parts are very complicated and somewhat imposing, very old and rather venerable; while its efficient part, at least when in great and critical action, is decidedly simple and rather modern. We have made, or rather stumbled on, a constitution which – though full of every species of incidental defect, though of the worst *workmanship* in all out-of-the-way matters of any constitution in the world – yet has two capital merits: it contains a simple efficient part which, on occasion, and when wanted, *can* work more simply and easily, and better, than any instrument of government that has yet been tried; and it contains likewise historical, complex, august, theatrical parts, which it has inherited from a long past – which *take* the multitude – which guide by an insensible but an omnipotent influence the associations of its subjects. Its essence is strong with the strength of modern simplicity; its exterior is august with the Gothic grandeur of a more imposing age. Its simple essence may, *mutatis mutandis*, be transplanted to many very various countries, but its august outside – what most men think it is – is narrowly confined to nations with an analogous history and similar political materials.

The efficient secret of the English Constitution may be described as the close union, the nearly complete fusion, of the executive and legislative powers. No doubt by the traditional theory, as it exists in all the books, the goodness of our constitution consists in the entire separation of the legislative and executive authorities, but in truth its merit consists in their singular approximation. The connecting link is *the Cabinet*. By that new word we mean a committee of the legislative body selected to be the executive body. The legislature has many committees, but this is its greatest. It chooses for this, its main committee, the men in whom it has most confidence. It does not, it is true, choose them directly; but it is nearly omnipotent in choosing them indirectly. A century ago the Crown had a real choice of Ministers, though it had no longer a choice in policy. During the long reign of Sir R. Walpole he was obliged not only to manage Parliament but to manage the palace. He was obliged to take care that some court intrigue did not expel him from his place. The nation then selected the English policy, but the Crown hose the English Ministers. They were not only in name, as now, but in fact, the Queen's servants. Remnants, important remnants, of this great prerogative still remain. The discriminating favour of William IV made Lord Melbourne head of the Whig Party when he was only one of several rivals. At the death of Lord Palmerston it is very likely that the Queen may have the opportunity of fairly choosing between two, if not three statesmen. But, as a rule, the nominal Prime Minister is chosen by the legislature, and the real Prime Minister for most purposes – the leader of the House of Commons – almost without exception is so. There is nearly always some one man plainly selected by the voice of the predominant party in the predominant house of the legislature to head that party, and consequently to rule the nation. We have in England an elective first magistrate as truly as the Americans have an elective first magistrate. The Queen is only at the head of the dignified part of the Constitution. The Prime Minister is at the head of the efficient part. The Crown is, according to the saying, the 'fountain of honour'; but the Treasury is the spring of business. Nevertheless, our first magistrate differs from the American. He is not elected directly by the people; he is elected by the representatives of the people. He is an example of 'double election'. The legislature chosen, in name, to make laws, in fact finds its principal business in making and in keeping an executive.

The leading Minister so selected has to choose his associates, but he only chooses among a charmed circle. The position of most men in Parliament forbids their being invited to the Cabinet; the position of a few men ensures their being invited. Between the compulsory list whom he must take, and the impossible list whom he cannot take, a Prime Minister's independent choice in the formation of a Cabinet is not very large; it extends rather to the division of the Cabinet offices than to the choice of Cabinet Ministers. Parliament and the nation have pretty well settled who shall have the first places; but they have not discriminated with the same accuracy which man shall have which place. The highest patronage of a Prime Minister is, of course, a considerable power, though it is exercised under close and imperative restrictions – though it is far less than it seems to be when stated in theory, or looked at from a distance.

The Cabinet, in a word, is a board of control chosen by the legislature, out of persons whom it trusts and knows, to rule the nation. The particular mode in which the English Ministers are selected; the fiction that they are, in any political sense, the Queen's servants; the rule which limits the choice of the Cabinet to the members of the legislature – are accidents unessential to its definition – historical incidents separable from its nature. Its characteristic is that it should be chosen by the legislature out of persons agreeable to and trusted by the legislature. Naturally these are principally its own members – but they need not be exclusively so. A Cabinet which included persons not members of the legislative assembly might still perform all useful duties. Indeed the peers, who constitute a large element in modern Cabinets, are members, now-a-days, only of a subordinate assembly. The House of Lords still exercises several useful functions; but the ruling influence – the deciding faculty – has passed to what, using the language of old times, we still call the lower house – to an assembly which, though inferior as a dignified institution, is superior as an efficient institution. A principal advantage of the House of Lords in the present age indeed consists in its thus acting as a *reservoir* of Cabinet Ministers. Unless the composition of the House of Commons were improved, or unless the rules requiring Cabinet Ministers to be members of the legislature were relaxed, it would undoubtedly be difficult to find, without the lords, a sufficient supply of chief Ministers. But the detail of the composition of a Cabinet, and the precise method of its choice, are not to the purpose now. The first and cardinal consideration is the definition of a Cabinet. We must not bewilder ourselves with the inseparable accidents until we know the necessary essence. A Cabinet is a combining committee – a *hyphen* which joins, a *buckle* which fastens, the legislative part of the State to the executive part of the State. In its origin it belongs to the one, in its functions it belongs to the other.

The most curious point about the Cabinet is that so very little is known about it. The meetings are not only secret in theory, but secret in reality. By the present practice, no official minute in all ordinary cases is kept of them. Even a private note is discouraged and disliked. The House of Commons, even in its most inquisitive and turbulent moments, would scarcely permit a note of a Cabinet meeting to be read. No Minister who respected the fundamental usages of political practice would attempt to read such a note. The committee which unites the law-making power to the law-executing power – which, by virtue of that combination, is, while it lasts and holds together, the most powerful body in the State – is a committee wholly secret. No description of it, at once graphic and authentic, has ever been given. It is said to be sometimes like a rather disorderly board of directors, where many speak and few listen – though no one knows.[1]

But a Cabinet, though it is a committee of the legislative assembly, is a committee with a power which no assembly would – unless for historical accidents, and after happy experience – have been persuaded to entrust to any committee. It is a committee which can dissolve the assembly which appointed it; it is a committee with a suspensive veto – a committee with a power of appeal. Though appointed by one Parliament, it can appeal if it chooses to the next. Theoretically, indeed, the power to dissolve Parliament is entrusted to the sovereign only, and there are vestiges of doubt whether in *all* cases a sovereign is bound to dissolve Parliament when the Cabinet asks him to do so. But neglecting such small and dubious exceptions, the Cabinet which was chosen by one House of Commons has an appeal to the next House of Commons. The chief committee of the legislature has the power of dissolving the predominant part of that legislature – that which at a crisis is the supreme legislature. The English system, therefore, is not an absorption of the executive power by the legislative power; it is a fusion of the two. Either the Cabinet legislates and acts, or else it can dissolve. It is a creature, but it has the power of destroying its creators. It is an executive which can annihilate the legislature, as well as an executive which is the nominee of the legislature. It *was* made, but it *can* unmake; it was derivative in its origin, but it is destructive in its action.

This fusion of the legislative and executive functions may, to those who have not much considered it, seem but a dry and small matter to be the latent essence and effectual secret of the English Constitution; but we can only judge of its real importance by looking at a few of its principal effects, and contrasting it very shortly with its great competitor, which seems likely, unless care be taken, to outstrip it in the progress of the world. That competitor is the Presidential system. The characteristic of it is that the President is elected from the people by one process, and the House of Representatives by another. The independence of the legislative and executive powers is the specific quality of Presidential government, just as their fusion and combination is the precise principle of Cabinet government.

First, compare the two in quiet times. The essence of a civilised age is, that administration requires the continued aid of legislation. One principal and necessary kind of legislation is *taxation*. The expense of civilised government is continually varying. It must vary if the Government does its duty. The miscellaneous estimates of the English Government contain an inevitable medley of changing items. Education, prison discipline, art, science, civil contingencies of a hundred kinds, require more money one year and less another. The expense of defence – the naval and military estimates – vary still more as the danger of attack seems more or less imminent, as the means of retarding such danger become more or less costly. If the persons who have to do the work are not the same as those who have to make the laws, there will be a controversy between the two sets of persons. The tax-imposers are sure to quarrel with the tax-requirers. The executive is crippled by not getting the laws it needs, and the legislature is spoiled by having to act without responsibility: the executive becomes unfit for its name, since it cannot execute what it decides on; the legislature is demoralised by liberty, by taking decisions of which others (and not itself) will suffer the effects.

In America so much has this difficulty been felt that a semiconnection has grown up between the legislature and the executive. When the Secretary of the Treasury of the Federal Government wants a tax he consults upon it with the chairman of the Financial Committee of Congress. He cannot go down to Congress himself and propose what he wants; he can only write a letter and send it. But he tries to get a chairman of the Finance Committee who likes his tax; – through that chairman he tries to persuade the committee to recommend such tax; by that committee he tries to induce the house to adopt that tax. But such a chain of communications is liable to continual interruptions; it may suffice for a single tax on a fortunate occasion, but will scarcely pass a complicated budget – we do not say in a war or a rebellion – we are now comparing the Cabinet system and the Presidential system in quiet times – but in times of financial difficulty. Two clever men never exactly agreed about a budget. We have by present practice an Indian Chancellor of the Exchequer talking English finance at Calcutta, and an English one talking Indian finance in England. But the figures are never the same, and the views of policy are rarely the same. One most angry controversy has amused the world, and probably others scarcely less interesting are hidden in the copious stores of our Anglo-Indian correspondence.

But relations something like these must subsist between the head of a finance committee in the legislature, and a finance Minister in the executive.[2] They are sure to quarrel, and the result is sure to satisfy neither. And when the taxes do not yield as they were expected to yield, who is responsible? Very likely the Secretary of the Treasury could not persuade the chairman – very likely the chairman could not persuade his committee – very likely the committee could not persuade the assembly. Whom, then, can you punish – whom can you abolish – when your taxes run short? There is nobody save the legislature, a vast miscellaneous body difficult to punish, and the very persons to inflict the punishment.

Nor is the financial part of administration the only one which requires in a civilised age the constant support and accompaniment of facilitating legislation. All administration does so. In England, on a vital occasion, the Cabinet can compel legislation by the threat of resignation, and the threat of dissolution; but neither of these can be used in a Presidential State. There the legislature cannot be dissolved by the executive Government; and it does not heed a resignation, for it has not to find the successor. Accordingly, when a difference of opinion arises, the legislature is forced to fight the executive, and the executive is forced to fight the legislative; and so very likely they contend to the conclusion of their respective terms.[3] There is, indeed, one condition of things in which this description, though still approximately true, is, nevertheless, not exactly true; and that is, when there is nothing to fight about. Before the rebellion in America, owing to the vast distance of other States, and the favourable economic condition of the country, there were very few considerable objects of contention; but if that government had been tried by English legislation of the last thirty years, the discordant action of the two powers, whose constant co-operation is essential to the best government, would have shown itself much more distinctly.

Nor is this the worst. Cabinet government educates the nation; the Presidential does not educate it, and may corrupt it. It has been said that England invented the phrase, 'Her Majesty's Opposition'; that it was the first Government which made a criticism of administration as much a part of the polity as administration itself. This critical opposition is the consequence of Cabinet government. The great scene of debate, the great engine of popular instruction and political controversy is the legislative assembly. A speech there by an eminent statesman, a party movement by a great political combination, are the best means yet known for arousing, enlivening, and teaching a people. The Cabinet system ensures such debates, for it makes them the means by which statesmen advertise themselves for future and confirm themselves in present Governments. It brings forward men eager to speak, and gives them occasions to speak. The deciding catastrophes of Cabinet governments are critical divisions preceded by fine discussions. Everything which is worth saying, everything which ought to be said, most certainly *will* be said. Conscientious men think they ought to persuade others; selfish men think they would like to obtrude themselves. The nation is forced to hear two sides – all the sides, perhaps, of that which most concerns it. And it likes to hear – it is eager to know. Human nature despises long arguments which come to nothing – heavy speeches which precede no motion – abstract disquisitions which leave visible things where they were. But all men heed great results, and a change of Government is a great result. It has a hundred ramifications; it runs through society; it gives hope to many, and it takes away hope from many. It is one of those marked events which, by its magnitude and its melodrama, impress men even too much. And debates which have this catastrophe at the end of them – or may so have it – are sure to be listened to, and sure to sink deep into the national mind.

Travellers even in the Northern States of America, the greatest and best of Presidential countries, have noticed that the nation was 'not specially addicted to politics'; that they have not a public opinion finished and chastened as that of the English has been finished and chastened. A great many hasty writers have charged this defect on the 'Yankee race', on the Anglo-American character; but English people, if they had no motive to attend to politics, certainly would not attend to politics. At present there is *business* in their attention. They assist at the determining crisis; they arrest or help it. Whether the Government will go out or remain is determined by the debate, and by the division in Parliament. And the opinion out of doors, the secret pervading disposition of society, has a great influence on that division. The nation feels that its judgment is important, and it strives to judge. It succeeds in deciding because the debates and the discussions give it the facts and the arguments. But under a Presidential government, a nation has, except at the electing moment, no influence; it has not the ballot-box before it; its virtue is gone, and it must wait till its instant of despotism again returns. It is not incited to form an opinion like a nation under a Cabinet government; nor is it instructed like such a nation. There are doubtless debates in the legislature, but they are prologues without a play. There is nothing of a catastrophe about them; you cannot turn out the Government. The prize of power is not in the gift of the legislature, and no one cares for the legislature. The executive, the great centre of power and place, sticks irremovable; you cannot change it in any event. The teaching apparatus which has educated our public mind, which prepares our resolutions, which shapes our opinions, does not exist. No Presidential country needs to form daily delicate opinions, or is helped in forming them.

It might be thought that the discussions in the press would supply the deficiencies in the Constitution; that by a reading people especially, the conduct of their Government would be as carefully watched, that their opinions about it would be as consistent, as accurate, as well considered, under a Presidential as under a Cabinet polity. But the same difficulty oppresses the press which oppresses the legislature. It can *do nothing*. It cannot change the administration;

the executive was elected for such and such years, and for such and such years it must last. People wonder that so literary a people as the Americans – a people who read more than any people who ever lived, who read so many newspapers – should have such bad newspapers. The papers are not as good as the English, because they have not the same motive to be good as the English papers. At a political 'crisis', as we say – that is, when the fate of an administration is unfixed, when it depends on a few votes yet unsettled, upon a wavering and veering opinion – effective articles in great journals become of essential moment. The *Times* has made many ministries. When, as of late, there has been a long continuance of divided Parliaments, of Governments which were without 'brute voting power', and which depended on intellectual strength, the support of the most influential organ of English opinion has been of critical moment. If a Washington newspaper could have turned out Mr. Lincoln, there would have been good writing and fine argument in the Washington newspapers. But the Washington newspapers can no more remove a President during his term of place than the *Times* can remove a lord mayor during his year of office. Nobody cares for a debate in Congress which 'comes to nothing', and no one reads long articles which have no influence on events. The Americans glance at the heads of news, and through the paper. They do not enter upon a discussion. They do not *think* of entering upon a discussion which would be useless.

After saying that the division of the legislature and the executive in Presidential governments weakens the legislative power, it may seem a contradiction to say that it also weakens the executive power. But it is not a contradiction. The division weakens the whole aggregate force of Government – the entire imperial power; and therefore it weakens both its halves. The executive is weakened in a very plain way. In England a strong Cabinet can obtain the concurrence of the legislature in all acts which facilitate its administration; it is itself, so to say, the legislature. But a President may be hampered by the Parliament, and is likely to be hampered. The natural tendency of the members of every legislature is to make themselves conspicuous. They wish to gratify an ambition laudable or blamable; they wish to promote the measures they think best for the public welfare; they wish to make their *will* felt in great affairs. All these mixed motives urge them to oppose the executive. They are embodying the purposes of others if they aid; they are advancing their own opinions if they defeat: they are first if they vanquish; they are auxiliaries if they support. The weakness of the American executive used to be the great theme of all critics before the Confederate rebellion. Congress and committees of Congress of course impeded the executive when there was no coercive public sentiment to check and rule them. But the Presidential system not only gives the executive power an antagonist in the legislative power, and so makes it weaker; it also enfeebles it by impairing its intrinsic quality. A Cabinet is elected by a legislature; and when that legislature is composed of fit persons, that mode of electing the executive is the very best. It is a case of secondary election, under the only conditions in which secondary election is preferable to primary. Generally speaking, in an electioneering country (I mean in a country full of political life, and used to the manipulation of popular institutions), the election of candidates to elect candidates is a farce. The Electoral College of America is so. It was intended that the deputies when assembled should exercise a real discretion, and by independent choice select the President. But the primary electors take too much interest. They only elect a deputy to vote for Mr. Lincoln or Mr. Breckenridge, and the deputy only takes a ticket, and drops that ticket in an urn. He never chooses or thinks of choosing. He is but a messenger – a transmitter; the real decision is in those who choose him – who chose him because they knew what he would do.

It is true that the British House of Commons is subject to the same influences. Members are mostly, perhaps, elected because they will vote for a particular Ministry, rather than for purely legislative reasons. But – and here is the capital distinction – the functions of the House of Commons are important and *continuous*. It does not, like the Electoral College in the United States, separate when it has elected its ruler; it watches, legislates, seats and unseats ministries, from day to day. Accordingly it is a *real* electoral body. The Parliament of 1857, which, more than any other Parliament of late years, was a Parliament elected to support a particular premier – which was chosen, as Americans might say, upon the 'Palmerston ticket' – before it had been in existence two years, dethroned Lord Palmerston. Though selected in the interest of a particular Ministry, it in fact destroyed that Ministry.

A *good* Parliament, too, is a capital choosing body. If it is fit to make laws for a country, its majority ought to represent the general average intelligence of that country; its various members ought to represent the various special interests, special opinions, special prejudices, to be found in that community. There ought to be an advocate for every particular sect, and a vast neutral body of no sect – homogeneous and judicial, like the nation itself. Such a body, when possible, is the best selector of executives that can be imagined. It is full of political activity; it is close to political life; it feels the responsibility of affairs which are brought as it were to its threshold; it has as much intelligence as the society in question chances to contain. It is, what Washington and Hamilton strove to create, an electoral college of the picked men of the nation.

The best mode of appreciating its advantages is to look at the alternative. The competing constituency is the nation itself, and this is, according to theory and experience, in all but the rarest cases, a bad constituency. Mr. Lincoln, at his second election, being elected when all the Federal States had set their united hearts on one single object, was voluntarily reelected by an actually choosing nation. He embodied the object in which every one was absorbed. But this is almost the only Presidential election of which so much can be said. In almost all cases the President is chosen by a machinery of caucuses and combinations too complicated to be perfectly known, and too familiar to require description. He is not the choice of the nation, he is the choice of the wire-pullers. A very large constituency in quiet times is the necessary, almost the legitimate, subject of electioneering management: a man cannot know that he does not throw his vote away except he votes as part of some great organisation; and if he votes as a part, he abdicates his electoral function in favour of the managers of that association. The nation, even if it chose for itself, would, in some degree, be an unskilled body; but when it does not choose for itself, but only as latent agitators wish, it is like a large, lazy man, with a small vicious mind, – it moves slowly and heavily, but it moves at the bidding of a bad intention; it 'means *little*, but it means that little *ill*'.

And, as the nation is less able to choose than a Parliament, so it has worse people to choose out of. The American legislators of the last century have been much blamed for not permitting the Ministers of the President to be members of the assembly; but, with reference to the specific end which they had in view, they saw clearly and decided wisely. They wished to keep 'the legislative branch absolutely distinct from the executive branch'; they believed such a separation to be essential to a good constitution; they believed such a separation to exist in the English, which the wisest of them thought the best Constitution. And, to the effectual maintenance of such a separation, the exclusion of the President's Ministers from the legislature is essential. If they are not excluded they become the executive, they eclipse the President himself. A legislative chamber is greeedy and covetous; it acquires as much, it concedes as little as possible. The passions of its members are its rulers; the law-making faculty, the most comprehensive of the imperial faculties, is its instrument; it will *take* the administration if it can take it. Tried by their own aims, the founders if the United States were wise in excluding the Ministers from Congress.

But though this exclusion is essential to the Presidential system of government, it is not for that reason a small evil. It causes the degradation of public life. Unless a member of the legislature be sure of something more than speech, unless he is incited by the hope of action, and chastened by the chance of responsibility, a first-rate man will not care to take the place, and will not do much if he does take it. To belong to a debating society adhering to an executive (and this is no inapt description of a congress under a Presidential Constitution) is not an object to stir a noble ambition, and is a position to encourage idleness. The members of a Parliament excluded from office can never be comparable, much less equal, to those of a Parliament not excluded from office. The Presidential Government, by its nature, divides political life into two halves, an executive half and a legislative half; and, by so dividing it, makes neither half worth a man's having – worth his making it a continuous career – worthy to absorb, as Cabinet government absorbs, his whole soul. The statesmen from whom a nation chooses under a Presidential system are much inferior to those from whom it chooses under a Cabinet system, while the selecting apparatus is also far less discerning.

All these differences are more important at critical periods, because government itself is more important. A formed public opinion, a respectable, able, and disciplined legislature, a wellchosen executive, a Parliament and an administration not thwarting each other, but co-operating with each other, are of greater consequence when great affairs are in progress than when small affairs are in progress – when there is much to do than when there is little to do. But in addition to this, a Parliamentary or Cabinet Constitution possesses an additional and special advantage in very dangerous times. It has what we may call a reserve of power fit for and needed by extreme exigencies. The principle of popular government is that the supreme power, the determining efficacy in matters political, resides in the people – not necessarily or commonly in the whole people, in the numerical majority, but in a *chosen* people, a picked and selected people. It is so in England; it is so in all free countries. Under a Cabinet Constitution at a sudden emergency this people can choose a ruler for the occasion. It is quite possible and even likely that he would not be ruler *before* the occasion. The great qualities, the imperious will, the rapid energy, the eager nature fit for a great crisis are not required – are impediments – in common times. A Lord Liverpool is better in everyday politics than a Chatham – a Louis Philippe far better than a Napoleon. By the structure of the world we often want, at the sudden occurrence of a grave tempest, to change the helmsman – to replace the pilot of the calm by the pilot of the storm. In England we have had so few catastrophes since our Constitution attained maturity, that we hardly appreciate this latent excellence. We have not needed a Cavour to rule a revolution – a representative man above all men fit for a great occasion, and by a natural legal mode brought in to rule. But even in England, at what was the nearest to a great sudden crisis which we have had of late years – at the Crimean difficulty – we used this inherent power. We abolished the Aberdeen Cabinet, the ablest we have had, perhaps, since the Reform Act – a Cabinet not only adapted, but eminently adapted, for every sort of difficulty save the one it had to meet – which abounded in pacific discretion, and was wanting only in the 'dæmonic element'; we chose a statesman, who had the sort of merit then wanted, who, when he feels the steady power of England behind him, will advance without reluctance, and will strike without restraint. As was said at the time, 'We turned out the Quaker, and put in the pugilist'.

But under a Presidential government you can do nothing of the kind. The American Government calls itself a Government of the supreme people; but at a quick crisis, the time when a sovereign power is most needed, you cannot *find* the supreme people. You have got a Congress elected for one fixed period, going out perhaps by fixed instalments, which cannot be accelerated or retarded – you have a President chosen for a fixed period, and immovable during that periods all the arrangements are for *stated* times. There is no *elastic* element, everything is rigid, specified, dated. Come what may, you can quicken nothing, and can retard nothing. You have bespoken your Government in advance, and whether it suits you or not, whether it works well or works ill, whether it is what you want or not, by law you must keep it. In a country of complex foreign relations it would mostly happen that the first and most critical year of every war would be managed by a peace Premier, and the first and most critical years of peace by a war Premier. In each case the period of transition would be irrevocably governed by a man selected not for what he was to introduce, but what he was to change – for the policy he was to abandon, not for the policy he was to administer. The whole history of the American Civil War – a history which has thrown an intense light on the working of a Presidential government at the time when government is most important – is but a vast continuous commentary on these reflections. It would, indeed, be absurd to press against Presidential government *as such* the singular defect by which Vice-President Johnson has become President – by which a man elected to a sinecure is fixed in what is for the moment the most important administrative part in the political world. This defect, though most characteristic of the expectations[4] of the framers of the Constitution and of its working, is but an accident of this particular case of Presidential government, and no necessary ingredient in that government itself. But the first election of Mr. Lincoln is liable to no such objection. It was a characteristic instance of the natural working of such a government upon a great occasion. And what was that working? It may be summed up – it was government by an *unknown quantity*. Hardly any one in America had any living idea what Mr. Lincoln was like, or any definite notion what he would do. The leading statesmen under the system of Cabinet government are not only household words, but household *ideas*. A conception, not, perhaps, in all respects a true but a most vived conception of what Mr. Gladstone is like, or what Lord Palmerston is like, runs through society. We have simply no notion what it would be to be left with the visible sovereignty in the hands of an unknown man. The notion of employing a man of unknown smallness at a crisis of unknown greatness is to our minds simply ludicrous. Mr. Lincoln, it is true, happened to be a man, if not of eminent ability, yet of eminent justness. There was an inner depth of Puritan nature which came out under suffering, and was very attractive. But success in a lottery is no argument for lotteries. What were the chances against a person of Lincoln's antecedents, elected as he was, proving to be what he was?

Such an incident is, however, natural to a Presidential government. The President is elected by processes which forbid the election of known men, except at peculiar conjunctures, and in moments when public opinion is excited and despotic; and consequently if a crisis comes upon us soon after he is elected, inevitably we have government by an unknown quantity – the superintendence of that crisis by what our great satirist would have called 'Statesman X'. Even in

quiet times, government by a President, is, for the several various reasons which have been stated, inferior to government by a Cabinet; but the difficulty of quiet times is nothing as compared with the difficulty of unquiet times. The comparative deficiencies of the regular, common operation of a Presidential government are far less than the comparative deficiencies in time of sudden trouble – the want of elasticity, the impossibility of a dictatorship, the total absence of a *revolutionary reserve*.
This contrast explains why the characteristic quality of Cabinet Governments – the fusion of the executive power with the legislative power – is of such cardinal importance. I shall proceed to show under what form and with what adjuncts it exists in England.

Anmerkungen

1 It is *said* that at the end of the Cabinet which agreed to propose a fixed duty on corn, Lord Melbourne put his back to the door and said, 'Now is it to lower the price of corn or isn't it? It is not much matter which we say, but mind, we must all say *the same*.' This is the most graphic story of a Cabinet I ever heard, but I cannot vouch for its truth. Lord Melbourne's is a character about which men make stories.

2 It is worth observing that even during the short existence of the Confederate Government these evils distinctly showed themselves. Almost the last incident at the Richmond Congress was an angry financial correspondence with Jefferson Davis.

3 I leave this passage to stand as it was written, just after the assassination of Mr. Lincoln, and when every one said Mr. Johnson would be very hostile to the South.

4 The framers of the Constitution expected that the *vice*-president would be elected by the Electoral College as the second wisest man in the country. The vice-presidentship being a sinecure, a second-rate man agreeable to the wire-pullers is always smuggled in. The chance of succession to the presidentship is too distant to be thought of.

2

RICHARD H. S. CROSSMAN

Contemporary Problems of British Government

Aus: »Introduction« to WALTER BAGEHOT, The English Constitution, 8. Aufl. London 1971, S. 39–51.

Die Ausgabe erschien zuerst 1963.
R. H. S. CROSSMAN ist Politikwissenschaftler und Labour-Politiker. Geboren 1907, war er 1930 bis 1937 Fellow und Tutor am New College, Oxford. Seit 1945 ist er Unterhausabgeordneter der Labour-Party für den Wahlkreis Coventry East. Er war 1964 bis 1966 Minister of Housing and Local Government, 1966 bis 1968 Leader of the House of Commons und 1968 bis 1970 Secretary of State for Social Services.

Party and Parliament

The growth of Party was of course directly related to the extension of the suffrage that began in the year *The English Constitution* was published. Once votes became too numerous to buy, organised corruption was gradually replaced by party organisation; and the voter was wooed not with offers of ready cash but with promises of state benefits to come. The party which, up to now, had been a weak organisation, functioning informally in the lobbies and political clubs, became a centralised, extra-parliamentary machine, constantly seeking to impose its discipline and its doctrine on the Member of Parliament as well as on the party worker. By the turn of the century, when the party caucuses were firmly entrenched, the efficient secret of the Constitution was no longer the fusion of the executive and the legislature, in that supreme committee of the House of Commons called the Cabinet, but the secret links that connected the Cabinet with the party on the one side and with the civil service on the other.

Of the modern party, Bagehot had not even a premonition – partly because he had never visited America where it was already dominant when he wrote. Throughout *The English Constitution,* he describes party organisation as weak at Westminster and almost non-existent outside. 'At present the member is free,' he remarks, 'because the constituency is not in earnest; no constituency has an acute, accurate doctrinal creed in politics'. One of his main reasons for opposing an extension of the suffrage was his correct premonition that this would bring as its consequence a growth of constituency government, i.e. party machines. 'Constituency government,' he observes, 'is the precise opposite of Parliamentary government. It is the government of immoderate persons far from the scene of action, instead of the government of moderate persons close to the scene of action'.
What he liked most about Parliament was the existence of a solid centre, composed of the majority of solid, sensible independent M.P.s, collectively able to make and unmake ministries, to defy when necessary their own whips, and above all to frustrate the growth of 'constituency government' outside. True, he emphasised the need for 'party' under a system where the government has to sustain its majority in order to endure. But the kind of party organisation he wanted was more like a club than a modern machine. It will work well, he remarks, precisely 'because it is not composed of warm partisans. The body is eager, but the atoms are cool. If it were otherwise, Parliamentary government would become the worst of governments – a sectarian government'. By Bagehot's standards, therefore, Parliamentary government has long since ceased to exist in this country. Ever since the party machines took over the 'electoral' powers previously exercised by the House of Commons, we have been living under 'sectarian government'.

The Modern Machine

The first impact of the modern mass party on classical parliamentary democracy was made by Joseph Chamberlain's Birmingham caucus.[1] But it was not until the rise of working class parties, based on trade unions and disciplined according to their canons of working class solidarity that the 'iron law of increasing oligarchy'[2] completed the transformation of the system. Until then, Parliament had been dominated by the middle classes, and parties had really been electoral organisations at the service of groups of M.P.s, still arguing within the social oligarchy. Though partially enfranchised, the working class were effectively though precariously excluded from government, which was still the monopoly of the aristocracy and the business community. When the Labour Party was formed at the beginning of the century, what Bagehot wrote in the introduction to his second edition* was still largely true:

"The issue put before these electors was, Which of two rich people will you choose? And each of those rich people was put forward by great parties whose notions were the notions of the rich – whose plans were their plans. The electors only selected one or two wealthy men to carry out the schemes of one or two wealthy associations.... They were just competent to make a selection between two sets of superior ideas; or rather – for the conception of such people are more personal than abstract – between two opposing parties, each professing a creed of such ideas.... They were competent to decide an issue selected by the higher classes, but they were incompetent to do more."

The irruption into politics of the Labour Movement ended this phase. In order to break down the walls of social oligarchy which surrounded Parliament, a battering ram was required and the Labour Party was created for this purpose. Its structure was determined by three conditions. First it must have very large funds at its disposal; hence the reliance on trade union financing which led to the sponsoring of Trade Union candidates by particular unions. Secondly, since it could not afford, like its opponents, to maintain a large army of paid party workers, the Labour Party required militants – politically conscious socialists to do the work of organising the constituencies. But since these militants tended to be 'extremists', a constitution was needed which maintained their enthusiasm by apparently creating a full party democracy while excluding them from effective power. Hence the concession in principle of sovereign powers to the delegates at the Annual Conference, and the removal in practice of most of this sovereignty through the trade union block vote on the one hand, and the complete independence of the Parliamentary Labour Party on the other. Thirdly, since its avowed aim was social revolution, the Labour Party from the first accepted the semi-military discipline of democratic centralism, based on the enforcement of majority decision. Hence its intolerance of minority opinion.

* veröffentlicht 1872

In any modern mass party, power tends to be concentrated in the hands of the parliamentarians, and the professional machine politicians. In working class parties, the spirit of trade unionism intensifies this process. The emergence of Labour as the alternative government had an important effect on its opponents. The Conservative Party was compelled in certain respects to copy it. Gradually it was transformed from an old-fashioned caucus, with old-fashioned electoral machinery, into a modern, carefully disciplined mass party. The two great machines began to resemble each other. In his *British Political Parties*, Robert Mackenzie has described in great detail this process of approximation. In so doing he seems to me to have very gravely under-estimated the differences both in social structure, group behaviour, organisation and discipline that still divide the Conservative and Labour Parties. Nevertheless the picture he painted in 1954 was in one important respect completely accurate. The British political scene was indeed dominated by two great party oligarchies which had usurped and divided between them most of the sovereign powers Bagehot ascribed to the Commons.

The Two-Party System

In order to see the difference between his English Constitution and that under which we now live, it may be useful to summarise these changes.

The effect of party on the individual M.P. In Bagehot's day, the private member was genuinely free to defy the whip, genuinely responsible to his own conscience and his constituents, and genuinely at liberty, within wide limits, to speak as he wished. It was this independence of the private member that gave the Commons its collective character and made it the most important check on the executive. Now the prime responsibility of the member is no longer to his conscience or to the elector, but to his party. Without accepting the discipline of the party he cannot be elected; and, if he defies that discipline, he risks political death. Even forty years ago it was still possible to cross the floor and survive. But today the member who loses the whip may win the next election, but after that the party machine will destroy him. Party loyalty has become the prime political virtue required of an M.P., and the test of that loyalty is his willingness to support the official leadership when he knows it to be wrong.

One result of the virtual disappearance of the M.P.'s independence is that the point of decision has now been removed from the division lobby to the party meeting upstairs. The debate on the floor of the House becomes a formality, and the division which follows it a foregone conclusion. It is what is said and done in the secrecy of the party meeting which is now really important – though the public can only hear about it through leaks to the press.

The effect of party on parliamentary control of the executive. Parliamentary control becomes a fiction with the disappearance of that solid centre of independent and independent-minded members, on which Bagehot relied to ensure that party government was always 'mild'. Once the party leadership runs a modern machine and can discipline its M.P.s, government control of Parliament and its business becomes absolute. The Commons, which in Bagehot's day had a real collective life and a general will, is split into two sectarian armies – the Cabinet with its phalanx of supporters, and the Shadow Cabinet also with its phalanx.

The effect of party on the task of Opposition. Theoretically, the task of checking and controlling the executive, which previously belonged in a real sense to the House as a whole, has now passed to the Opposition. But the Opposition is incapable of adequately fulfilling it. For with good management and even a moderate sized majority, any modern government can survive, whatever the Opposition may do, until the Prime Minister decides to dissolve. Modern Oppositions are often accused of ineffectiveness, and rebuked for shadowboxing. But this is all they can do – unless they are willing over a period of months to obstruct legislation and so halt the process of government. But by taking opposition to this level, an Opposition lays itself open to the charge of extremism and irresponsibility, and may well lose the support of that mass of floating voters which it must hope to win in order to turn out the government. Hence the tendency of the modern Opposition to play safe.

It is not the Opposition but the electorate whose views, as revealed in by-elections and gallup polls, the government solicitously watches, and is often ready to appease. Indeed the Opposition normally has less power to exert a check on the executive, or to modify government policy, than a dissident group on the government's back benches. The government knows that it could be undermined from inside by the dissident group, whereas it cannot be defeated by an attack across the floor from the opposite front bench. That is why a government tends to pay much more attention to the private approaches from its own back-benchers, than it does to the public onslaught of the Opposition. For even if the Shadow Cabinet triumphs in the debates day after day, the Government knows that it cannot be brought down except by disloyalty among its own supporters. Thus is it no exaggeration to say that, very often at Westminster, more effective opposition can be exercised by dissident groups of Government supporters than by Her Majesty's Loyal Opposition.

The effect of party on the struggle for power. Just as the important debates have been removed from the floor of the Commons to the secrecy of the committee rooms upstairs, so the struggle for power which gives meaning to democratic politics has also been hidden from the public eye. Today the struggle for real power takes place secretly inside the government party, and for shadow power inside the Opposition. Driven underground by the requirements of party discipline, it is normally a conspiratorial matter of cliques and cabals. Groups are formed to fight for causes or uphold principles, only to be disintegrated from above by threats of expulsion and offers of preferment. In our modern party politics, there is no 'loyal' way either of removing a disastrous leader or of promoting to power a saviour at loggerheads with the machine.

In the classical parliamentary system, the debates were public, the issues were known and the personal struggle for power could take place on the floor of the House or on the hustings. The elector could see something at least of the issues at stake in the clash of personalities. In our modern system, all he can usually see is the shadow fight between the selected champions of the two party phalanxes on the floor of the chamber. Of the struggle between personalities and the conflict of ideas that takes place inside each great party machine, he can only hear the garbled versions leaked to the press by interested parties. Thus he can never know for certain why a Cabinet has been suddenly reconstructed, why a policy defended for years is now dropped, and what importance should really be attached to the various items in a programme. Politics is inevitably personified and simplified in the public mind, into a battle between two super-leaders – appointed for life or until they are removed by intra-party *coup d'état.*

The effect of party on ministerial responsibility. So long as parties were little more than electoral caucuses, the responsibility of the minister to Parliament was an important check on bureaucratic incompetence competence become rare. Indeed the incompetent minministers disagreed with their colleagues, they could resign without losing caste. But now that the Government party controls Parliament, both resignations on principle and dismissals for incomeptence competence become rare. Indeed the incompetent minister with a departmental muddle to cover up may be kept in office for years; and the louder the demand for his dismissal, the more loyally the party oligarchy will usually support him, rightly calculating that more votes will be lost in a general election by admitting ministerial incompetence than by concealing ist.

The reduced rôle of Parliament. The Commons still have a useful job to do. But today it is not very much more useful than the job allotted by Bagehot to the House of Lords. If the peers provide one reservoir from which governments are drawn, the House of Commons is a much more important one. Although a Premier can co-opt an outsider to his Cabinet, anyone ambitious for a political career is still well-advised to obtain a seat in the Commons, and there to prove his suitability for high office by a longish period of safe party speeches and loyal adherence to the party line. In the sense that both Cabinet and Shadow Cabinet are steeped in parliamentary tradition, and manned overwhelmingly by loyal party men who are also loyal parliamentarians, we can still call our system of government 'parliamentary democracy'. We can still be proud of Question Time and of the work of the Public Accounts and Estimates Committees. We can still claim that even a government with a substantial majority must remain sensitive to the climate of parliamentary opinion. But the fact remains that in a period when effective power in all spheres of life – economic, social, political – is being concentrated in fewer and fewer hands, parliamentary control of the executive has been steadily decreasing, without being replaced by other methods of democratic control.

The danger into which we are drifting has been well described by one acute French observer. In his *Political Parties*, M. Duverger reminds us how far we have moved from the system described by Bagehot:

"Officially Great Britain has a parliamentary system ... in practice the existence of a majority governing party transforms this constitutional pattern from top to bottom. The party holds in its own hands the essential prerogatives of the legislature and the executive ... Parliament and Government are like two machines driven by the same motor – the party. The regime is not so very different in this resped from the single party system. Executive and legislature, Government and Parliament are constitutional facades: in reality the party alone exercises power."

In this passage, M. Duverger no doubt was being deliberately one-sided in order to point out a very real danger. What makes his description unbalanced is the existence of a second countervailing factor, rivalling that of the modern party, which was given just as little importance in *The English Constitution*. This factor is the vast apparatus of power and public service which the state now administers centrally and locally, and whose emergence Bagehot failed to foresee. As Parliament has been reduced to a new and more submissive rôle by the modern party machine, so the powers of the Cabinet have been eroded by the growing ascendancy of Whitehall. Bagehot, as we have seen, was profoundly suspicious of J. S. Mill's proposal to create an administrative *élite*, selected strictly by competitive public examination, which would take over the job of state management. No business, he tells us, selects its personnel in this way. And though the argument sounds naïve to-day, it seemed conclusive enough to a Victorian banker who liked the Cabinet precisely because it functioned like a board of directors.

The truth, is that a skilled bureaucracy – a bureaucracy trained from early life to its special avocation – is, though it boasts of an appearance of science, quite inconsistent with the true principles of the art of business.... One of the most sure principles is, that success depends on a due mixture of special and non-special minds – of minds which attend to the means, and of minds which attend to the end.

Bagehot believed that a civil service of the kind Mill desired would very soon arrogate to itself the common-sense business decisions which in *The English Constitution* are reserved to the inexpert minister in his department, and to the secret informal meetings of the Cabinet. He did not deny that Napoleon in France and Frederick the Great in Germany had created far more efficient public administration than anything we knew in Britain. Indeed, he was prepared to admit that any dictatorial or revolutionary régime 'is likely, whatever be its other defects, to have a far better and abler administration than any other Government.... The dictator dare not appoint a bad Minister if he would.... He will know how to mix fresh minds and used minds better; he is under a stronger motive to combine them well.' But he concluded very firmly 'that the revolutionary selection of rulers obtains administrative efficiency at a price altogether transcending its value'.

Cabinet government of this type could only function so long as state activity and the public services remained on a very small scale. Even so, as Bagehot frankly admitted, the price the business community paid for freedom from bureaucratic tyranny was the fantastic degree of incompetence revealed in the Crimean War. After 1868 both the powers of the state and the efficiency of the civil service increased very rapidly; and if Cabinet government of the classical type lasted far longer into this century than the parliamentary system to which it was linked, the reason is to be found in the readiness of the business community to tolerate, at least in peace-time, a high degree of incompetence in the highest places.

The first major change in the system was the ending of Cabinet informality by the creation of a secretariat to keep the minutes and circulate papers. This took place in World War I when Lloyd George was leading a small war Cabinet, in which all important decisions were centralised. But oldfashioned Cabinet government was reestablished in the 1920's in a form not very different from that described in *The English Constitution.* In describing the Labour Government of 1929, where he had his first experience as a Cabinet minister, Lord Morrison makes it clear that normally decisions were still taken collectively by the full Cabinet. He also suggests – probably rightly – that this was one cause at least of the Labour Government's failure to cope with the economic crisis.[3]

Already, in fact, by 1931 Cabinet Government in Bagehot's sense of the word had become an anachronism. It finally disappeared under the Churchill war régime. Once Sir Winston had accepted the leadership of the Conservative Party, his ascendancy became unchallengeable. As party leader, he controlled the Conservative machine inside and outside Parliament, and could therefore dictate his terms, not merely to the House of Commons but to the Labour members of his Cabinet. As Prime Minister and Minister of Defence, he was the apex of a pyramid of power, exerting a personal control over the whole of the war effort through a vastly expanded Cabinet secretariat, and a network of Cabinet committees, under the chairmanship of ministers who had become his agents. Over wide fields of policy and administration Cabinet Government lapsed altogether, and the informal discussions of policy which had been its lifeblood now took place exclusively between the Premier and his entourage.

When Mr. Attlee took over in 1945, he was determined that there should be no 'return to normalcy' as there was in 1918. Under his Premiership, a well-organised system of centralised decision-taking replaced the rather haphazard personal autocracy of Sir Winston. Despite his mild appearance, however, Mr. Attlee had no intention of becoming the chairman of a large traditional Cabinet. The war-time centralisation of power in the person of the Premier was in no way reduced by Mr. Attlee; and under him the enlarged Cabinet secretariat and the eleborate system of Cabinet committees were maintained and reorganised for peace-time purposes. In this way, the point of decision, which in the 1930's still rested inside the Cabinet, was now permanently transferred either downwards to these powerful Cabinet committees, or upwards to the Prime Minister himself.

The same forces which produced these changes in the structure and functions of the Cabinet were simultaneously responsible for an equally important but far less noticeable revolution in Whitehall. Since 1919 the civil service has been subjected to a double process of expansion and centralisation, which has transformed it from a collection of self-recruiting and autonomous departments into an ever more homogeneous bureaucracy controlled by a closely knit central directorate with its centre in the Treasury.

Until the end of World War I, the civil service had remained decentralised. Young men who joined a department expected to stay there. Moreover, because each department recruited its own staff under a Permanent Under-Secretary responsible to and appointed by the Departmental Minister, there was no difficulty in adding to the non-specialist civil servants recruited by the normal examination experts, technicians, and other specialists from outside.

All this was changed as the result of a decision promulgated by Lloyd George on September 4th, 1919.[4] Apparently the wartime Premier was persuaded by the then Secretary of the Treasury, Warren Fisher, that the only way of making available the best talents of all departments for post-war reconstruction was to unify the service, and recognise the Secretary of the Treasury as its Head. This ruling was followed by a further regulation laying down that the consent of the Premier (which in practice meant the head of the civil service) would be required in all departments to the appointment of the permanent heads and their deputies.

As a result of these two regulations, it has by now become the exception rather than the rule for the head of a department to be a man with life-long service within it. A circulation of *élites* from Ministry to Ministry has replaced vertical promotion to the top of a single Ministry. Instead of a cluster of departments, each with its own traditions, characteristics, and standards of recruitment, there has emerged a new horizontal stratification, with the heads forming a single, like-minded group of super bureaucrats, each confident that he can take charge at a few weeks' notice of a Ministry of which he has had no previous experience. One inevitable by-product of this process has been the tendency to give technicians and experts a lower status, and to resent any attempt by a minister to introduce 'outsiders' even into his privat office. The system is more democratic if by democracy we mean the possibility of rising from the humblest clerical work to a Permanent Under-Secretaryship. But the price to be paid for this democracy is the surrender of leadership in Whitehall to 'the Treasury mind', and an ever increasing uniformity of outlook and resistance to outside influences and new ideas.

Unification and centralisation have had two important political effects. Firstly, they have made it even more difficult for departmental ministers to get their way against their senior officials, or where necessary to dismiss them. In our new kind of civil service, the minister must normally be content with the rôle of public relations officer to his department, unless the Premier has appointed him with the express purpose of carrying out reforms. Secondly, the centralisation of authority, both for appointments and for policy decisions, under a single head of the civil service (quite recently the task has been given to a committee of three) responsible to Downing Street, has brought with it an immense accretion of power to the Prime Minister. He is now the apex not only of a highly centralised political machine, but also of an equally centralised and vastly more powerful administrative machine. In both these machines, loyalty has become the supreme virtue, and independence of thought a dangerous adventure.

Anmerkungen

1 This is described by Ostrogorski in his *Democracy and the Organisation of Political Parties.*

2 First described by Michels in *Political Parties,* 1915.

3 See *Government and Parliament,* p. 17.

4 On this topic I have closely followed '*The Apotheosis of the Dilettante*', by Dr. Thomas Balogh *(The Establishment* [1959]).

3

L. S. Amery

The Essential Nature of the Constitution

Aus: Thoughts on the Constitution, Oxford Paperback London 1964, S. 10–21, 22–32.

Das Buch erschien zuerst 1947.

L. S. Amery (1873–1955) war 1897 Fellow of All Souls College, Oxford, und über dreißig Jahre lang Unterhausabgeordneter der Konservativen Partei. Er hatte eine Reihe von Regierungsämtern inne, darunter Colonial Secretary, Secretary of State for Dominion Affairs, First Lord of the Admiralty, Secretary of State for India and Burma.

Our Constitution is still, at bottom, based on a continuous parley or conference in Parliament between the Crown, i.e. the Government as the directing and energizing element, and the representatives of the Nation whose assent and acquiescence are essential and are only to be secured by full discussion. The whole life of British politics, to quote Bagehot, 'is the action and reaction between the Ministry and the Parliament'. One might almost say to-day 'between the Ministry and the Opposition', for it is the latter upon which has devolved most of the original critical function of Parliament.
Montesquieu was not, in fact, so wide of the mark as is sometimes thought when he made the division and equipoise of powers in our Constitution its chief characteristic and the secret of its success. It must be remembered that when he published his *Esprit des Lois* in 1748 the solution of ensuring stable majorities for the Crown in Parliament by entrusting office to those who could guarantee those majorities had not been fully explored. In any case he was contrasting the English give and take between independent and coequal political forces and the independence of our judges – the natural and logical consequence of our conception of the reign of law – with the rigid centralization of all power in the French Monarchy. To that extent he was only in line with Blackstone's dictum; 'herein consists the true excellence of the English government that all the parts of it form a natural check upon each other'.[1]

Where Montesquieu went astray was in treating the division as one between the executive and legislative functions, abstractions bearing no relation to the reality of our political life. Parliament is not, and never has been, a legislature, in the sense of a body specially and primarily empowered to make laws. The function of legislation, while shared between 'King, Lords and Commons in Parliament assembled', has always been predominantly exercised by Government which, indeed, has never allowed Parliament as such to take any initiative in one of its most important fields, that of finance. The main task of Parliament is still what it was when first summoned, not to legislate or govern, but to secure full discussion and ventilation of all matters, legislative or administrative, as the condition of giving its assent to Bills, whether introduced by the Government or by private members, or its support to Ministers.

Montesquieu's error remains of interest, for on it the Fathers of the American Constitution based a constitutional structure which they believed reproduced the best features of the British Constitution. The practical inconveniences resulting from this artificial severance between functions which, in the nature of the case, are largely interdependent is an obvious weakness of the American Constitution. On the other hand, the President's freedom from the vagaries of parliamentary interference and his fixed tenure of office were, no doubt, in the past steadying factors in a young community continuously absorbing new elements with no common tradition. The Fathers of the American Constitution were, however, under no illusion as to one essential difference in the character of the two constitutions. Inspired in part by the republican tradition of the Puritans and even more by current individualist theories of the foundation of the State, they made the individual citizen the starting-point and motive power of the political process, the creator both of the President as the embodiment of the citizen's executive authority and of Congress as the embodiment of his power over legislation. On that issue they knew they were departing directly from the British tradition. It may, indeed, be said that for the underlying British conception of balance and adjustment between two coequal elements, each enjoying original and independent authority, they substituted the citizen voters, or the numerical majority of citizen voters, as the antecedent and ultimate source of authority.

More serious in its consequences, not so much for ourselves, perhaps, as for other countries, was the misreading of the essential nature of our Constitution in the last century by writers of the dominant Liberal individualist school, of whom Bagehot was the typical or, at least, most popular exponent. Interpreting the parliamentary situation of their own time in the light of their general prepossessions, they persuaded themselves that our Constitution had, in fact, become what they thought it ought to be, namely a system based on the delegation of authority by the electorate to a Parliament which, in its turn, delegated the day-by-day exercise of that power to a Cabinet which was, in substance, only a committee – to use Bagehot's phrase – of the parliamentary majority. That reinterpretation, though queried by eminent authorities like Seeley and Lowell, and contested fundamentally by so thoughtful a constitutionalist as Hearn, became the prevalent text-book theory, and still colours most current journalistic and political phraseology.[2]

There was, indeed, much in the external circumstances of the time to encourage their assumptions. The mutual interlocking of Government and Parliament had by then been fully achieved. The *laissez-faire* theories of the age in economic matters and the absence of any serious external menace since Trafalgar and Waterloo had reduced the active work, both of administration and of legislation, to a minimum. A few broad issues of general policy could be spread over prolonged and eloquent debates. Parliamentary debate as such dominated the attention of the public and created the great parliamentary figures of that day. In the comparatively evenly balanced and less strictly disciplined Parliament of the time, with both parties and the electorate itself drawn from a limited social stratum, it was not unnatural to conclude that Parliament, which so frequently upset Government, was in fact the body which governed and did so in response to the positive wishes of an actively interested electorate.

What was not foreseen by the Radical reformers of those days was that the progressive extension of the franchise, on the one hand, and the continuous increase in the volume of government work, on the other, would, by leading to stronger party organization in the country and to stricter party discipline in Parliament, reinforce the inherent tendency, in our system, for government, as such, to reassert itself whenever the opportunity or the need might arise. As for the fears of Conservative critics, whatever dangers or disadvantages may, or may not, have resulted from the spread of democracy in this country, the weakening of government has not been one of them. The strength of the innate tendency of our governmental tradition has been sufficient to overcome the danger which Burke foresaw in democracy, as preached by the individualist school, when he wrote:[3]

'No legislator has willingly placed the seat of active power in the hands of the multitude; because then it admits of no control, no regulation, no steady direction whatever. The people are the natural control on authority; but to exercise and to control together is contradictory and impossible.'

In that respect our Constitution has throughout conformed to that principle of balance between initiative and control which Burke laid down. It has never been one in which the active and originating element has been the voter, selecting a delegate to express his views in Parliament as well as, on his behalf, to select an administration conforming to those views. The startingpoint and mainspring of action has always been the Government. It is the Prime Minister who, in the name of the Crown, makes appointments and confers honours without consulting Parliament. It is the Prime Minister, in the name of the Crown, who summons Parliament. It is the Government which settles the programme of parliamentary business and directs and drives Parliament in order to secure that programme. If Parliament fails to give sufficient support it is the Government, or an alternative Government, which, in the name of the Crown, dissolves Parliament.

At a general election the voter is not in a position to choose either the kind of representative or the kind of government he would like if he had a free choice. There is a Government in being which he can confirm or else reject in favour of the alternative team. The candidates before him – the only candidates worth taking seriously – are either supporters of the team in office or of its rivals for office. It is within those narrow limits that his actual power is exercised. He may be influenced by the personality of the candidates, still more by that of the leaders of the parties, by a Government's record or by its opponents' promises, by sheer party loyalty or lighthearted desire for a change. No doubt, too, he has had his continuous share in the making of that public opinion which helps to shape parties and influence governments. But by the time it comes to an actual decision his function is the limited and essentially passive one of accepting one of two alternatives put before him.

Our whole political life, in fact, turns round the issue of government. The two-party system is often referred to as if it were the happy result of an accidental historical development, or as the consequence of a natural division between two types of mind.[5] Both statements contain a substantial element of truth. But the decisive and continuous influence has been the fact that a governing team with a majority in Parliament can normally only be displaced by another team capable of securing an alternative majority. Parties which are not in a position to make their own government may, like the Labour party in the early years of the century, represent the intrusion of a new school of political thought, content to make its voice heard and its influence felt, pending the day when they can take office for themselves. Or, like the Liberal party to-day, they may be survivals of a past political alinement, not yet despairing of resuscitation or at least of influence as a balancing factor. But they are essentially transition phenomena. The two-party system is the natural concomitant of a political tradition in which government, as such, is the first consideration, and in which the views and preferences of voters or of members of Parliament are continuously limited to the simple alternative of 'for' or 'against'. It is only under the conditions created by such a tradition that there can be any stability in a government dependent from day to day on the support of a majority in Parliament. It is precisely on that issue that the nineteenthcentury Liberal exponents of our constitutional system so grievously misled the outside world. They created the belief that it was possible successfully to combine the British form of Constitution with the prevalent continental conception, derived from the French Revolution,[6] of political power as a delegation from the individual citizen through the legislature to an executive dependent on that legislature. That conception naturally involves the widest freedom in the citizen's choice of party regarded as the end in itself. In many countries it has led to the almost indefinite multiplication of parties.[7] Another consequence has been the adoption of systems of proportional representation, usually based on party lists, in order to secure for the individual voter or individual party their fair share of the composition of the legislature. It equally implies the right of the legislature to the initiative in all respects, including finance, and the denial to the Government of the power of dissolution. All these logical deductions have, indeed, been asserted as self-evident consequences of popular and parliamentary sovereignty by the great majority of those who have been engaged in drafting the new French Constitution.

Such a system of government, not in and with Parliament, but by Parliament, is bound, by its very nature, to be weak and unstable, subject to the continual shifting and reshuffling of coalition ministries and to the influence of personal ambitions. Face to face with the growing need of the age for more governmental action and more definite leadership, it has almost everywhere broken down. The rise of dictatorships and of oneparty governments has been the almost inevitable consequence of the ineffectiveness of constitutions which reproduced the outward form of the British Constitution without that spirit of strong and stable government which is of its essence. The danger in Europe to-day is that we seem to be laying all our emphasis on urging the reproduction everywhere of those same externals, and asserting that same misinterpretation of the character of British 'democracy', instead of laying stress on the need for strong and stable government first and then leaving it to each country in the light of its particular conditions to find the way to reconciling that essential with public opinion and popular consent. We may thus be only too successful in paving the way for the spread of Communism or of some variant of Fascism that will offer what Europe most needs and what we seem unable to supply. Nor is the danger confined to Europe. All over the East and, not least, within our own Empire, we have created a demand for constitutional forms which can only work in a homogeneous community like ours and under a tradition in which all the emphasis lies on the strength and stability of government. We have never tried to think out alternative forms which could preserve the real character of our Constitution adapted to wholly different conditions.[8]

Democratic government based, in principle, at least, on delegation from below can, no doubt, be made to work. But in order to do so, the Government, however chosen, must enjoy a real measure of independence and for a reasonably long period. The United States affords one example. An even better example is Switzerland, where the executive is directly elected by the legislature and reflects its composition, but once elected, remains independent for the lifetime of the legislature. In France General de Gaulle, with a just insight into the weakness of the existing French political outlook, has recently proposed, in order to ensure continuity and as the only safeguard against the danger of dictatorship, a blend of the American and British systems in which executive power and initiative are effectively centred in the President and the Ministry and not in the Chamber.[9] What cannot work, as Mill[10] himself admitted, and as Cromwell decided somewhat more forcibly before him, is government by an elected assembly or subject to continual direct dictation and interference by such an assembly. In any case that is not the kind of government under which we live ourselves. Our system is one of democracy, but of democracy by consent and not by delegation, of government of the people, for the people, with, but not by, the people.

How far astray the prevalent mid-Victorian theory of our Constitution was from the reality even of that age, and still more so of ours, may be seen if we compare Bagehot's definition of the Cabinet as a committee of Parliament, or rather of the majority in Parliament, with the actual process by which Cabinets come into being and are, in fact, constituted. A committee usually implies definite appointment in detail by the parent body. Nothing of the sort takes place in the creation of a British Cabinet. The starting-point is the selection by the Monarch of a Prime Minister. The Monarch's choice, like that of the voter, may in most cases be very limited...

Far wider is the field of choice open to a newly appointed Prime Minister. No doubt he has to consider the claims and views of lead-in members of his party in both Houses. But, subject to Parliament putting up with his selection of his colleagues and his arrangement of offices, he has a very free hand in shaping his government according to his own view of what is likely to work best and according to his personal preferences. It is for him to decide on the size of the cabinet and what Ministers to include in it. He may consult a few leading colleagues or the Chief Whip or his personal cronies. In 1929 Mr. MacDonald settled his chief appointments in consultation with Messrs. Snowden, Clynes, Henderson, and Thomas. What formal or informal consultations may have taken place in the formation of the present Cabinet is not within my knowledge. Hitherto, in this country, at any rate, the Prime Minister has never been under any sort of direct dictation either from Parliament or from a Party Executive outside in making up his government. He may go outside the party ranks, or even outside Parliament, to choose someone whom he may think specially fitted for a particular post. Thus in 1903 Mr. Balfour offered the Colonial Office to Lord Milner, who was then still High Commissioner in South Africa and had never played any part in parliamentary life. In 1923 Mr. Baldwin offered the Chancellorship of the Exchequer to Mr. McKenna, a Liberal ex-Cabinet Minister, who declined on grounds of health, while Mr. MacDonald in 1924 made Lord Chelmsford, a non-party ex-Viceroy, First Lord of the Admiralty. Even more remarkable in its disregard of his party's views was Mr. Baldwin's appointment in that same year of Mr. Churchill to the Exchequer. At that time Mr. Churchill was almost the last person to whom Conservatives would have dreamt of entrusting that key position, not only because he had until only quite recently been a political opponent, but because he was known still to be vehemently opposed to the main constructive policy of the

Party. But the appointment was made and the Conservative Party in Parliament, though never quite reconciled to it, grumbled and submitted.

Few dictators, indeed, enjoy such a measure of autocratic power as is enjoyed by a British Prime Minister while in process of making up his Cabinet. In France or in any other continental country which has imitated the outward form, but not the essentials, of our Constitution, newly appointed Prime Ministers have had to go round hat in hand to appeal for co-operation from political rivals each determined to make his own bargain as to the particular office he might wish to hold or as to the filling of other offices, and by no means sure that he might not do better for himself by holding back and waiting for the next ministerial reshuffle. With us there has been no instance of a Prime Minister failing to form a government owing to the irreconcilable claims or views of party colleagues since Russell's failure to form a government in 1845 because Grey would not serve with Palmerston. It was, indeed, widely bruited about in 1905 that Sir Henry Campbell-Bannerman could not form a workable government in face of the anticipated refusal of the Liberal Imperialist leaders, Asquith, Grey, and Haldane, to serve under him. But when it came to the point the strength of the Prime Minister's position easily asserted itself and they joined unconditionally. In 1916 Mr. Asquith resigned in the confident but, as the event proved, mistaken belief that, except for Mr. Bonar Law and Sir Edward Carson, no Conservative or Liberal of any standing would be willing to serve under Mr. Lloyd George.

A British Prime Minister may, no doubt, while forming his Cabinet, be besieged by insistent candidates for this or that office, but rarely is such a candidate prepared to reject the Prime Minister's final allocation. Refusal may mean exclusion from office, not merely for that Parliament, but for good and all. In 1924 Sir Robert Horne, who had been a successful President of the Board of Trade and Chancellor of the Exchequer, refused the Ministry of Labour which Mr. Baldwin offered him. He was never considered for office again. It is only exceptionally forceful or fortunate political rogue elephants that, once extruded from the governing herd, can find their way back into it, as both Mr. Churchill and your present lecturer discovered for a decade after 1929.

This power of the Prime Minister to appoint, reshuffle, or dismiss his colleagues continues throughout his term of office. It is, no doubt, mainly influenced by considerations of administrative or parliamentary success or failure. But it is a purely personal authority and makes the Prime Minister something very much more than a *primus inter pares* in the Cabinet. His exact position must always depend in large measure upon his own personality and that of his colleagues in the Cabinet, as well as upon parliamentary and party influences outside. But he is, in effect, both captain and man at the helm, enjoying, as undisputed working head of the State, a power far greater than that of the American President – so long as he does not actually forfeit the allegiance of naturally deferential and loyal colleagues in the Cabinet or of his followers in Parliament.

The fact that Parliament does not appoint but accepts a Prime Minister and a Cabinet is even more strikingly evident in time of war or acute crisis. Mr. Asquith's Coalition Cabinet of 1915 resulted immediately from Lord Fisher's resignation as First Sea Lord and from consequent negotiations with the Conservative leaders. It may, however be said to have conformed to a general desire on the part of the House of Commons that he should strengthen his government by including the leaders of the Opposition. But the Lloyd George War Cabinet at the end of 1916 was not one that could have emerged from any method of ascertaining the wishes of Parliament beforehand. Few Liberals and still fewer Conservatives would have actually chosen Mr. Lloyd George as Prime Minister. Nor was there any demand, outside a very small circle, for a drastic change in the structure and working of the Cabinet as such. The whole affair was, in effect, a Palace Revolution brought about by a handful of men in the inner circle of the Asquith Government who were convinced that the war could not be won under the existing leadership and by the existing methods.

Still more notable, in that respect, was the formation of the MacDonald-Baldwin-Samuel Coalition of 1931. It is doubtful whether a Gallup poll taken in advance in favour of that particular solution would have secured even 10 per cent. support from either Socialists or Conservatives in Parliament. The bulk of the Socialist party, indeed, broke away as soon as it was formed, and the Conservatives only acquiesced on the most explicit assurances given by Mr. Baldwin to a party meeting that the emergency arrangement would be terminated the moment a balanced budget had been passed. By then, however, Ministers had begun to feel at home in their offices and to persuade themselves that the economic emergency still called for a 'National Government'. Unable to agree upon any policy to meet the emergency, they appealed to the country for a 'doctor's mandate'. The public, impressed by the vigour of the effort to balance the budget, and persuaded by a vast consensus of political and non-political 'expert' authority of the imminent danger of inflation and soaring prices, gave, by its vote, a majority in Parliament of ten to one, not so much for the Coalition, as against the unhappy and bewildered rump of the Socialist party. The subsequent necessity of having some sort of positive economic policy was met, for several months, by the fantastic expedient of certain Ministers dissociating themselves from the collective repsonsibility of the Cabinet and voting against its measures, and by their resignation after the Ottawa agreements.

The change of government in 1940 was, indeed, the direct result of a parliamentary demonstration of dissatisfaction with Mr. Neville Chamberlain's war leadership, and Mr. Chamberlain's recommendation to the King to send for Mr. Churchill coincided with the general feeling that the latter had the gifts which the occasion needed. As the basis of his government Mr. Churchill started with a more or less conventional interparty coalition. But he freely enlarged and strengthened his administration by bringing in able outsiders to political life, fixing them up with seats in one or other House of Parliament as might be convenient.

I have purposely dwelt at some length on these particular instances in order to make it clear that, however essential it may be for a British government, once formed, to be sufficiently acceptable to Parliament to secure support in the division lobbies, its formation is in no sense the result of a parliamentary initiative and that its composition may bear little relation to the wishes and views of Parliament at the time. They are the result of an independent process beginning with the Monarch and carried on by the Prime Minister. It is still the Monarch who selects the individual who is likely to make the most effective Prime Minister and that individual who acts on his own responsible judgement of the situation. The Cabinet which he has formed then unite to support him to the best of their ability in administration and in debate, while those useful adjuncts to the Cabinet system, the Government Whips, fulfil their day-by-day duty of exhortation, encouragement, or discreet menace, in order to maintain the disciplined support of the back benches.[11] Government and Parliament, however closely intertwined and harmonized, are still separate and independent entities, fulfilling the two distinct functions of leadership, direction, and command, on the one hand, and of critical discussion and examination on the other. They start from separate historical origins, and each is perpetuated in accordance with its own methods and has its own continuity.

The continuity of government in our system is symbolized in the person of the Monarch. But it is also maintained in substance by the fact that the vast majority of the servants of the Crown carry on their duties permanently. What we call a change of government is, in fact, only a change in that small, if important, element which is required to direct the general policy, while securing for it parliamentary and public support or at least acquiescence. A change of government, to quote Hearn, means that:

'The vigour and uniform action of the Executive are maintained; but the direction of its forces is altered according to the wishes of the legislature ... the vessel of state is entrusted to other hands and proceeds upon a different course. But it is essential to the success of the operation both that the crew should be skilled in their work and that they should render due obedience to their commander for the time being, whoever he may be.'

The parallel, perhaps, suggests a much greater freedom than does in fact exist to change the ship's course – or, rather, the course of a fleet composed of a number of separate ships. Each of our great departments of State has its own tradition and policy, founded on long experience. Its crew has an accumulated knowledge of wind and weather, of reefs and shoals, by which a new captain is inevitably guided. It has its own private cargoes and destinations which a new captain soon tends to make his own and to advocate with vigour and conviction at the captains' conference. It may have projects for which the last captain could not secure that conference's assent and may return to the charge with better hope. In any case by far the greater part of the field of administration, and even of policy, is governed by factors which cannot be changed by party theories or prepossessions, or at any rate not to the extent which Ministers may have thought or said when in Opposition. The advent of a Socialist Government has not noticeably softened the heart of M. Molotov, or overcome the antagonisms of Hindu and Moslem in India or of Jew and Arab in Palestine. Housing raises the same issues of materials and man-power, of the relation of the central government to the local authorities, of the wishes of the people to be housed, whatever the political complexion of a government. The emphasis may be changed, new methods introduced. But much of whatever is done has to be a continuation of what was done before.

Our system of government is usually described as Parliamentary

Responsible Government. It would be difficult to find a better description. But it must be remembered, first of all, that Parliamentary Government means government, not by Parliament, but to use the old phrase, government 'by the King in Parliament'. Secondly, that the responsibility is not merely one towards the majority in Parliament. Ministers on taking office accept a first and dominant responsibility to the Crown, as representing the unity and continuity of the life of the nation and of the Empire, for defending the wider national and Imperial interest. They accept, as I have pointed out just above, a corresponding individual responsibility towards the particular services over which they have been called to preside. As members of a Cabinet they accept, over and above their individual ministerial responsibility, a responsibility to and for their colleagues which is the basis of the collective responsibility of the Cabinet. As members of Parliament themselves they are responsible to Parliament as a whole and to the nation for the effective working of Parliament as the centre of our national life, for the maintenance of full and free discussion of every aspect of government policy, and for support of the Speaker in upholding the dignity and impartiality of debate. It is only subject to these wider responsibilities that, as party leaders, they owe a responsibility to their own party for promoting its particular views and forwarding its interests.

The word 'responsibility' has, however, two senses. It connotes not only accountability to an outside or final authority. It also connotes a state of mind, which weighs the consequences of action and then acts, irrespective, it may be, of the concurrence or approval of others. It is the strength of our constitutional system that it encourages and fosters responsibility in that higher sense. A British government is not merely responsible to those who have appointed it or keep it in office in the sense in which an agent is responsible to his principal. It is an independent body which on taking office assumes the responsibility of leading and directing Parliament and the nation in accordance with its own judgement and convictions. Members of Parliament are no mere delegates of their constituents, but, as Burke pointed out, representatives of the nation, responsible, in the last resort, to their own conscience.

Nor in the responsibility of the Opposition in these various respects any less than that of the Government and of its supporters. On the Opposition rests the main responsibility for what was once the critical function of Parliament as a whole, while at the same time it directs its criticisms with a view to convincing public opinion of its

own fitness for office. It is with the importance of this responsibility in mind that Lowell in his *Government of England* said that:
'The expression "His Majesty's Opposition" ... embodies the greatest contribution of the 19th century to the art of government, that of a party out of power which is recognised as perfectly loyal to the institutions of the State and ready to come into office without a shock to the political traditions of the nation.'
The same point was made by Lord Simon:[12]
'Our parliamentary system will work as long as the responsible people in different parties accept the view that it is better that the other side should win than that the constitution should be broken.'
The combination of responsible leadership by government with responsible criticism in Parliament is the essence of our Constitution. Our aim must be to preserve it through the inevitable changes which the needs and demands of each generation bring about in its outward structure and in the adjustment of its parts.

Anmerkungen

1 So, too, Hearn argues that the classification of governments by external form, e.g. monarchical, oligarchic, democratic, gives no clue to their real character, and points out the danger to freedom involved in any system of government which places an undivided sovereignty in any one hand or set of hands: 'The distinctive character of a free or constitutional government is the composite character of its sovereignty and not the plurality of sovereigns. The distinctive character of Imperialism (i.e. Caesarism or dictatorship) is the unity of its power, not the individuality of the person in whom it is vested .... If the whole power of the State be centred in one body, if thought and speech and action depend upon the will of one person or one set of persons, that Government ... is an absolute Government.' – *The Government of England.*

2 How little real importance the writers of that period assigned to the part played by the Crown, as embodied officially in the Cabinet, is indicated by the fact that not one of the eighteen chapters of Mill's *Representative Government* is devoted to the functions of the Cabinet. So stalwart a survivor of the mid-Victorian Liberalism as my old chief Lord Courtney of Penwith, in his *Working Constitution of the United Kingdom,* writing as late as 1901, could still dismiss the Cabinet in five pages out of nearly 200 devoted to Parliament, and could speak of the 'absolutely unqualified supremacy of Parliament' as 'embodying the supreme will of the State' to which 'every partial authority must yield'. In this respect the Socialist party has inherited many of the theoretical misconceptions of its Liberal precursors and Mr. Laski himself has referred to the executive as a 'Committee of the Legislature'.

4 *Appeal from the New to the Old Whigs.*

5 The actual shape of the Chamber with its direct confrontation of the two Front Benches at close range helps to emphasize the continuous conflict between two sets of competitors for office. The case for its retention was eloquently stated by Mr. Churchill in the debate on the rebuilding of the House of Commons in January 1945.

6 Disraeli's phrase, 'the Anglo-Gallic scheme', shrewdly summarized both the conception and the absurdity of its application to any and every country, regardless of its traditions or social structure. 'If the barren adoption of a form of government by France, styled by courtesy the English Constitution, must be classed among the prime follies of human conduct, what language are we to use when the Anglo-Gallic scheme is gravely introduced to the consideration of the lazzaroni of Naples and the hidalgos of Spain; we seem to have arrived at the climax of human absurdity.' – *Vindication of the English Constitution*, ch. vii.

7 There were twelve parties in the Italian Parliament before the Fascist Revolution and, at one time, over thirty in Germany and in Czechoslovakia.

8 The point is one made by Burke in his letter to a Member of the French National Assembly: 'When I praised the British Constitution and wished it to be well studied, I did not mean that its exterior form and positive arrangement should become a model for you or for any people servilely to copy. I meant to recommend the principles from which it has grown and the policy on which it has been progressively improved out of elements common to you and to us.'

9 'Executive power cannot issue from the... Parliament exercising legislative power without degenerating into a confusion of functions in which the Government would in a short time be nothing but a collection of delegations.... Executive power must therefore emanate from the Head of the State, placed above parties and elected by the electoral college which includes Parliament but is wider than Parliament.... It is his function to name Ministers and above all to name the Prime Minister who is called upon to direct the policy and work of the government. It is the function of the Head of the State... to preside at Cabinet meetings and exercise there that influence of continuity which no nation can do without. It is his function to serve as arbitrator above political contingencies, either nominally through the Cabinet or in moments of serious confusion, by inviting the country to express its sovereign decision in elections.' – General de Gaulle, Bayeux, 16 June 1946.

10 'Instead of the function of governing, for which it is radically unfit, the proper office of a representative assembly is to watch and control the government:... To be at once the nation's Committee of Grievances and its Congress of Opinions.... Nothing but the restriction of the function of representative bodies within these rational limits, will enable the benefits of popular control to be enjoyed in conjunction with the no less important requisites (growing ever more important as human affairs increase in scale and complexity) of skilled legislation and aministration.' – J. S. Mill, *Representative Government.*

11 The Cabinet is an autocracy exerted with the utmost publicity, under a constant fire of criticism, and tempered by the force of public opinion, the risk of a vote of lack of confidence and the prospects of the next election.' – Lowell, *Government of England.*

12 In an address to the Empire Parliamentary Conference in 1937.

4

A. H. Brown

Prime Ministerial Power

Aus: Public Law, incorporating The British Journal of Administrative Law. London 1968, S. 28–51, 96–118.

A. H. Brown –, früher Lecturer im Department für Politikwissenschaft und Soziologie der Universität Glasgow, ist jetzt Fellow am St. Antony's College in Oxford.

Discussion of the Prime Minister's powers is not a new subject for academic writers on politics, but it has been taken up with a renewed gusto in recent years and has become a familiar theme of journalism. It would be going too far to say it has been a subject of debate, for whatever the reservations many academics may have had about the thesis propounded, for example, in R. H. S. Crossman's introduction to the 1963 edition of *Bagehot,* they have been in no hurry to commit them to print, other than implicitly. Prominent among those who have taken issue with the thesis are D. N. Chester[1] and G. W. Jones.[2] But the fashionable view would still appear to be that the Prime Minister's powers have greatly increased in recent years.

According to Crossman, "the post-war epoch has seen the final transformation of Cabinet Government into Prime Ministerial Government."[3] Bertrand de Jouvenel has devoted attention to what he calls "contemporary regimes where the body politic is in fact vested in one man" and he believes that the British system has joined the trend in that direction[4]. A former senior civil servant in the Cabinet Office, Sir George Mallaby, has written: "Whatever the constitutional position of the Prime Minister, in practice he is infinitely more than *primus inter pares.* The deference accorded to any British Prime Minister is very striking indeed." Cabinet ministers "will pay special attention to his views and his leadership, with a strong inclination to sink their own opinions and defer to his."[5] F.

W. G. Benemy, in his study of prime ministerial power, goes so far as to conclude that "the Prime Minister is sovereign – that is to say, he governs with an absolute authority, whereas in theory he is at bottom a Member of Parliament at the mercy of Parliament."[6] More recently, the presidential thesis has been fully accepted by Humphry Berkeley, who argues that there has been a great increase in the individual power of the Prime Minister in the past fifty years and regards this as the central problem facing parliamentary reformers.[7]
But if the notion of prime ministerial government is particularly popular at the moment, there is nothing especially new in the idea that the Prime Minister is obtaining an ever-increasing power. This view has been advanced periodically throughout the present century. Sidney Low argued that "the Premier is acquiring the attributes of an Imperial Chancellor, and ... he is performing certain duties to which the 'collective responsibility' of the Cabinet cannot easily be applied. The point was emphasised when the Imperial Conference of 1907 resolved that in future the Prime Minister, not the Colonial Secretary, should be the ex officio president."[8] For Ramsay Muir the Prime Minister was a "potentate who appoints and can dismiss his colleagues. He is, in fact, though not in law, the working head of the State, endued with such a plenitude of power as no other constitutional ruler in the world possesses, not even the President of the United States."[9] But, in Muir's view, the Prime Minister holds this power "so long as he controls a majority in the House of Commons" and "it is necessary that he should carry his colleagues in the Cabinet, or a large majority of them, along with him."[10] These qualifications are of major importance[11] and if they still hold good, they make nonsense of the description of the Prime Minister as a wielder of "autocratic" power. Leo Amery, in his Chichele lectures of 1946,[12] was another who took an ample view of the Prime Minister's powers, but he was also acutely conscious of how much the exercise of power varied according to personality. Many of Amery's arguments are those used by more recent writers to illustrate the Prime Minister's great and growing powers, despite the fact that Amery was not in a position to take post-Second World War experience into account when he formulated them.[13] Harold Laski, in his last published work,[14] though he took issue with Amery on a number of points, much more precisely anticipated the modern prime ministerial government theory, while employing more evidence both to qualify and to substantiate his argument than is advanced by some of his successors. He believed that "a Prime Minister with a will of

his own has the same power over the business of the Cabinet as the Cabinet, in its turn, has over the business of the House"[15] and argued that "there is a problem of some real significance involved in this growth of the Prime Minister's power."[16] He did not welcome this development (as he saw it) and cited Chamberlain's conduct of foreign policy in support of his opposition. One will not, however, find either Amery or Laski guilty of the kind of crude *non sequitur* of a more recent observer: "Since a prime minister without a majority in the House of Commons is an impossibility, he is in a position to make any law he thinks fit."[17] This statement not only exaggerates the power of the Executive, but could scarcely be more question-begging in its assumptions about the Prime Minister's role in policy-making. The belief that "government" and "Prime Minister" are terms which can be used synonymously is much too simple.

Very few people, of course, would suggest that the Prime Minister is only *primus inter pares*, even in Morley's sense – still less with the emphasis on the *pares*. To attack this view of the Prime Minister's powers is to attack a virtually undefended position. As party leader, as head of the government (and thus appointing and dismissing ministers), as the ultimate co-ordinating minister, as chairman of the Cabinet, and as the member of the government who receives most publicity on radio and television and in the Press, the Prime Minister possesses a formidable set of advantages.

But if a Prime Minister has an influence and authority greater than that of any one of his colleagues (and few would argue with such a statement), it is by no means equally clear that this is a recent development. Whether there has been significant change in the importance of, and the powers attached to, the office of Prime Minister since the Second World War (perhaps even in the present century) is debatable. In the late nineteenth century, as now, a Prime Minister's power depended largely upon his relative standing in the Cabinet and in the parliamentary party. The modern office of Prime Minister, together with the modern position of the party leader, really dates from the extension of the suffrage in the second half of the nineteenth century. It was not until after the Second Reform Act that a Prime Minister could begin to rely upon a parliamentary majority. It became increasingly necessary for members of a government and their back-bench supporters to co-operate and to maintain a mutual loyalty in order to retain the confidence of the electorate. As this was a two-way loyalty, in some respects a Prime Minister's freedom of action was curtailed. In addition, it should not be overlooked that even before the Second Reform Act there is no shortage of cases of Prime Ministers playing a decisive part in the making of particular policies. There is no need to rely upon the example of such an outstanding Prime Minister as the Younger Pitt. Even a comparatively lethargic one like Melbourne could, when he roused himself, change the minds of his Cabinet.[18] If the evidence of Parkes, one of the leading radicals, is to be accepted, this was true of the franchise provision of the Municipal Corporation Act of 1835. Parkes anticipated strong opposition from the Cabinet. Writing to Durham in October 1836, Parkes stated that "they swore in my presence that they would never agree to Household Municipal Franchise. But Ellice and I convinced Lord Melbourne and he converted them."[19] With Melbourne this was perhaps less than a common occurrence. In the person of Peel, the Prime Minister was very much stronger. Peel was able to exercise a detailed control over government business which the scope and complexity of governmental activity was later to render impossible. As one of the abler members of Peel's government put it: "We never had a minister who was so truly a first minister as he is. He makes himself felt in every department, and is really cognisant of the affairs of each. Lord Grey could not master such an amount of business. Canning could not do it. Now he is an actual minister, and is indeed *capax imperii.*"[20] Gladstone, in his farewell interview with Peel, said to him: "Your government has not been carried on by a cabinet, but by the heads of departments each in communication with you."[21] In agreeing, Peel criticised the Melbourne government as "a mere government of departments without a centre of unity."[22] Queen Victoria believed that not only was Peel "completely *master* of his Cabinet" but that "the Prime Minister *ought* to be," and in this respect she coupled the names of Derby and Palmerston with that of Peel.[23]

It is not necessarily the case that the Prime Minister who ignores minute detail is less powerful than one who becomes engrossed in it. If a particular Prime Minister can impose his will on Cabinet colleagues on the most important matters, he may reasonably be regarded as very powerful. As Robert Blake has written of Disraeli: "What made him emphatically a strong Prime Minister was that he seldom relinquished his purpose, or failed to get his way when he had decided on a policy. Of course, he did not always have a policy, but this was not a sign of inability to persuade or direct his Cabinet, rather of ill health, weariness and old age."[24] (Blake's second sentence touches on the tricky question of a Prime Minister's *latent power*, and the implications of this notion are sometimes carried too far. It is advisable to base an assessment of the Prime Minister's powers on what Prime Ministers do and do not do, rather than upon speculation about what they might hypothetically do, if only they chose to.) The possibility of a Prime Minister's *detailed* control over *certain areas* of policy in the last quarter of the nineteenth century was illustrated when Gladstone held the office of Chancellor of the Exchequer as well as that of Prime Minister from 1880 to 1882 and Salisbury on three occasions held jointly the offices of Prime Minister and Foreign Secretary.[25]

If a graph could be constructed to illustrate prime ministerial power from the time of the Second, or even of the First, Reform Act to the present day, it would show nothing as consistent as a steadily (far less rapidly) rising curve. It would be a picture of ups and downs, in which it would be possible to imagine a Prime Minister in the early 1840s appearing at a higher point than one in the mid-1930s and one in the early 1920s above one in the mid-1960s. Unfortunately, however, the question of prime ministerial power cannot be tackled in this way. By a selective use of evidence, as plausible a case could be made for the general proposition that the Prime Minister's power has declined as for the view that it has increased. It depends upon which of his "powers" one is talking about.[26] If progress is to be made, it becomes necessary to isolate the major variables and to attempt to distinguish the growth points in the Prime Minister's power from the aspects in which it has remained the same or has even declined.

The power of the Executive

There is no more important variable than that of the power of the Executive as a whole. A good deal of confusion arises through a failure to make a distinction between the position of the Prime Minister in relation to his government colleagues, on the one hand, and the increasing role of government in society (and its strengthened position in relation to Parliament) on the other. It is generally agreed that the powers and functions of the Executive in Britain have increased. There is a fairly general acceptance of the mixed economy, of governmental regulation of the economy, and of the "Welfare State" with the enormously expanded functions of government departments which it entails. Many who accept that this expansion has taken place argue that, as a consequence, individual ministers are less able to run their departments than they were in the past. Somewhat paradoxically, this point has been linked with the view that the Prime Minister's control has increased. As a matter of fact, it was precisely because the government as a whole did less over a century ago that Peel, for instance, was able to do more in the way of controlling policy within the various departments than a modern Prime Minister could hope to attempt. As the scope of governmental activity has broadened, so the Prime Minister has come to *share* in an increased governmental power. But given the number of departments now in existence, and the nature and extent of their responsibilities, it is extremely difficult for the Prime Minister to get into the policy-making process at an early enough stage to exert influence. He does not have time to participate in policy-making within each department to anything like the extent of either the individual responsible minister or of the ablest Prime Minister of an earlier generation.

There has been a slightly paradoxical trend towards greater governmental power, of which one major beneficiary is the Prime Minister, while, at the same time, an increasing number of decisions are being taken of which the Prime Minister knows nothing (or which are presented to him as a *fait accompli*) for the very simple reason that an increasing number of governmental decisions are being taken. In so far as he participates in decisions about redistribution of industry and employment, the Prime Minister is doing things which his nineteenth century predecessors could not contemplate. But if increased power is, in this respect, a concomitant of changing functions, the problems which new functions pose for the Prime Minister in the form of proliferating ministries (keeping abreast with their manifold activities) should not be overlooked. The roles of extra-departmental bodies within the Executive (*e.g.*, the public corporations, the National Economic Development Council, and the Prices and Incomes Board) further diffuse power, as, indeed, does the part played in the policy process by the organised interests, whose numbers have considerably increased during the present century.

Appointments

There is a strong case for regarding the Prime Minister's right to appoint ministers, to dismiss them and to advise the monarch to dissolve Parliament as definite growth points in his power. But more far-reaching conclusions have frequently been reached about the power that the exercise of these functions has placed in the Prime Minister's hands than the evidence will support. So far as the actual appointing of ministers is concerned, this is a growth point in the Prime Minister's power only in the sense that there is a growing number of governmental posts to be filled. To that extent, his patronage has increased, but what the implications of this are for his control of personnel needs to be carefully argued, rather than merely asserted. In other respects the power is not a new one. The distinctions which Bagehot made in his discussion of Cabinet appointments still essentially hold good. That is to say, there is still a distinction between those ministers who, because of their party standing, the Prime Minister must include, and those whose presence in the Cabinet is not vital to the security and acceptability of the Prime Minister and in relation to whom he has a larger element of real discretionary power.[27] Similarly, Bagehot was perfectly correct in suggesting that the Prime Minister has a greater freedom in deciding to which office a minister will be sent than in deciding who will be left out of his Cabinet. G. W. Jones, in his stimulating article, examines Harold Wilson's Cabinet appointments of October 1964, and concludes that "the Prime Minister has not a free hand in the choice of his colleagues or the allocation of their offices."[28] It is one thing, however, to accept that in practice a Prime Minister does not have complete freedom of choice in selecting a Cabinet[29] and quite another to hold that he is virtually obliged to send certain ministers to particular offices. Jones writes of Wilson that "the actual offices to which he allocated the individuals showed very few surprises and suggested that he had not much freedom to manoeuvre. Most went to offices to which they had already staked a claim, as members of the Shadow Cabinet, as front-bench spokesmen, and because they had some expertise or interest in the subject."[30] If, however, many ministers went to the ministry they had "shadowed," quite a few did not. Mr. Michael Stewart, who had been Shadow Minister of Housing immediately before the election, went, first, to Education, then to the Foreign Office, and then to the Department of Economic Affairs. The present Leader of the House, Mr. Richard Crossman, Shadow Secretary for Education, went to the Ministry of Housing. But much more basic is the question: who allocates the "shadow" duties? It is, in fact, the Leader of the Opposition. When the party leader becomes Prime Minister it is natural enough that he should not completely change his mind concerning what are appropriate duties for a particular person. His liberty to send a minister to whatever office he likes is certainly to some extent checked by the prudential consideration that it would be unwise to put a colleague of high party standing in low-status office. But this does not bind him to give an M.P. a particular office. Of course, when the range of jobs which a senior minister would be prepared to accept is a narrow one, to that degree, the Prime Minister's choice is narrowed. Thus Wilson was able to give George Brown, initially, not the Foreign Office which he wanted, but one of the two major economic ministries. At the reshuffle he had less room for manoeuvre, and Brown got the Foreign Secretaryship which Wilson had shown marked reluctance to grant him. On the other hand, throughout his premiership, Macmillan successfully ignored the obvious qualifications of R. A. Butler for the Foreign Office, and for a considerable time kept Hailsham out of major office, despite the fact that he was later to support him in the struggle for succession to the party leadership.

But much more drastic implications are commonly drawn from the Prime Minister's power of appointment than a mere recognition that some ministers more than others owe their position to the Prime Minister, and that the Prime Minister has a certain amount of liberty to place them in the office of his choice. It is frequently asserted that unless an M. P. shows complete loyalty to the Prime Minister and toes the party line, he stands a poor chance of promotion. It is argued that an able man may be kept out of the government because he has been too much of a rebel or because of a personal quirk on the part of the Prime Minister. It is contended that a minister may be kept out of higher office because he has not been an ally of the Prime Minister in the past or has subsequently failed to cultivate his friendship. But there is little evidence to suggest that men of real ability, well qualified for office in every respect, are being kept out on account of the purely personal disfavour of the Prime Minister. Where personal dislike enters in, the feeling is often mutual. It is true, to take an example, that Mr. Macmillan did not give office to Mr. Robin Turton and that some personal animosity apparently existed between them. But since Mr. Turton disliked Mr. Macmillan as much as Macmillan disliked Turton, it is doubtful if the latter would have been prepared to serve.

Up to a point it could be argued that, so far as the ranks of junior minister are concerned, a conformist of mediocre ability will be more likely to achieve promotion to this level than the mediocre rebel. But there is little evidence to suggest that people of outstanding qualities do not achieve office because they are rebels. Even in the filling of junior posts, a Prime Minister, when forming a government, tries to achieve some kind of balance between different strands of party opinion. This has the effect of bringing in rebels and potential rebels from both right and left. In a reshuffle a Prime Minister will be governed by the overriding requirements of introducing men of promise and of consolidating the government's standing with those sections of the party and country with which it is in most need of improving its position. These factors were operative in Mr. Wilson's ministerial reshuffle of early 1967, a reshuffle which further illustrated the point that deviation from the party line is by no means an obstacle in the path of the able back-bencher. Orthodoxy is not necessarily the road to promotion, and even for junior posts (in cases where the person may be expected to go still higher), ability, and the qualities of mind and personality worthy of ministerial office, count for more than an M.P.'s loyalist or deviationist record. On the January 1967 reshuffle, the lobby correspondent of *The Guardian* reported that "some ministers have ... been mildly surprised at the political complexion of the tiny band of entirely new Ministers."[31] Of the five new ministers, Mr. Fernyhough, Mr. Buchan and Mr. Freeson could be regarded as being distinctly left of centre and Mr. Hattersley as being on the right wing of the party. Some of Mr. Wilson's other appointments (and retentions) have also been criticised on the different ground that there are men probably superior in administrative ability languishing on the back benches. This is not such a devastating criticism of a Prime Minister as is sometimes imagined. A Prime Minister cannot simply abide by the dictates of smooth public administration. He is leader of a party as well as head of the government. An unwillingness to lose friends and stir up resentments which could have political consequences is at least as much a characteristic of the successful Prime Minister as the overrated attribute of being a "good butcher."

At the top there is also evidence which suggests a poor correlation between rebelliousness and an unsuccessful career. It is noteworthy that four of the last five British Prime Ministers (Churchill, Eden, Macmillan and Wilson) were, at different points of their careers, very prominent rebels within their party. Rebellious tendencies do not lead to the automatic rejection of able men. A Prime Minister will be judged, not only by the way in which he plays his personal part within the government, but by how his government as a whole performs. This gives him a very strong incentive to disregard purely personal friendships or dislikes and to concentrate on ability and balance. The search for men of ability and the attempt to maintain harmony in the party will inevitably lead the Prime Minister into rebel territory.

Dismissing Ministers

A Prime Minister's ability to dismiss colleagues as well as to promote them might be regarded as one of the growth points in his power. Though, on such a clear case as Palmerston's failure to act in accordance with agreed Cabinet policy over the Louis Napoleon *coup d'état*, Russell was able to insist upon the Foreign Secretary's resignation, much later in the nineteenth century Gladstone met with strong resistance on one occasion when he tried to engineer a minister's resignation. In the words of Harcourt: "I know that he tried it in one case for convenience of reconstruction: he was point blank refused, and acquiesced."[32] Harcourt was referring to the case of Lord Carlingford, whom Gladstone wished to remove from his office of Lord Privy Seal in order to bring Lord Rosebery into the Cabinet in 1884. But writing some years later, Harcourt exaggerated when he said that Gladstone "entertained great doubts as to the right of a Prime Minister to require a Cabinet Minister to resign."[33] The practical considerations regarded as relevant in 1884 were not so very different from those taken into account by Prime Ministers today. *If*, however, a Prime Minister's constitutional right to dismiss ministers could be doubted in the late nineteenth century, it can hardly be questioned today. The premierships of Attlee and Macmillan did much to underline this point. But the Macmillan purge of July 1962 proves less than is sometimes claimed for his action. Dismissing colleagues has its dangers for the Prime Minister. Those ministers who found themselves on the back-benches at very short notice were not all able to disguise their discontent, a discontent which was shared by a section of their parliamentary colleagues and by a considerable number of Conservative Party supporters in the country.[34] One of the ministers who retained his place during those July Days, Reginald Bevins, expressed his puzzlement strongly: "This was making enemies on a grand scale, enemies of those dismissed, enemies of their friends in Parliament, and shattering confidence in the Party at large."[35] He even added: "Of one thing I was then convinced: no Conservative Prime Minister could behave like that and still survive. In July 1962 Harold Macmillan committed political suicide more certainly than if he had himself resigned."[36] Lord Butler, making the same point less dogmatically, agreed that an action such as this could help to stimulate countervailing forces within the government party "because all the people who go out have friends who mobilise round them."[37] In Macmillan's case, the Prime Minister's reputation did suffer as a result of such large-scale dismissals, and there was particular back-bench resentment at the way he had rewarded the loyalty of Selwyn Lloyd. A Prime Minister's constitutional right to dismiss ministers is not in dispute, but the idea that a Prime Minister can get rid of ministers more or less at will is an over-simplification. Everything depends upon the minister and upon the circumstances. If a minister is very inefficient, or if he is being run by his department, this will be known to other ministers. When the Prime Minister demotes or sacks the man who is not up to the job, he can rely upon the tacit approval of his colleagues and the cheerful acquiescence of those who hope to take the place of the departing minister. But to dismiss a man of high party standing, or one held by a large section of the parliamentary party to be doing a good job, remains a procedure so dangerous that a Prime Minister can seldom contemplate it.

The corollary of the exaggerated idea of the Prime Minister's practical political freedom to *dismiss* a minister is the notion that a Prime Minister can now face the *resignation* of even important ministers without much need for worry. Macmillan's placid acceptance of the resignations from his Cabinet of Mr. Peter Thorneycroft and of Lord Salisbury is sometimes cited as evidence in support of such a view. It is true that these were senior ministers and that the Macmillan government survived their departure without much difficulty. But Thorneycroft had been Chancellor for less than a year and was not quite the major party figure which the office he held would suggest. Salisbury, who was important, made a deliberate decision to go quietly. He was out of sympathy with Cabinet policy over quite a wide area and deliberately withdrew on the relatively minor issue of the release of Archbishop Makarios from imprisonment. The effect of a resignation depends not only upon the importance of the person who resigns, but on the issue, the timing, and the state of party feeling.

Though it has sometimes been argued that the Prime Minister's power to force a minister to resign helps him to get his own way on matters of policy, it is an observable fact that Prime Ministers do not normally ask for a minister's resignation because they disagree with the minister's policy. It is more likely to be because of the minister's administrative failings or, in some cases, because of the department's bad image.[38] In a resignation over policy, the initiative is much more likely to come from the minister himself, rather than from the Prime Minister. In these circumstances, it becomes a case of the minister having failed to get his way *in Cabinet* rather than one of divergence from the policies of the Prime Minister. In the case of the Thorneycroft resignation from the Treasury, all the spending ministers as well as Macmillan were firmly ranged against the Chancellor. It would be argued, of course, that spending ministers will normally disagree with the Chancellor and that the Prime Minister, therefore, has a special duty to back him up; that not to do so is, perhaps, to acquiesce in his resignation. But this is not wholly true. During a good part of Mr. Selwyn Lloyd's Chancellorship, Macmillan, an ardent economic expansionist, was opposed to Treasury deflationary policy. The Chancellor could certainly not rely on Macmillan's support for his policies. But when Selwyn Lloyd objected to a policy on the grounds of its cost, he frequently carried the day. Even with the Prime Minister and most of the Cabinet ranged against him, Lloyd on a number of occasions made it clear that he regarded the issue as a resigning matter, and the Prime Minister and spending ministers gave way.[39] By the time the Chancellor became one of the seven Cabinet ministers asked by Macmillan to resign in July 1962, there was some relief on both sides, since their views had become so divergent. But it is probable that Macmillan by this time, if not earlier, had a party and Cabinet majority on his side over the issue of taking the risks involved in economic expansion. Earlier Macmillan clearly felt that a second resignation by a Chancellor during his premiership on the grounds that the Prime Minister and Government were pursuing an inflationary policy was something more than he could risk. He was prepared to give way gracefully until such time as he felt a large-scale reorganisation of the Government could no longer be postponed. Selwyn Lloyd's eventual departure was in the context not of new policy differences, but of the drastically extensive dismissals aimed at bringing new blood into the Government and at improving the party image.

Similarly, Harold Wilson took very seriously George Brown's attempts to resign from office in July 1966; so seriously that he gave him the office of Foreign Secretary which Brown had always wanted. The last person that a Prime Minister wishes to see given the freedom of the back-benches is a potential rival. If it be true that

Harold Wilson has never really been in great danger, one reason for this is precisely that he takes seriously the threat of discord involved in letting major party figures go or in neglecting important sectors of party opinion. Wilson apparently regretted the departure of Frank Cousins in spite of the fact that Cousins had been less than strict in his adherence to the conventions of collective responsibility, and even though his position in the parliamentary party was much less broadly based than Brown's. Cousins' front-bench performances, moreover, had not enhanced his standing. His resignation, accordingly, did not stimulate widespread back-bench discontent.

Dissolution

The right of the Prime Minister, rather than of the Cabinet as a whole, to advise the monarch to dissolve Parliament is, as Geoffrey Marshall has argued,[40] largely a twentieth century development. This may reasonably be held to be a growth point in the Prime Minister's power – which is not the same thing as holding, with Marshall, the view that the Cabinet has the better constitutional entitlement to take this decision. Be that as it may, the more important point about dissolution as one of the Prime Minister's powers is that it is a power in relation to the Opposition – not power *vis-à-vis* his own colleagues. There is surely little life left in the idea that the Prime Minister's power to advise the Queen to dissolve Parliament is an important weapon which can be used against rebels in his own party. To fight an election when his party is openly disunited would be to do so at a most disadvantageous time for the Prime Minister, who, after all, has much to lose. A good time for the Prime Minister to call an election tends simply to mean a good time for his party. Their interests in this case are identical. Where dissolution *is* an important power is in relation to the Opposition. If a Prime Minister is right in thinking that a particular time will suit the Government party, it follows that it will not be the best time for his opponents. This tactical advantage in the hands of the Prime Minister has gained in importance with the development of techniques capable of ensuring at least short-term economic expansion (an important aid in creating a favourable electoral climate) and the advent of opinion polling, which enables a government to assess its current popularity. Indeed, towards the end of the thirteen years in which Conservative Governments held office, the argument was being put forward that this was too great an advantage for the Prime Minister and government to possess, and a system of fixed election dates was suggested. If the Conservatives had won again in 1964, pressure for this reform would undoubtedly have mounted.

Narrow tactical advantage is not always, however, the decisive factor. Nor, despite the tendency towards making the decision to dissolve the Prime Minister's, is it always the voice of the Prime Minister which is most influential. The decision to hold the 1950 General Election in February rather than in May was pressed upon Attlee and a reluctant Cabinet by Sir Stafford Cripps. Cripps, as Attlee has pointed out,[41] was opposed to postponing the election, since this would mean having a Budget in the meantime, and the last thing he wanted to do was to produce a specifically election Budget. He had not forgotten the unfair aspersions cast upon his integrity over devaluation and the allegations that he had misled the country. Attlee's point that the choice of election date was essentially Cripps' (though he does not blame him for it) is underlined by Douglas Jay when he notes that Hugh Gaitskell did not "favour Cripps' disastrous determination (opposed by all his colleagues) to hold the 1950 election in February rather than in May."[42] But 1950 is something of an exceptional case. Most modern Prime Ministers have been less willing than Attlee to share responsibility for deciding the most suitable moment for the party to fight. Certainly, Eden, Macmillan, Douglas-Home and Wilson took these decisions themselves.

Personality variable in Policy-Making

A Prime Minister's power over the appointing and dismissing of ministers, though subject to limitations, and his modern right to choose the date of a general election, are relatively straightforward matters in comparison with the question of his power in policy-making and his role in the Cabinet. The variables, only some of which I can discuss, are almost infinite in number. So far as decision-making within formal Cabinet meetings is concerned, there are far more difficulties for the student of politics than those imposed by lack of access to recent Cabinet minutes. When there is a near consensus in the Cabinet (and it is by no means uncommon), the difficulties of isolating the inputs which contribute to that consensus are almost insuperable. There is also the problem of *apparent* agreement. As a rule, Prime Ministers do not like to appear in the minority in Cabinet and so there are occasions when a Prime Minister will keep his views to himself rather than indulgently identify himself with the losing side. No defeat for the Prime Minister will be registered – even in the Cabinet minutes. Only one or two of his colleagues who happen to know the Prime Minister's private views on the question will detect that he did not get his way.

If there is one element in the problem the importance of which cannot be overstressed, it is the extent to which "style" of government and the location of key decision-taking varies according to the personality of the Prime Minister and the experience and ability of the members of his Cabinet. The extent of the variation from one Prime Minister to another is remarkable and scarcely supports the notion that in the period since the Second World War, prime ministerial power has been greater than ever before. When Tom Jones spoke of the Prime Minister "who is a dexterous, perhaps brilliant, autocrat" who "feels intuitively the invisible and inaudible reasoning going on in the minds of his colleagues, knows when to insist, when to give way, and when to adjourn," who "will concede in matters of no consequence, develop a stiff resistance to compromise when big issues are at stake, postpone rather than be defeated and thus secure time for private persuasion,"[43] he was thinking primarily of Lloyd George, with whom he was most closely acquainted. The contemporary example of Neville Chamberlain may also have been in his mind. But no Prime Ministers in the twentieth century have exercised greater personal power than Lloyd George and Chamberlain. None have been more willing to interfere with, or completely by-pass, their Cabinet colleagues. Nor is it entirely coincidence that both came to a sticky end. Tom Jones (who knew Baldwin well) recognised that there were also Prime Ministers "who appeared, except on critical occasions, to allow matters to take their course and to be indifferent to the decision reached or evaded. They preside but they do not prescribe. If agreement is not forthcoming, there is always escape by means of a committee, the matter is shelved and the next item called."[44]

The Prime Minister's power in relation to government policy has not, in fact, followed a steady course. In the period since Lloyd George's premiership, it cannot be said to have increased either sharply or gradually. It has varied from time to time, according to the strength, style and aptitudes of the individual Prime Minister, and the ability, experience and determination of his colleagues. A closer look at the prime ministerial style of Lloyd George and of

Neville Chamberlain is instructive, for it would be difficult to find any post-Second World War Prime Minister treating important colleagues with a comparable degree of disrespect. If the term "autocratic" can be applied to any British Prime Minister in modern times (and it can be applied only in a severely qualified sense), it should be reserved for these two men.

Lloyd George's purely personal authority stands out among twentieth-century Prime Ministers. Since he was a Prime Minister without a party, he became, as Ramsay MacDonald was later to become, dependent upon Conservative support. But he was prepared to take far greater liberties with his Conservative colleagues than MacDonald ever did. He not only kept patronage firmly under his own control, but used it to fill the coffers of his Political Fund, which, ostensibly for Liberal Party use, also remained under his personal jurisdiction. It can be argued (as Dalton argued[45]) that Lloyd George was not such a strong war leader as Churchill, inasmuch as he was far less in control of the generals and did not dare to fire them. But the generals had powerful support[46] from the King, Press and public, as well as in the House of Commons, and Lloyd George's power as Prime Minister cannot be adequately judged by concentrating on this special case.

More important was the fact that Lloyd George attempted to maintain his wartime style of government after the Peace, and interfered with his ministers to the extent of taking policy decisions without their knowledge through the medium of his personal secretariat. This secretariat was unusually large for a British Prime Minister and, in addition to it, Lloyd George made some use of the Cabinet Office to promote his policies. His most extreme interference was in foreign affairs, for war and the post-war conferences had accustomed him to being the supreme authority in this field. It is remarkable that not only did the Prime Minister conduct departmental policy other than through the departments, but that he actively pursued policies with which his Cabinet disagreed – over Russia, for instance.

When Lloyd George wished to come to an economic and political settlement with the new Communist régime in Russia, he took with him Lord Swinton, then the Secretary for Overseas Trade, rather than Lord Curzon, who, as Foreign Secretary, might have been expected to conduct the negotiations and who was, at the very least, entitled to be present. Swinton recognised this, and once said to Lloyd George: "'If you treated me as you do Curzon I would quit. I cannot understand why Curzon does not resign.' Lloyd George replied: 'Oh, but he does, constantly. But there are two messengers in the Foreign Office: one has a club foot, he comes with the resignation: the other is a champion runner, he always catches him up.'"[47] Curzon liked office too much to carry his numerous threats of resignation into action. He contented himself with letting off steam to his wife and close friends. "Girlie," he wrote to Lady Curzon, "I am getting very tired of trying to work with that man. He wants his Forn. Sec. to be a valet, almost a drudge..."[48] But Lloyd George's by-passing of the Foreign Office served to weaken his own prospects of survival. Curzon, naturally, was not inclined to take a strong line for keeping the Lloyd George Coalition going. But, more important, the Prime Minister's treatment of Curzon and, to a lesser extent, Balfour was the decisive factor in keeping out of the Coalition the one man whose return might have saved it. Bonar Law was on three occasions – unknown to the Foreign Secretary – offered Curzon's job, once in 1921 and twice in 1922. But he refused, telling Birkenhead (who had conveyed the third offer) "that the Foreign Office was out of the question. His view was that if he undertook the task he would not be in the position to control foreign policy."[49]

One reason why Lloyd George was so dominant was, of course, the sheer force of his personality. For even in a Cabinet which included brilliant men, none seemed to rival the brilliance of the Prime Minister. The predominance of Neville Chamberlain is, from one perspective, more surprising, for Chamberlain had much less personal magnetism than Lloyd George. On the other hand, Chamberlain was not surrounded by outstandingly able ministers. There were no Churchills or Birkenheads (and those who regard Macmillan as having extended prime ministerial power over appointment should recall that Chamberlain kept out a bigger man in Churchill than anyone rejected by his successors[50]). There was neither a clear second-in-command to Chamberlain within the government, nor an obvious successor.[51] When he was Chancellor of the Exchequer under MacDonald, and later Baldwin, and nominally number three after Baldwin and MacDonald, Chamberlain in fact could be regarded (and he regarded himself) as the strong man of the government. But he was dissatisfied with the amount of power he possessed, and the kind of Prime Minister he intended to become is foreshadowed in his comment to his sister in March 1935: "As you will see I have become a sort of Acting P. M. – only without the actual power of the P. M. I have to say 'Have you thought' or 'What would you say' when it would be quicker to say 'That is what you must do.'"[52]

When Chamberlain became Prime Minister, circumstances dictated that he devote a great deal of his time to foreign policy, but he was not content to run *only* foreign policy.[53] He ensured his strong influence on major domestic policy by taking the chair at all the important domestic Cabinet Committees.[54] Chamberlain had strong views and he wanted his government and entire administration to reflect them. Accordingly, he showed little interest in bringing in able critics such as Churchill, Leo Amery or Macmillan. On Eden's resignation, the Earl of Swinton (who was himself sacked by Chamberlain from his office of Secretary of State for Air) has written: "Eden rightly resented the secrecy with which Chamberlain surrounded his personal contacts, his hush-hush messages from and meetings with mysterious go-betweens. It was an increasingly impossible position for a Foreign Secretary to be in, especially for one as sensitive about his importance and private feelings of pride as Eden was. . . . Neville was running a one-man band, and became angry if anyone appeared to question his judgment. All the negotiations and secret or official contacts with Mussolini were his own. Munich was his own. He was convinced that he, and he alone, could understand and get on with the dictators and secure a peaceful settlement with them."[55]

Chamberlain's successor was in some respects a special case. Many factors combined to give Churchill in wartime great power and authority. But his very preoccupation with the conduct of the war meant that he had to delegate authority on home affairs to Attlee and Sir John Anderson. In his second period of office as Prime Minister, Churchill still benefited from his wartime record and public prestige. Yet, partly no doubt because of his declining health, and partly because of his regard for constitutional propriety, his role in policy-making in the 1951–55 Government does not appear to have been extensive. He remained in full charge, however, at Cabinet meetings and took pleasure, for instance, in impressing his colleagues with analogies drawn from his experience as a minister in 1910! The fact that in the course of his long political career Churchill had held many offices was, arguably, one of his advantages, compensating in some measure for his failing physical and mental powers. Attlee, as Prime Minister, interfered little with his ministers and this partly reflected his own inclinations, but it was also a reflection of the strength and experience of many of his Cabinet colleagues. When the supposed "prime ministerial government" of Wilson is contrasted with the Attlee administration, the outstanding difference is not an accretion of power to the office of Prime Minister. Nor are even the differences in the personality and ability of the men the most relevant factors. More important is the relative strength and experience of their Cabinet colleagues. Attlee was surrounded by men like Bevin, Cripps, Morrison, Bevan and Dalton, formidable personalities, who, with the notable exception of Aneurin Bevan, had already gained ministerial experience in the wartime coalition. In addition, these were men of great experience in the Labour Movement and people of unusual ability. Bevin, Cripps, Morrison and Bevan were also, in their different ways, politicians with strong support in different sections of the party and they could command a great deal of personal loyalty. The contrast between these men and Mr. Wilson's Cabinet is a notable one. There are able men in the Wilson Cabinet who, in time, could acquire a political position comparable with some of those who surrounded Attlee. But George Brown is no Bevin, Callaghan stands much less high in party esteem than did Cripps, and Anthony Greenwood, who on past form may be regarded as the most left-wing member of the Cabinet, does not bear comparison with Bevan. As regards previous experience, only Gordon Walker, apart from Wilson himself, held important office in the Attlee government, and Gordon Walker's party standing is simply not comparable with that, say, of Herbert Morrison. Morrison, moreover, joined the Attlee Cabinet with his intimate knowledge of London government behind him, in addition to his period of office as Home Secretary and membership of the wartime Cabinet. In the circumstances, it would be scarcely surprising if Harold Wilson, though a comparatively young Prime Minister, found himself in a stronger-than-average position in relation to his colleagues. In experience as well as in political ability he has no party rival to compare with him. His previous experience – as wartime member of the Cabinet Secretariat, as President of the Board of Trade, as "shadow" Chancellor, as "shadow" Foreign Secretary, as Chairman of the Public Accounts Committee, and as Leader of the Opposition – could scarcely have been a more apposite apprenticeship, short of further experience of actual government office which, in the circumstances of Conservative electoral success from 1951 onwards, was not possible.

Among the other post-Second World War Prime Ministers, Eden's high party and national standing, and the great respect in which he had been held as Foreign Secretary, enabled him to become a domineering Prime Minister. But even before his Suez policy collapsed in ruins, this style of government had begun to irritate his colleagues and alienate support. Eden was also disadvantaged as Prime Minister by his unusually one-sided political background. He had spent his political life almost exclusively in foreign affairs. In valuable contrast, Macmillan had experience of the Treasury and the Ministry of Housing, as well as Foreign Affairs and Defence. Sir Alec Douglas-Home, however, suffered, like Eden, from relative lack of familiarity with the problems of home (and, in particular, economic) departments. Though there are ministers who served under Douglas-Home and Macmillan who regard the former as the better Cabinet chairman, his position *vis-à-vis* his colleagues was not as strong as was Macmillan's, following the election victory in 1959. Macmillan's assets, the electoral success apart, were his wide political experience, tactical acumen and sheer intellectual ability. Douglas-Home could not compete in these respects and could scarcely hope to dominate the policies of a Cabinet which included several men with political experience at least as great as his own (for example, Mr. Quintin Hogg and Mr. Selwyn Lloyd), one whose experience was considerably greater (Mr. R. A. Butler), and able, younger men who had already held important office, and whose further political ambitions had been given encouragement during the leadership crisis of 1963 (Mr. Maudling and Mr. Heath).

While the differences among twentieth century British Prime Ministers are necessarily a recurring point in this discussion, it is scarcely less important to take note of certain ministers who did not become Prime Minister but who carried great weight in the Cabinets in which they served and played an important role outside it. While there is no lack of evidence of the Prime Minister's importance (which no serious student of politics would wish to ignore), acceptance of the "prime ministerial government" notion may foster a tendency to overlook the role of other leading ministers, some of whom have had a more important influence on the course of British politics than a number of those who became Prime Minister. Ernest Bevin, Herbert Morrison, Aneurin Bevan and R. A. Butler are post-war names that spring to mind. Lord Butler's influence on policy-making within his party was a remarkable one for a single individual. Lloyd George, Neville Chamberlain and Harold Macmillan were prepared to argue in Cabinet and win many rounds *before* they became Prime Minister. A Prime Minister, as well as other ministers, may be bound by collective responsibility to support a policy he does not like. Macmillan was forced to defend two credit squeezes which his Chancellors imposed and which he heartily disliked.

Cabinet Chairman and Cabinet Agenda

As Cabinet chairman, the Prime Minister undoubtedly enjoys an advantage in the discussion. He has more opportunities to express his views, for if any other minister ventured opinions on such a wide range of issues, he would be regarded as a dangerous bore. When a Prime Minister also possesses considerable intellectual and political ability (true, for example, of Macmillan and Wilson, among recent Prime Ministers), there will be no question as to who is the most powerful man in the Cabinet. Yet the power which the chairmanship bestows on the Prime Minister may too easily be exaggerated. Many of the decisions which are taken in Cabinet have effectively been taken elsewhere and it will be very difficult for the Prime Minister to change them at this late date. If he wishes to do so, he must carry his Cabinet with him. The same applies to any policy initiative that he may take it upon himself to bring before them. The Conservative bid to enter the Common Market during Macmillan's premiership is a good illustration of the strength and limitations of prime ministerial initiative, given an able Prime Minister. The initiative and drive came from Macmillan, but it was not a policy he could simply impose on his Cabinet. On a number of occasions, he raised the Common Market question, but was forced to adjourn the discussion because there was insufficient agreement. Only after a tough and fairly long drawn-out struggle was he able to get something approaching consensus.[56] It is certainly the case, as G. W. Jones has argued,[57] that a Prime Minister cannot sum up against the sense of the meeting. His ability to affect the sense of the meeting will depend upon a number of variables, including his own personality and talents, the strength of feeling the issue arouses, and the standing of the ministers opposed to him.

The Prime Minister's power to determine the Cabinet agenda has frequently been misinterpreted. Dr. Mackintosh is wrong in suggesting that "the Prime Minister ... can keep any item off the agenda indefinitely."[58] This is greatly overstating the case. Nor is the Prime Minister's control over Cabinet business adequately demonstrated by the example of Neville Chamberlain wanting to discuss reform of the House of Lords at a Cabinet meeting in June 1929. "It was *not on the agenda*[59] and though he did try to bring it up at the end of the listed business, Baldwin rose and walked out of the room, thus ending the Cabinet."[60] There is a standard procedure for getting a matter discussed in Cabinet which is to submit the item in advance to the Cabinet Secretariat, who draw up the Cabinet agenda. This, in turn, requires the Prime Minister's final approval. But it is not in a Prime Minister's interest to keep matters off the agenda which his colleagues want to discuss. If a minister feels particularly strongly about a matter which has been decided against him at Cabinet Committee or at inter-departmental level, he has the right to bring the issue before a full meeting of the Cabinet. If he does not, of course, always do so, it is because the ministers most concerned will have been involved in the earlier discussions, and, therefore, the chances of the decision being overturned are slim. Nevertheless, as Enoch Powell has asserted,[61] "a minister clearly has a right to bring a matter to his colleagues if he wants to. The very nature of collective responsibility implies that if a man wants his colleagues' assent or advice he can have it."[62]

Though the principal co-ordinating committee (and ultimate decision-taking body in the event of disagreement at lower levels) is still the Cabinet,[63] the Prime Minister does have a special role in the co-ordination of policy. He is the ultimate co-ordinating minister. As Harold Wilson has put it: "... any decision which is not going through smoothly, possibly because two different departments do not see eye to eye, if it cannot be resolved by a Cabinet sub-committee, or an *ad hoc* get together – *which is what usually happens*[64] – comes to the Prime Minister."[65] The Prime Minister must draw a careful line between observing a watchful general oversight and constantly interfering in his ministers' work. To know what is going on and to be able to intervene when things look as if they may soon go wrong is an attribute of a successful Prime Minister. Constant meddling with the business of his colleagues is not normally successful. Of recent Prime Ministers, the one most given to such interference was Sir Anthony Eden, who thoroughly irritated many of his colleagues in the process. From the beginning of Macmillan's premiership, wrote the Earl of Kilmuir, there was "a new 'feel' about the Government. Eden's chronic restlessness, which had sensibly affected all his colleagues was replaced by a central calmness which provided a wonderful contrast with 1955–56."[66] It may not be too fanciful to see a connecting link between Eden's interference and overwork, his subsequent bad health, the ill-conceived Suez policy, and his ultimate resignation.

One of the most important developments in the machinery of government in the twentieth century has been the establishment of a system of Cabinet Committees – both permanent functional committees and *ad hoc* committees. It has sometimes been argued that these strengthen the position of the Prime Minister and give him a larger role in policy-making. But though this may from time to time happen, as it probably did in the case of Eden's Suez Committee, it does not necessarily follow. Cabinet Committees are a logical extension of the Cabinet rather than of prime ministerial power. The Prime Minister is not a member of all of these specialised committees, and where he is not, the members of the committee are likely to have a greater influence on the final shape of policy than he. Not many Prime Ministers have, like Chamberlain, attempted to run everything. Though Chamberlain was Leader of the House as well as Prime Minister and, especially following Eden's resignation, bore the brunt of foreign affairs questioning in the Commons, he continued to exercise strong influence over home policy through his chairmanship of Cabinet Committees. As Cabinet Committees have proliferated, this has become a more difficult thing for any Prime Minister to do. The spread of Cabinet Committees is no argument for the passing of the Cabinet system. Though members of the Cabinet Committees are appointed by the Prime Minister, to a large extent the members (of, for example, the Overseas Policy Committee, Social Services Committee or Economic Affairs Committee) pick themselves in accordance with the departmental responsibilities of the ministers concerned. In the autumn of 1965 even such an important Cabinet Committee as the Economic Committee was being chaired not by Harold Wilson (the first economist to become Prime Minister), but by the Minister of Economic Affairs and First Secretary of State, George Brown.[67] Arguably, the extension of Cabinet Committees has strengthened all ministers. It keeps them informed of the sphere most relevant to their work, and gives them a greater opportunity to participate at the highest level of decision-making than they could hope to have in a meeting of the full Cabinet. There, with over twenty members present and time limited, each individual member must weigh carefully the likely effect of making too many contributions. It may also be argued that Cabinet Committees have, in particular, strengthened the party hierarchy – not only the Prime Minister, but his leading colleagues who now share the chairmanship

of committees with him. The chairmanship of Cabinet Committees strengthened the power, for instance, of Sir John Anderson in Churchill's wartime coalition, of Herbert Morrison in the Attlee Government, and of R. A. Butler in more than one Conservative government. (A minister's party standing and his influence within the government on policy do not always coincide. Both Morrison and Butler, for instance, had an influence in excess of their popularity in the party. With some ministers, this position is reversed. Different again, of course, may be popularity in the country and popularity within the party. Butler's prominent position in the Churchill, Eden and Macmillan governments, together with his appeal to the centre of the British political spectrum, made him the clear public opinion poll, if not party, favourite to succeed Macmillan to the Conservative Party leadership.) It has not been sufficiently recognised that Cabinet Committee chairmen are very important people and that, though a Prime Minister will keep in close touch with these half-dozen or so key men and doubtless exert some influence, this is not a fully effective substitute for chairing every meeting himself. Indeed, the latter course might appeal to a Prime Minister intent on short-term maximisation of his power, but it is no longer a practical possibility. In the long run it would be damaging to both the efficiency of, and contentment within, his government. There is no need to doubt the realism of the present Prime Minister when he chose to regard "the first essential in any Prime Minister" as "the ability to keep a good team working together."[68]
The development of the Cabinet Office and of the Prime Minister's Private Office are also twentieth century developments, but the latter has not gone very far. Indeed, it is doubtful if the Prime Minister's private office has ever at any time reached the importance it had under Lloyd George.[69] Though nowadays a highly efficient private office in terms of secretarial and personal services, it is absolutely minimal as an advisory body. Indeed, there are politicians with ministerial experience who regard it as quite inadequate if the Prime Minister is to comprehend departmental matters when they come to the Cabinet and when ministers go to him. Macmillan's advisers, it is said, were able to talk "globally," but did not have the skills required to sharpen the issues. The Prime Minister does not have in his Private Office anyone of the seniority, ability and experience of the abler Permanent Secretaries – of men such as Sir Douglas Allen or Sir William Armstrong, for instance.

On the other hand, the Secretary to the Cabinet (and to a lesser extent the Joint Permanent Secretary at the Treasury responsible for Civil Service establishment) normally enjoys a close relationship with the Prime Minister. It is through the Cabinet Office that the Prime Minister must largely work if he wishes to be well informed about the conduct of government departments. Avoiding Churchillian precedents, Harold Wilson, when he decided to use Dr. Balogh and Sir Solly Zuckerman in an advisory capacity, gave them appointments in the Cabinet Office rather than in his Private Office. Balogh was given the title of "Economic Adviser to the Cabinet," even though most of the briefs he prepared were for the attention of the Prime Minister. The latter fact is not surprising. Departmental ministers have their own specialised staff and, if the minister is capable of running his department, he will normally be able to get the information he requires from his subordinate officials, and will thus be in much less need than the Prime Minister of the services of the Cabinet Office. If he wishes to find out more about aspects of government policy beyond the scope of his own departmental work, it is open to him to use the facilities of the Cabinet Office, though only the most enterprising of ministers do so.

The Cabinet Secretariat, however, through the circulation of agenda, minutes and background information, has enabled ministers to come to the Cabinet very much better informed about the business on hand than they could easily be before the creation of the Secretariat during the First World War.[70] There is a myth of a golden age of Cabinet government which is just as misleading as the myth of the golden age of the House of Commons, when the House was allegedly the scene of free, vigorous and well-informed discussion. (In fact, one of the distinguishing marks of fairly recent recruits to the House of Commons is not only their greater professionalism and representativeness, as compared with their nineteenth-century predecessors, but their greater *awareness* of ignorance and the need for better sources of information.) Some Cabinets are greatly superior to others in talent, and Asquith's, for instance, may compare favourably with some more modern specimens. But most Cabinets include members who try to keep themselves informed over a wide range of policy, as well as those who leave themselves time for nothing but the problems of their own department. If the extension of governmental activity has made the individual minister's job a more exacting one, the development of the Cabinet Office has had a compensatory effect, enabling the abler and less myopic ministers to keep in touch with the work of their colleagues. In spite of the Prime Minister's continuous use of the Cabinet Office, it is incorrect to regard it as no more than a glorified Private Office of the Prime Minister. The Cabinet Office acts as guardian of correct Cabinet procedure, is professionally concerned with the distribution of information to ministers, and would be unwilling to go on record (especially now that the records are to be published after thirty years!) with a deliberate by-passing of Cabinet ministers. Even if the Secretary to the Cabinet works more closely with the Prime Minister than with any other politician (and is, indeed, the *only* high official in constant touch with the Prime Minister), men such as Lord Bridges, Lord Normanbrook and Sir Burke Trend have been conscious of their duty towards the Cabinet as a whole and could not readily be suspected of supporting an autocratic tendency on the part of the Prime Minister.

The fact that the Prime Minister is political head of the Civil Service is of some importance, in so far as it indicates his considerable role in the initiation of changes in the machinery of government, including substantial power in the creation and winding up of departments.[71] The Prime Minister has a special responsibility in these matters, though this does not mean that he is quite free to follow his vision of administrative rationality. There are generally political pressures to be absorbed, loyal colleagues to reward, and potentially disloyal colleagues to be accommodated.

R. H. S. Crossman has argued that "the centralisation of authority, both for appointments and for policy decisions, under an single head of the civil service (quite recently the task has been given to a committee of three)[72] responsible to Downing Street, has brought with it an immense accretion of power to the Prime Minister. He is now the apex not only of a highly centralised political machine, but also of an equally centralised and vastly more powerfull administrative machine. In both these machines, loyalty has become the supreme virtue, and independence of thought a dangerous adventure."[73] It is true that high civil service appointments and, most notably, permanent secretaryships require the Prime Minister's consent. But Crossman's argument would carry more conviction if Prime Ministers had acquired the habit of pressing their own nominees for these posts. This has not in fact happened. The practice has been for Prime Ministers to give their official blessing to the choice made by the permanent heads of the civil service machine. The real discretionary power exercised by the Prime Minister over these appointments is not much greater than that of the Queen when she is presented with a list of ministers for approval. Arguably, it could be a greater power, for the Prime Minister might refuse to endorse the "machine's" candidate. But to do so, other than in the most exceptional circumstances, would be to alter radically the nature and structure of the higher civil service. Conceivably this should be done, but demonstrably it has not happened yet.

As things stand, civil servants are in general appointed by civil servants and on the comparatively rare occasions when a Permanent Secretary is rejected by a politician (or transferred at his behest), the initiative comes from the departmental minister. Indeed, when a new Permanent Secretary is being appointed to a department, the minister has a *de facto* right of veto. It is not often exercised, for few ministers are equipped with knowledge which enables them to judge the relative merits of possible candidates for the job.

During the period of Mr. Wilson's prime ministership, there have, however, been several cases of ministers objecting to their Permanent Secretaries, though this has been done succesfully only when an imminent retirement has brought about the need for a change. Somewhat ironically, the most notable ministerial victory was Mr. Richard Crossman's. When Dame Evelyn Sharp retired as Permanent Secretary to the Ministry of Housing, her job (to the consternation of Whitehall) remained vacant for seven months while the determined Mr. Crossman refused to accept the choice of successor that the "machine" had ordained for him. The Prime Minister, as usual, supported the Civil Service Establishment view and quite a tussle ensued. For Crossman not only named the civil servant he did not want, but said whom he did want. There was an eventual compromise in which a third person (neither the "machine's" original choice nor Crossman's) was appointed to the Permanent Secretaryship. The process confirmed the departmental minister's right of veto in the case of a new appointment, but failed to establish his right to choose his own chief adviser.[74]

Area of Policy

A distinction of some importance may be made between the role and influence of the Prime Minister in certain areas of policy as compared with others. Prime Ministers, by convention, have special responsibilities in the field of foreign policy, defence and national security.

Though it is true that they also have an overall responsibility for the conduct of the government, their special interest in foreign affairs, the demands made by the speed of modern communications and the tendency towards conduct of diplomacy at head of government level simply do not leave them with time to participate so knowledgeably or so frequently in the work of other departments.

The Prime Minister's role in foreign policy is subject, of course, to the same qualifying factors as affect his conduct of government generally. The personality and strength of the Foreign Secretary are highly relevant, as are the interests and aptitudes of the Prime Minister himself. The variations from one government to another over the past fifty years have been considerable. The case of Lloyd George has already been mentioned. Not only was Balfour excluded from his small War Cabinet, but Curzon was in general treated with even greater disdain when Lloyd George became peacetime Prime Minister. MacDonald, reverting to a practice by no means unknown to earlier Prime Ministers, became his own Foreign Secretary. Baldwin's Foreign Secretaries, on the other hand, enjoyed as much independence as any other departmental minister (indeed, rather more[75]), while, in contrast, Neville Chamberlain reverted to a policy of by-passing the Foreign Office which was reminiscent of Lloyd George's tactics. Churchill during the war was a special case, but in the period from 1951 to 1955 Anthony Eden had a great deal of freedom as Foreign Secretary.[76] This may be attributed in part to Churchill's failing powers, of which Lord Moran has provided ample evendence.[77] It also reflects Churchill's "constitutionalism," his belief in the importance of the Cabinet[78] and the rights of individual ministers, as well as his respect for the judgment and experience of his particular Foreign Secretary.[79] The importance of the last point should not be underestimated. Eden's position as heir apparent, his seniority within the party and long experience in foreign affairs made him the major figure in foreign policy-making, just as Ernest Bevin had been before him. Somewhat similar factors were operating in the Attlee-Bevin relationship. Bevin was an experienced minister, one of the outstanding successes in Churchill's small War Cabinet, and a tremendous figure in the Labour and Trade Union Movement. Attlee had the greatest respect for him and, in turn, Attlee's safety when conspiracy threatened depended much upon Bevin's loyal support.

Bevin and Eden, accordingly, had a position and power within their governments which Eden's successor, Selwyn Lloyd (a junior and inexperienced politician by comparison), could not be expected to command.

Given, however, that personalities matter, foreign affairs remains one area of policy where it is almost impossible for a Prime Minister to keep out. If Baldwin dabbled no more in foreign policy than he had to, it is arguable that he did less than he ought. Certainly the pressures to participate are great. Against this it can be argued, and with support from the findings of public opinion polls, that the handling of foreign policy comes low on the electorate's list of priorities and that a Prime Minister may, therefore, be unwise to spend too much time on it. The exigencies of the situation, however, frequently dictate his course of action. The frequency and speed of modern international consultation, the fact that diplomacy at the highest level now means diplomacy carried out by heads of executive in many countries with which Britain has important dealings, brings the Prime Minister in, whether he likes it or not. In foreign affairs such quick action is frequently required that the Cabinet cannot be consulted until after the Foreign Office has made an important move. In these circumstances, a Foreign Secretary will often welcome the opportunity of consultation with the Prime Minister and the possibility of sharing the burden and responsibility.

Sometimes the Prime Minister will take important initiatives in foreign policy, though in the period since the Second World War these have always been taken in consultation with the Foreign Secretary (and often with a Cabinet Committee as well). There ist, however, at least a case for arguing that the Cabinet as a whole have not always been adequately informed. The examples which are invariably used in support of such a contention (and, more generally, to promote the view that Prime Ministers have increased their power) are those of Attlee and the manufacture of the British atom bomb, and of Eden and Suez policy.

The use of these examples has not been entirely fortunate. In so far as they are pathological cases, they may be misleading, and the extent, furthermore, to which they demonstrate the Prime Minister's individual power has almost certainly been exaggerated. It seems fairly clear that Attlee was strongly in favour of the manufacture of the atom bomb and that he exerted a strong influence in this decision in his role as chairman of the Defence Committee of the Cabinet.[80] The minutes of the committee were, however, circulated to Cabinet members and if none of them chose to raise the issue within the Cabinet, this may be interpreted either as acquiescence or negligence (a failure to read the minutes with due care), but it cannot convincingly be interpreted in terms of the by-passing of the Cabinet by the Prime Minister.[81] Nor has any evidence been produced to show that a majority of members of the Labour Cabinet at that time were opposed to the decision taken.

A more thoroughly researched case is the Suez crisis of 1956. In this instance, a good deal of evidence is now available, though there is still ample room for difference of interpretation. One of the conclusions of a recent diligent investigator is that "Suez was a good example of how a single individual can affect events. It showed the almost limitless power of a Prime Minister in present circumstances, particularly when supported by a powerful group of Minister."[82] Both Hugh Thomas and Anthony Nutting[83] describe convincingly how Eden arried his Foreign Secretary, Selwyn Lloyd, along with him, even though Lloyd had doubts about the wisdom of hitting back at Nasser in the way Eden and the French intended. Suez was a pathological case, not only because Eden deliberately misled the House of Commons, the country, the United States and the United Nations, but because he by-passed the normal machinery of government. The Middle Eastern specialists in the Foreign Office were not fully aware of what was afoot. Anyone who might have been in a position to offer expert advice against the Suez adventure was deliberately not consulted. This was the Prime Minister's decision. Even the British Ambassador in Egypt was not told of the ultimatum to Egypt until it was delivered. He, like almost everyone else in the diplomatic service, including Sir William Hayter, the British Ambassador in Moscow, was strongly opposed to the venture. Eisenhower was just as opposed as was Dulles, and so the Americans were not told what was going on. For all this, Eden must bear a good deal of individual responsibility.

Yet it would be wrong to suppose that Eden by-passed his Cabinet in the way in which he largely ignored the Foreign Office specialists and his allies. The Cabinet Committee which considered the Suez policy included the major figures in the Cabinet who were departmentally involved – für example, Harold Macmillan as Chancellor, Selwyn Lloyd (the Foreign Secretary), Lord Home, Lennox-Boyd, and Anthony Head, as well as (for some of the time) R. A. Butler. In addition, the Cabinet as a whole took the vital decision on August 2, 1956, that "force would be used if negotiations failed within a measurable time."[84] Though Lord Butler has gone on record[85] as suggesting that the Cabinet was not consulted as much as it might have been, he has also pointed out that "the Cabinet could have blown up if it had wanted to, but the Cabinet had confidence in Eden at the time and what doubts there were were not expressed until, I think, a later stage." Furthermore, "the party in the House at the time of Suez was on the whole behind the Prime Minister and very indignant with Nasser; so there wasn't the seed-bed for opposition to the policy in the Conservative Party in the House that you would expect if the Prime Minister was acting contrary to the general line of what the back-benchers thought."[86] Another senior minister at that time has said: "We all bear some responsibility.... There is a slight element of a scapegoat in making Eden responsible for Suez."[87] It is also of some significance that Eden did not by-pass his Foreign Secretary in the way in which Lloyd George by-passed Curzon, nor in the way in which he himself was by-passed by Neville Chamberlain. He had, on the contrary, persuaded Selwyn Lloyd of the rightness of his policy, and others, for instance, Macmillan, Lennox-Boyd, and Anthony Head, needed no persuading. Macmillan, indeed, played a crucial role. Though Chancellor of the Exchequer, he paid little attention to the position of sterling until the Suez attack had already been mounted and there was tremendous pressure on the pound. He then changed overnight from being the most enthusiastic advocate of the use of force to being the minister who most strongly insisted that there must be a cease-fire. Hugh Thomas has regarded Suez as illustrating "the almost limitless power of a Prime Minister in present circumstances." It is true that Eden played a positive and vital role in the whole affair, and it is possible that if he had advocated a non-violent course of action, he could have carried the Cabinet with him. But, then, if other ministers had acted differently, it is probable that they also could have prevented the use of force. If the Foreign Secretary, for example, had been determined to oppose Eden's plans, the outcome could have been different. If Macmillan, who was personally a more senior minister than Lloyd and held a key office as Chancellor of the Exchequer, had opposed the use of force from the start, it is also unlikely that armed intervention would have taken place. Professor Thomas's own observations on Macmillan's role may be found to be somewhat at variance with his views concerning the Prime Minister's dominance. On the decision to use force, there is an important implication in Thomas's question: "Eden's masterful handling of foreign affairs no doubt swept the Cabinet along; but did Macmillan sweep Eden along?"[88] On the cease-fire, he writes: "Macmillan was the strong man of this Cabinet by now and it seems to have been really his advice as a man not as a Minister that brought the fighting to an end.... Macmillan now became the leader of those who wished to halt the operation, leading also what was basically a rebellion against Eden's leadership."[89] There is a suggestion that Eden may have been persuaded somewhat against his will to accept the cease-fire.[90] It is also by no means clear that Eden was in favour of the subsequent withdrawal of British forces from Egypt. There is no denying that the present Earl of Avon was a Prime Minister who liked his own way and who interfered with his colleagues. It is equally clear that in 1956 he became convinced that Nasser must be overthrown or humiliated and that he used his full weight in Cabinet and out of it to convince his celleagues. But the view that this constituted some kind of prime ministerial dictatorship is a great over-simplification. There was neither one decisive moment nor only one decisive voice in the crisis, but something close to a consensus in the Conservative Party (in favour of force) to which many sectors of party opinion, and most of the leading men in the Cabinet, contributed.

Though there is a case for regarding Eden's Suez role as one in which a Prime Minister played an unusually large and sustained part in the policy-making process, similar examples can be found in an earlier part of this century. The military conversations with the French after 1905, for example, were kept from the whole Cabinet by Campbell-Bannerman and Sir Edward Grey, though one or two closely concerned ministers were informed. The Cabinet as a whole was certainly by-passed more completely than it was at the time of Suez, and indeed the looser form of Cabinet organisation prior to the First World War reforms made settlements between the Prime Minister and Foreign Secretary (or between the P.M. and any other departmental minister), to the exclusion of the Cabinet, probably more common than they are today. At present, by convention the first item on the formal agenda is a report on developments in foreign affairs, and the circulation of minutes both of Cabinet Committees and of meetings of the full Cabinet enables those ministers who avoid getting too immersed in the detailed work of their departments to keep themselves informed.

The case of the first British attempt to join the Common Market which has already been touched upon, is a good example of the possibility of prime ministerial initiative in the field of foreign policy. It involved no deals behind the Cabinet's back. On the contrary, a decision to seek membership of the EEC required a major Cabinet decision, and though Macmillan devoted himself with some passion to the task of persuading his Cabinet colleagues, agreement was not immediately forthcoming. Only after many meetings held over several months was something like a consensus obtained. A long and tactful process of persuasion was necessary before influential doubters (who included R. A. Butler) could be won over. The final result of Macmillan's pressure and the Cabinet deliberations illustrates three points which may be offered as generalisations.

First, the Prime Minister has the power to give a lead to his colleagues on a major issue of policy – in particular, on overseas policy. This oppertunity (perhaps duty) is most clearly the Prime Minister's when the issue affects almost every department and is the exclusive responsibility of none. Secondly, if the Prime Minister has (in the terms which Richard Neustadt applies to the President of the United States) "the power to persuade," the Cabinet remains the principal body which must be persuaded. This is no mere formality, as Macmillan found out. Thirdly, and this point is linked with the second, in the course of long deliberation on a policy in Cabinet and Cabinet committee, the policy becomes modified and hedged with qualifications as part of the process of obtaining consensus. In the case of the Common Market dispute, this may have turned Macmillan's success into something of a Pyrrhic victory. Such were the concessions that had to be made to Cabinet opponents of British membership in the EEC and to those who were only prepared to give markedly qualified support that Heath and his negotiating team were left with little room for maneouvre. It is arguable that even without de Gaulle's help, the opponents and less than wholehearted supporters of Macmillan's policy within the Cabinet (who reflected important sections of Conservative Party and national opinion) had effectiveley scuppered the policy.[91] They had certainly restricted the options open to Macmillan and his supporters. If the case of the Conservative government and the Common Market is compared with the Suez policy of 1956, it would appear that Eden made fewer concessions and that the details of the execution of the policy (up to and including the landing of British troops in Egypt) were virtually as he had ordained. This may owe something to the difference in style of government of Eden and Macmillan, but it owes more to the difference in degree of dissension within the Conservative Party and government on the two occasions. Even those members of the Cabinet in 1956 who were most sceptical about the use of force failed to give firm voice to their doubts. Doubtless they were inhibited by their assessment that party opinion would be behind Eden. In the case of the Common Market, Cabinet dissent was vocal and persistent, and in this instance strengthened by the knowledge that it was in line with a substantial sector of party opinion.

Home Policy

Regardless of who has taken the initiative and of how successful they have been in implementing their policies, foreign affairs and defence have engaged the continuous interest of all post-Second World War British Prime Ministers. While this does not absolve them of responsibility for the smooth running and success of the government as a whole, it does go some way towards restricting the part they can play in domestic policy-making. There are, as has already been mentioned, many Cabinet Committees in the home policy field which are not chaired by the Prime Minister, and where important decisions are being taken in the Prime Minister's absence. While he may give the committee chairmen the benefit of his advice, it is carrying the prime ministerial government notion too far to believe that committee chairmen (normally experienced politicians of some party standing) are the Prime Minister's puppets or that his ubiquitous spirit will dominate colleagues in his absence. There are whole areas of major domestic concern, such as health and education, in which the Prime Minister seldom attempts to be a policy-maker. There are many good reasons for this. One is that the policy-making process in departments such as these tends to be a long-drawn-out affair involving argument and consultation with interested parties and a fair measure of acquired expertise on the part of the minister. The Prime Minister is not in a strong position to sustain an argument on policy with, say, his Minister of Education.[92] No doubt, like everyone else, Prime Ministers reckon they know a good deal about education. But in fact none since Balfour has had real expertise on the subject or departmental experience of it. Able as they are to devote only sporadic attention to education and being, in comparison with the departmental minister, generally under-briefed by the Cabinet secretariat or their Private Office, Prime Ministers *may* be able to successfully probe into a minister's policies, but will be unlikely to dominate them. Perhaps it is not surprising that Churchill in wartime was not much concerned with education. It is significant, nonetheless, that a measure of the importance of the 1944 Education Act was prepared and introduced by the minister, R. A. Butler, in complete independence of any views the Prime Minister may have had on the subject. The educational reform had already been a matter of discussion between the Board of Education and the local authorities before the new minister moved in. As Butler has expressed it: "... therefore there was a plan which I could consider. What was not considered was the whole of what is called the religious settlement under the Act between the churches – that was the biggest bit of negotiation which I had to do myself; with the aid of my colleague, Mr. Chuter Ede, who was then the Under Secretary. It was only at the later stages, when we wanted authority, that we went to a government committee to get authority for it."[93]

When a Prime Minister does take an interest in a matter within the province of a particular departmental minister, reaction will obviously depend very much on the personalities involved and the relationship between them. But it would be abnormal and unwise for a minister not to take an interest in a departmental matter which has attracted the attention of the Prime Minister. If the P.M. wishes to question what is being done, the departmental minister, if he is up to his job, should be able to supply the answer. So far as senior ministers, at least, are concerned, there is no question of prime ministerial dictation. The Prime Minister makes suggestions rather than issuing orders. A former Conservative Chancellor of the Exchequer told me that he received about a suggestion a week from the Prime Minister. He (and the Treasury) looked into them all, but found objections to most of them. Perhaps half a dozen in the course of a year were accepted.

Even fairly junior ministers, given a will of their own, may reject the Prime Minister's advice. Lord Hill of Luton owed his appointment as chairman of the Independent Television Authority to Reginald Bevins, who was Postmaster General at the time. Macmillan suggested two alternatives whom he regarded as preferable to Hill, but Bevins stood firm on his original choice.[94] On a more minor matter, another Postmaster General defeated Macmillan. When the M.P. for Ayrshire South, Emrys Hughes, was conducting his compaign for the issue of a commemorative stamp to celebrate the bicentenary of the birth of Robert Burns, his battle with Macmillan on this point made for some of the brighter moments at Question Time. Behind the scenes, however, Macmillan was trying to persuade his Postmaster General, Ernest Marples, to accede to the demand for the stamp.[95] In this, he showed a good deal more political acumen than his junior colleague, for in spite of its apparent triviality, the issue generated some heat and passion in Scotland. But Marples stuck to his view and Emrys Hughes had to wait until early 1966 for the Burns stamp.[96]

In a more important ministry such as the Home Office, interference by the Prime Minister is not common, nor is his influence generally great. As ever, time and knowledge are necessary prerequisites of influence, and the Home Office is a demanding and complex department. It is, moreover, usually in the hands of a fairly important minister. The fluctuations in Home Office policy under, say, Mr. Henry Brooke, Mr. R. A. Butler, Sir Frank Soskice and Mr. Roy Jenkins reflect the differences of view and of ministerial style among these Home Secretaries rather than the attitudes of Prime Ministers. Indeed, under the same Prime Minister, Home Office policy changed quite radically when Soskice was succeeded by Jenkins. The reforming zeal of the Home Office under Jenkins and its support of causes which Jenkins has long espoused are a good illustration of the extent to which an able political head can still influence the work of his department.

The power of Prime Ministers over major economic decisions is difficult to determine, but this is one area of domestic policy in which Prime Ministers cannot avoid close involvement. The importance of economic strength for every other government policy, its electoral significance, and the fact that the Prime Minister will sometimes be forced to answer economic questions in the House of Commons and on television are among the main reasons for his continuous interest. Certain Prime Ministers are, of course, very much better equipped for this aspect of their role than others. Both Sir Anthony Eden and Sir Alec Douglas-Home were relativeley ignorant of economic matters and neither had experience of an economic ministry, though Home had been a junior minister in the Scottish Office. Harold Macmillan, in contrast, had been Chancellor of the Exchequer and had long taken an interest in economic policy and organisation. Harold Wilson not only began with the advantage of being the first professional economist to become Prime Minister, but he had his years of experience as President of the Board of Trade and as Chairman of the Public Accounts Committee behind him.

Macmillan's memories of the inter-war years made him a steadfast and ardent economic expansionist. His Chancellors did not always feel able to share his expansionist views, and Macmillan's relationship with the four Chancellors of the Exchequer who served under him was not entirely easy.[97] In particular, he had to put up with two credit squeezes (imposed by Thorneycroft and Selwyn Lloyd) which he heartily disliked. Though supporting them in public, he argued against them in Cabinet. Eventually defeat in the Cabinet led to Thorneycroft's resignation, but, as has already been mentioned, Selwyn Lloyd was able to win many Cabinet arguments when he made it clear that he regarded the issue as a resigning one. On the other hand, much as Macmillan detested Selwyn Lloyd's pay pause, Lloyd and the Prime Minister saw eye to eye on several of the important organisational developments which took place during Lloyd's period at the Treasury. They were in agreement, for instance, on the setting up of N.E.D.C., though Samuel Brittan has argued that the Chancellor, rather than the Prime Minister, should be regarded as the Founding Father.[98] The setting up of the National Incomes Commission was a clearer case of the comparatively rare instance when a Prime Minister takes matters into his own hands and plays a basic part in sponsoring a new development and determining the ultimate decision. Brittan, in his careful study, writes: "In the end Macmillan lost his patience with the argument and delay and himself summoned a group of officials, including Sir Laurence Helsby, to Admiralty House in the spring of 1962 to hammer out the main lines of N.I.C. – an extremely unconventional kind of initiative for a British Prime Minister to take."[99]

On Augst 28, 1967, the present Prime Minister took personal charge of the Department of Economic Affairs, thus becoming the first Prime Minister since Gladstone to add a major economic ministry to his office as Prime Minister. Wilson's new role in the D.E.A. underlines the point that he is more of an interventionist than the average Prime Minister and more powerful *vis-à-vis* his colleagues, for reasons I have suggested, than most. It is perhaps unlikely, though, that his control over the detail of economic policy will be as great as was Gladstone's when he combined the offices of Chancellor of the Exchequer and Prime Minister. The take-over is less complete. Mr. Peter Shore has, after all, been given the title of Secretary of State for Economic Affairs and promoted to the Cabinet, where, admittedly, his closeness to Wilson could be useful for the Prime Minister. Wilson may, however, be storing up diffculties for himself if he becomes strongly identified with the views of one department which has been known to be in frequent disagreement with another. It will not be easy simultaneously to take command of the D.E.A., and to achieve a prime ministerial perspective on inter-departmental disputes, and to play an adjudicating role as chairman of the Cabinet and its economic committee.

The change suggests that Mr. Wilson was dissatisfied with the amount of influence over economic policy that can be wielded by a Prime Minister as such. At the same time, it is an interesting and unusual use of his power of appointment to extend his control in this sphere. How it will affect the Prime Minister in the performance of other duties, and most notably in foreign affairs, remains to be seen. As an overlord in economic affairs and new chairman of N.E.D.C., Wilson would appear to be switching some of his interest away from foreign policy. (The presence of a strong minister in the Foreign Office, as well as the persistence of economic problems, may have something to do with this.) But since, in modern conditions, no Prime Minister can afford not to be well briefed on overseas and defence policy, the Prime Minister is imposing a heavy burden upon himself. One conjecture might be that his D.E.A. move is no more than a rescue operation to combat Treasury influence – and unemployment – in the immediate future, and to give the D.E.A. new strength and hope in the losing battle it has been fighting with the Treasury. My own view is that the Prime Minister's command of the D.E.A. can be no more than a temporary measure and that he will relinquish the task within eighteen months or, at the most, two years. The alternative would be to become a mere figurehead – and let Peter Shore do *all* the work. But if the Prime Minister is to collect full blame when things go wrong (as now he must), it is in his political interest to be a real head of the department which he formally commands.

Be that as it may, it remains true that in the eyes of the spending minister power is seen to lie, first, with the Treasury and, secondly, with the Cabinet (or its appropriate committee). These are the bodies he must persuade, since they have the power to frustrate or facilitate his good intentions. The Prime Minister's importance to the spending minister lies in the fact that he is normally the most important single ally he can secure for a fight with the Treasury. If the Treasury has stood firm against a spending department at the inter-departmental official committee and Cabinet Committee level, a determined minister may want to carry the matter further and put it on the Cabinet agenda. His chances of winning his point in Cabinet are improved if the Prime Minister is on his side. Many – probably most – of the informal meetings between ministers and Prime Ministers take place on the initiative of a departmental minister seeking advice and influential support. It is virtually unknown, for example, for the Prime Minister to take the initiative in interfering with the Scottish Office. But it is not uncommon for a Secretary of State for Scotland to attempt to win the Prime Minister's support. Macmillan was an invaluable ally for the Scottish Office against the Treasury, not only because he was a thoroughgoing expansionist, but since he was strongly in favour of special treatment for the less developed areas of the country. (The regional policy which has become a commonplace today was bitterly opposed by Treasury officials and academic economists as recently as seven or eight years ago.)

But, helpful though he may be, the Prime Minister can only defy a Cabinet majority at his own peril and by putting the fate of his government in the balance. (It was this risk which Eden was not prepared to take at the time of the Suez cease-fire.) There is nothing unusual about a Prime Minister in the course of Cabinet discussions being forced to modify his views, compromise, or keep his mouth shut. It is when the Cabinet is fairly evenly divided on an issue that the Prime Minister's views gain in importance, for he would not be where he is if his opinions and judgment did not command a more than average respect. It was within the context of a rather evenly divided Cabinet that Macmillan was sometimes able to help a spending ministry such as the Scottish Office to win points from the Treasury, and that Sir Alec Douglas-Home was able to exercise significant influence in favour of the abolition of resale price maintenance. The latter case was a good example of a Cabinet split down the middle with influential members on both sides. When Home succeeded Macmillan, it helped to tilt the balance in favour of the abolitionists, for Macmillan (whose experience as a publisher may have been an influence) was not notably sympathetic towards their cause.

A variable factor in the Prime Minister's power which should be touched upon briefly is the exigency of the situation. Exigency, as has already been argued, helps to account for the Prime Minister's greater role in foreign than in home affairs. It means, too, that he will play a more powerful role in war than in time of peace. But even in peacetime an emergency situation can lead to the Prime Minister exercising a more than normal personal power (with the tacit acquiescence of his colleagues). This was true of Baldwin, who was not given to asserting himself, during the General Strike and the Abdication crisis. It would apply to the present Prime Minister over the Rhodesia crisis, the economic crisis of July 1966,[100] and the handling of the Seamen's Strike. The corrollary of such extraordinary activities on the part of a Prime Minister is his corresponding, temporary neglect of other areas of governmental activity. (Baldwin indeed implied in conversation with R. A. Butler that one reason why he did not devote more attention to the growing international crisis in his last year of office was the extent to which that period was occupied with the problems of the Abdication.[101]) For while the Prime Minister is devoting most of his attention to one matter, other activities in Whitehall do not grind to a halt. Life – and the political process – goes on.

P.M.'s Party Standing

It is arguable that one of the most important variables affecting the Prime Minister's power is his relative party standing. The point cannot be ignored here. Neither can it be fully explored. The relationship between a Prime Minister and his party (parliamentary party, constituency parties, Central Office permanent officials, and mass support) could quite easily form the subject of a book-length study.[102]

The roles of party leader and of Prime Minister (when the party is in office) are so interwoven that they are exceedingly difficult to disentangle. At the level of formal powers, it is possible to distinguish those which are explicitly associated with the office of Prime Minister from certain party responsibilities. Where the right to make appointments is concerned, the distinction may be especially clear. The extent to which a Prime Minister's influence over policy or assertiveness *vis-à-vis* his colleagues is affected by his party standing is more difficult to determine. Harold Laski, in the course of his academic career, changed his mind on this issue. In his inter-war writings, he argued that the Prime Minister's power rested entirely on his position in the party. In his last published work, he took the view that very considerable power was attached to the actual office of Prime Minister.

It is not necessary to deny the last point in order to regard party standing as an important variable. For though no Prime Minister's power is ever negligible, the same Prime Minister may be stronger at some periods than others. The variation is largely due to his party standing. Macmillan's ministerial colleagues, back-bench M.P.s and constituency party supporters were inclined to give the Prime Minister a good deal of personal credit for the recovery of party morale

after Suez and the subsequent sweeping victory in the 1959 general election. In the period immediately following the election, Macmillan's influence was at its height, and it may be surmised that the Conservative Party would have "put up" with more from him than they were prepared to tolerate three years later. The "July purge," for instance, might have gone through much more smoothly from this earlier position of strength than in 1962 when Macmillan's popularity with party and public was on the decline. It was on the high tide of his post-1959 popularity that Macmillan was able to float his most controversial policies and those most likely to alienate traditional Conservative support – for instance, the coming to terms with African nationalism which followed Lennox-Boyd's departure from the Colonial Office[103] and his Common Market initiatve. Douglas-Home, in contrast, at no time enjoyed such a position of strength *vis-à-vis* his party. There were always sceptics who had doubts about his ability or popular appeal, and eventually, of course, the rumblings of discontent were sufficiently loud to force his resignation from the party leadership. In his (admittedly short) period as Prime Minister, he was not able to give any strong and distinctive lead on major policy. On the other hand, it could well be argued that Harold Wilson's great popularity within the Labour Party (and the remarkable extent to which he had succeeded in unifying the Parliamentary Party) from the time of his election to the party leadership until immediately after the 1966 General Election enabled the government to carry policies into effect which would have caused a much greater commotion (if not a major crisis) under the leadership of Gaitskell. The retention of British nuclear weapons, support for the Americans in Vietnam, sustained deflation and the wage freeze, as well as the second British bid for Common Market membership, are cases in point. As a corollary, if dissent within the Labour Party grows and the popularity of the Prime Minister begins to decline, fewer options will be open and major concessions may be made to back-bench opinion. M.P.s (and even rank and file party members) are notably reluctant to change their party allegiance, but they can in the last resort, change their leaders, and the leaders know it.
G. W. Jones has argued that dissension in the party makes for dissatisfaction in the leadership, for support tends to coalesce around the Prime Minister's principal colleagues. In Jones's view: "There is no loyalty at the top because the Prime Minister's colleagues are his rivals, eager to replace him, and he is engaged in a constant battle to fend them off."[104] But this is not acceptable as a generalisation.

Much still depends upon the Prime Minister's party standing which is sometimes so high that there are no rivals in sight and at other times quite the reverse. Douglas-Home had serious rivals and Wilson has not. Also of relevance is the Prime Minister's health and age. Macmillan had no rivals in 1959, but plenty in 1962–63. Between 1951–55, there were attempts (eventually successful) to unseat Churchill, though in this case there was little rivalry, since the heirdom was not in dispute. The Prime Minister's leading colleagues tend to have temporary, rather than permanent followings. They are not rivals in the sense that they are constantly engaged in conspiratorial activities. But alternative Prime Ministers are important in that they are there – even if they choose only to stand and wait.

Some Conclusions

One of the difficulties in discussing "prime ministerial government" is to know exactly what the notion entails, for it appears to mean different things to different people. It seems, however, to include the following propositions: 1. A Prime Minister has the effective power to give office only to those of whom he personally approves, and his ministers have been "reduced to the rank of lieutenants that he can dismiss as he wishes." 2. Control of the machinery of government ensures the Prime Minister's preponderant influence over his colleagues. Through his "control" of the Cabinet Office and of Cabinet Committees he can manipulate the Cabinet collectively and prevent ministers from putting items on the Cabinet agenda. 3. More generally (and most basic to a meaningful definition of prime ministerial government), major policy decisions are taken or dominated by the Prime Minister. He dominates Cabinet deliberations to such an extent that he can rarely, if ever, be defeated in Cabinet.[105] Formal meetings apart, he may also intervene at will to dominate the policies of any department he chooses to take an interest in. 4. These points constitute a great *increase* in the Prime Minister's power within the government, and are developments that date from the First World War (or, as some believe, from the Second). They are changes sufficiently important to warrant the use of a new term, "prime ministerial government," to describe the British political system.[106]
One may doubt the validity of these propositions and still hold that such areas of decision-making as appointments, dismissals and dissolution have been growth areas in a Prime Minister's power. But

(as has already been emphasised), a modern Prime Minister has greater power over *appointment*, as compared with Prime Ministers of over fifty years ago, only in the limited sense that there are more jobs to be filled. If his power to *dismiss* a minister is unquestioned, one has to go back much further than fifty years to find a time when it was not. More important, severe practical constraints limiting his ability to dismiss ministers still persist. Even Macmillan dismissed no potential Prime Ministers and sacked his friends rather than prospective rivals. If dissolution is more of a personal prerogative of the Prime Minister than it was formerly, it might still quite appropriately be classified under power of the executive. It is certainly not a power of the Prime Minister over his colleagues. Proposition one, it would appear, is a misleading overstatement of the case. The second proposition is also misguided. Changes in governmental organisation (such as the development of the Cabinet Secretariat and Cabinet Committees) have strengthened the central machinery of control, but not the hand of the Prime Minister alone. The Cabinet agenda is finalised by the Prime Minister, but its contents are dependent upon the wishes and interests of his Cabinet colleagues. The idea that the Prime Minister is the policy-maker *par excellence* both inside the Cabinet and out of it (proposition three) is, to put it at its mildest, an oversimplification. *Area* of policy is relevant here, as are such variable factors as the aptitudes and experience of particular Prime Ministers,[107] the experience and ability of their colleagues, the Prime Minister's party standing, and the exigency of the situation. The view (proposition four) that the Prime Minister's powers *vis-à-vis* his colleagues have been growing in the twentieth century, especially since the First World War or even (and much more implausibly) since the Second, rests upon rather weak foundations. In a sense, Lloyd George and Neville Chamberlain provide the best examples of "prime ministerial government." But it is difficult to regard them as evidence of a *trend* – for three reasons. Firstly, the examples are from almost fifty years ago in the one case; almost thirty in the other. Secondly, the power exercised by Lloyd George and Chamberlain was exceptional. Thirdly, their arrogation of more than usual power to themselves worked only in the short term. It helped to hasten their political eclipse.

"Prime ministerial government" is but the latest of many shorthand expressions which have been coined to convey the essence of the British system of government. "Parliamentary democracy" and "Cabinet government" were predecessors and remain rivals. Each phrase contains an element of truth, but none is an adequate brief description of the political system. There is much to be said for eschewing all three. In very general terms it may be said that a Prime Minister who is autocratic pays the penalty not only in terms of policy failures but party rebellion and, in all probability, ultimate dismissal. He stands where he is because his party put him there and he must continue to satisfy them broadly if he is to remain. Should he be deficient in important respects, there are good precedents (especially in the Conservative Party) for his replacement as party leader and, accordingly, as Prime Minister. "From him that hath not shall be taken away even that which he hath." Even when a strong and able Prime Minister, and one popular with his party, is in office, effective policy-making power is much more widely diffused than the idea of prime ministerial government would suggest. The increase in powers and functions of the executive has done little to simplify the Prime Minister's task. It has done much, in fact, to exacerbate the difficulties in the way of his effective supervision and intervention. As government becomes more complex and the range of governmental activity continues to expand, a Prime Minister has to run fairly hard simply to stay in the same place.

Anmerkungen

1 D. N. Chester, "Who Governs Britain?" *Parliamentary Affairs*, 1961–62, Vol. XV, pp. 519–527. This is a review of John P. Mackintosh's important historical study, *The British Cabinet*, 1962.

2 G. W. Jones, "The Prime Minister's Power," *Parliamentary Affairs*, Spring 1965, pp. 167–185.

3 Walter Bagehot, *The English Constitution* (Fontana edition, 1963). Introduction by R. H. S. Crossman, p. 51. There is a fair measure of common ground between Crossman and J. P. Mackintosh. However, Mackintosh's more detailed study is also a more heavily qualified statement of the prime ministerial government case. There would also appear to be a difference of emphasis in the time scale adopted by Mackintosh and Crossman. For Mackintosh, prime ministerial government is essentially a post-First World War development, and for Crossman a continuation of the "system of voluntary totalitarianism" which was accepted during the Second World War.

4 Bertrand de Jouvenel, "The Principate," pp. 20–51 of *The Political Quarterly*, London, January–March, 1965, p. 21.

5 Sir George Mallaby, *From My Level: Unwritten Minutes*, 1965, p. 59.

6 F. W. G. Benemy, *The Elected Monarch: the Development of the Powers of the Prime Minister*, 1965, p. 245. This is one of only two books exclusively devoted to a study of the position of British Prime Minister. Of these, the more scholarly and better balanced is B. E. Carter's *The Office of Prime Minister*, London, 1956.

7 "I accept that we are now operating a presidential system; to do otherwise would be unrealistic. Let us concede the Prime Minister presidential powers and equip ourselves with safeguards" (*The Listener*, August 25, 1966).

8 *The Governance of England*, Revised Edition, 1914, p. xxii. The change was, in fact, made because the self-governing colonies resented having to deal with the British Government through the Colonial Office in the same way as governments of Crown Colonies.

9 *How Britain is Governed*, 1930, p. 83.

10 *Ibid.* 1930, p. 83.

11 This was pointed out in 1935 by Reginald Bassett in a brief reply to Ramsay Muir in his work (a more central preoccupation of which is the refutation of Laski's *Democracy in Crisis*) *The Essentials of Parliamentary Democracy*, 2nd edition, 1964 pp. 19–25. (Without accepting Bassett's arguments *in toto*, one might wish that his perceptive book were better known.)

12 *Thoughts on the Constitution*, 1947: second edition (1953) with new introduction, Oxford, 1964.

13 *Ibid.* especially pp. 22–27. Morley's "*primus inter pares*" has become too popular and easy an Aunt Sally. Amery prefers to cite Morley's less ambiguous and (on the common interpretation of "*primus inter pares*") contrasting remark: "The 'Keystone of the Cabinet Arch,' to quote Lord Morley, is the Prime Minister, with powers always great and in an emergency 'not inferior to those of a dictator'" (p. 73).

14 *Reflections on the Constitution*, 1951, especially pp. 95–120.

15 *Reflections on the Constitution*, 1951, p. 103.

16 *Ibid.* p. 117.

17 R. W. K. Hinton, "The Prime Minister as an Elected Monarch" in *Parliamentary Affairs*, Vol. 13, 1959–60, p. 298.

18 One aspect of the pre-1867, and especially the 18th century, situation must, however, be noted. The very real power of the monarch in the earlier period contrasts strongly with more recent times. Thus, even a Prime Minister who dominated his Cabinet was less powerful in an important sense than his modern successors who do not in fact accept instructions (though they may sometimes accept advice) from the Crown.

19 J. K. Buckley, *Joseph Parkes of Birmingham*, 1926, p. 121. (Quoted in G. B. A. M. Finlayson, *The Municipal Corporations Act, 1835*, Oxford B.Litt. thesis, 1959, pp. 78–79).

20 Sir James Graham, quoted in Morley's *Life of Gladstone*, Vol. 1, p. 248.

21 *Ibid.* Vol. p. 298.

22 Gladstone gave his strong approval to Peel's style of government on more than one occasion. For example: "In a perfectly organised administration such for example as was that of Sir Robert Peel in 1841–46, nothing of great importance is matured,

or would even be projected, in any department, without his personal cognisance; and any weighty business would commonly go to him before being submitted to the Cabinet": Gladstone, *Gleanings*, pp. 242–243. (Quoted in Arthur Berriedale Keith's *The British Cabinet System*, p. 65).

23 A. Ponsonby, *Henry Ponsonby*, p. 195 (quoted in Sir Ivor Jennings, *Cabinet Government*, 3rd ed., Cambridge, 1959, p. 360).

24 Robert Blake, *Disraeli*, 1966, p. 542. Hicks Beach recalled: "I have known Lord Beaconsfield enforce his own view on the Cabinet after all its members but one had expressed a different opinion: Lord Salisbury frequently allowed important matters to be decided by a small majority of votes, even against his own opinion" (Lady Gwendolen Cecil, *Life of Robert, Marquis of Salisbury*, 1931, Vol. III, p. 169. Cited by J. P. Cornford, "The Parliamentary Foundations of the Hotel Cecil," pp. 268–311 of Robert Robson (ed.), *Ideas and Institutions of Victorian Britain*, 1967, p. 305). In making the contrast with Salisbury, Hicks Beach attributes to Disraeli a power which has more in common with that of President Lincoln *vis-à-vis* his Cabinet ("Noes seven, ayes, one. The ayes have it") than with any known feat of a Prime Minister of the present generation.

25 Salisbury was Prime Minister and Foreign Secretary throughout the period of his first Cabinet, 1885–86. In his second Cabinet he had a short spell as Prime Minister only, but early in 1887 succeeded Iddesleigh as Foreign Secretary and held both offices until 1892. From 1895 until October 1900, he was again both Prime Minister and Foreign Secretary.

26 Or, as Robert A. Dahl puts it. "When one hears that X is highly influential, the proper question is: 'Influential with respect to what?'" (*Modern Political Analysis*, 1963, p. 45). Analytically, *power* and *influence* may be fairly clearly separated when the Prime Minister's formal institutional powers are being considered. Elsewhere the distinction becomes blurred. Thus, one tends to speak of *power of appointment*, but of *influence* over *policy*. For practical purposes, it is possible in the latter case to use *influence* and *power* almost interchangeably.

27 *Party* was a less solid part of the political scene that Bagehot was interpreting, and as he formulated this point, it is "*Parliament and the Nation*" who "have pretty well settled who shall have the first places; but they have not discriminated with the same degree of accuracy which man shall have which place" (*The English Constitution*, 1963 ed., p. 67).

28 G. W. Jones, *op cit.* p. 179.

29 He has least room for manoeuvre in the case of coalition government when bargains must be struck with other party leaders. (For a valuable reassessment of the place of coalition government in British political life, see Alan Beattie, "British coalition government revisited," in *Government and Opposition*, Vol. 2, No. 1, October 1966–January 1967, pp. 3–34.)

30 Jones, *op. cit.* p. 179.

31 Ian Aitken, *The Guardian*, January 9, 1967, "Some ministers," reported *The Guardian*, feared that Mr. Wilson's "selection for ministerial office might encourage other young backbenchers to take the view that vice rather than virtue was most likely to be rewarded in the present Parliament."

32 A. G. Gardiner, *Life of Sir William Harcourt*, i. 508, ii. 610 (quoted in A. B. Keith, *The British Cabinet System*, 2nd ed., 1952, p. 79).

33 *Ibid.* There were practical political difficulties in the way of *demanding* Carlingford's resignation. First, he was Irish, and as Granville wrote to Gladstone: "I believe it would be much better for Rosebery to come in without a popular man, the only Irishman in the Cabinet, being turned out for him." Secondly, there was a Press leak. The *Pall Mall Gazette* announced that Carlingford was about to be replaced by Rosebery. Granville, counselling caution, wrote: "I believe that Sir R. Peel said it was a serious matter putting a man into a Cabinet, but a more serious one to put him out. I am afraid after Carlingford's letter that it would be a question of turning him out. It was most unlucky the line *Pall Mall* has taken." Gladstone's reply suggests delicacy of feeling and a weighing of the political consequences rather than giving the impression that he did not have the *power* to remove a minister: "To proceed in the matter with Carlingford is something, I admit and feel, of a butchering business but yet I feel that under the circumstances our case is strong and the thing just. I hope you will not disapprove of it. I talked it through again and again with Harcourt and saw my way clearly. You say truly that it is not easy to put a man out of a Cabinet: but something depends on the questions 1. whether he can rise higher *in* it. 2. whether he is simply shelved or has a great office offered" (Agatha Ramm (ed.) *Gladstone-Granville Correspondence, 1883–1886*, 1962, Vol. II, pp. 247, 248, 249, 251, 253).

34 In the words of one of those dismissed, Dr. Charles Hill, the Minister of Housing and Local Government: "I find no pleasure in the reflection that, because of the way these changes were made, much of the advantage of bringing new blood into the Cabinet was thrown away, or that there was no marked improvement in the Government's image in the year which followed" (Lord Hill of Luton: *Both Sides of the Hill*, 1964, p. 248).

35 Reginald Bevins, *The Greasy Pole*, 1965, p. 137.

36 *Ibid.* p. 138.

37 Lord Butler of Saffron Walden, *The Listener*, September 16, 1965, p. 409.

38 There was, for example, no difference over policy between Mr. Wilson and Mr. Tom Fraser at the time (December 1965) when the Prime Minister asked for Mr. Fraser's resignation as Minister of Transport.

39 My source is a very senior member of Macmillan's Cabinet at that time.

40 Geoffrey Marshall, "Advice to Dissolve," *The Guardian*, March 8, 1966.

41 Francis Williams, *A Prime Minister Remembers*, 1961, p. 228.

42 W. T. Rodgers (ed.), *Hugh Gaitskell, 1906–1963*, 1964, p. 95.

43 Thomas Jones, *Of Prime Ministers and Cabinets*, B. B. C. Publication, 1938, pp. 26–27.

44 *Ibid.*

45 Hugh Dalton, *Memoirs, Vol. 1, "Call Back Yesterday,"* 1953, p. 90.

46 See, *e.g.*, Richard Lloyd George, *Lloyd George*, 1960; and Lord Beaverbrook, *The Decline and Fall of Lloyd George*, 1963, especially pp. 206, 302.

47 The Earl of Swinton, *Sixty Years of Power*, 1966, p. 49.

48 Lord Beaverbrook, *The Decline and Fall of Lloyd George*, p. 40.

49 Beaverbrook, *op. cit.* p. 172.

50 It is also the case, of course, that MacDonald and Baldwin kept Churchill out of office in the thirties. But in the earlier part of that period, in particular, Churchill was in disgrace with the moderate sector of the Conservative Party over his attitude to India. Baldwin, when he first became Prime Minister in 1924, had, on the other hand, given Churchill the Treasury because "He would be more under control inside than out."

51 See Sir Keith Feiling's *Life of Neville Chamberlain*, 1946, esp. p. 305.

52 Iain Macleod, *Neville Chamberlain*, 1961, p. 165.

53 Shortly after Chamberlain became Prime Minister, Thomas Jones wrote of him: "He told Nancy" (Lady Astor) "last week that he meant to be his own Foreign Minister and also to take an active hand in co-ordinating ministerial policy generally, in contrast with S. B. We shall see" (Thomas Jones: *A Diary with Letters, 1931–1950,* 1954, p. 350).

54 Macleod, *op. cit*, pp. 200–201.

55 Swinton, *op. cit.* p. 116.

56 More recently, Harold Wilson has argued that "the Common Market is of such transcendent importance to Britain that the whole Cabinet must be involved, and that is the way I am playing it." In the first part of 1966 the Common Market question was considered by a Cabinet Committee. But in the autum of that year and again in 1967 the Common Market became a major subject of discussion at a hole series of Cabinet meetings ("The Prime Minister on the machinery of government," Part. II, Harold Wilson, M. P., interviewed by Norman Hunt, *The Listener*, April 13, 1967, p. 483).

57 G. W. Jones, *op. cit.* p. 181.

58 John P. Mackintosh, *The British Cabinet*, 1962, p. 394.

59 My italics.

60 Mackintosh, *op. cit.*

61 In a radio interview with Norman Hunt, *Whitehall and Beyond*, B. B. C., 1964, p. 59.

62 Among ministers with whom I have spoken, the definite consensus of opinion is that a minister can get an item on the agenda if he wants to. A minister may occasionally be told that there is no room left on the Thursday agenda and that discussion of the question he wishes to raise will have to be held over until the following Tuesday, but there is no question of keeping an item off indefinitely.

63 There is, however, a tendency, as Michael Shanks (after two-and-a-half years in the Department of Economic Affairs) argues, "to accept compromises for the sake of peace" and issues may even be "fudged at official level to stop them going to the top executive committee, which is the Cabinet" ("'Positive government' – a contradiction in terms?" *The Times*, August 14, 1967, p. 19). Settlements at this level, it may be added, leave the Prime Minister as much in the dark as the Cabinet.

64 My italics.

65 Harold Wilson, in an interview with Kenneth Harris, *The Observer* Colour Supplement, October 24, 1965, p. 21.

66 *Political Adventure, The Memoirs of the Earl of Kilmuir*, p. 308.

67 Several ministers have confirmed that George Brown was a powerful Committee Chairman. A dispute which found the Minister of Economic Affairs and the Chancellor of the Exchequer on one side and a spending minister and the Prime Minister on the other was regarded as a very good match.

68 In an interview with Gerald Kaufman, *New Statesman*, March 5, 1965.

69 A possible exception is Churchill's Private Office in his wartime coalition government.

70 How difficult it was for the individual minister to make an *informed* judgment prior to the development of the Cabinet Secretariat is noted by Mackintosh, *op. cit.* pp. 311–312.

71 The constraints upon this power are fewer at the time when a Prime Minister is first forming his government than they are later.

72 Crossman's summary is slightly misleading. For a brief but more precise account of the present arrangements, see Lord Bridges: *The Treasury*, 2nd ed., 1966, pp. 161, 164–165, 176–177.

73 Crossman, Introduction to Bagehot, *op. cit.* p. 51.

74 For a variety of views on the desirability of this, see Nora Beloff, "The mandarins win again," *The Observer*, February 13, 1966; *The Guardian* leader, "The right to choose your own adviser," February 17, 1966; and James Margach, "A High Wind in Whitehall," *The Sunday Times*, February 20, 1966.

75 See *The Life and Letters of Sir Austen Chamberlain*, ii, p. 246, quoted in Sir Ivor Jennings, *Cabinet Government*, 3rd ed., p. 189.

76 See, *e.g.*, *Political Adventure, The Memoirs of the Earl of Kilmuir*, 1964, p. 193.

77 Moran, *Winston Churchill: the Struggle for Survival, 1940–65*, 1966.

78 In April 1953, Churchill remarked: "We had 110 Cabinet meetings in the past year; while the Socialists had only 85 in a year – and that in a time of great political activity. I am a great believer in bringing things before the Cabinet. If a Minister has got anything on his mind and he has the sense to get it argued by the Cabinet he will have the machine behind him" (*ibid.* p. 404).

79 Occasionally, however, Churchill felt he should be consulted more. "Anthony tells me nothing," he complained to Moran in June 1954. "He keeps me out of foreign affairs, treats them as a private preserve of his own" (*ibid.* p. 553).

80 "Defence," Lord Avon has written "is very much a Prime Minister's special subject. He presides over the meetings of the Defence Committee which are attended by the Chiefs of Staff. He may, on occasion, hold informal meetings with the Minister of Defence and the Chiefs of Staff, or with these and the Service Ministers as well. The Prime Minister is ultimately responsible for all important decisions on defence. This is how it should be" (*The Memoirs of Sir Anthony Eden: Full Circle*, p. 367). The point is perhaps made a shade dogmatically, reflecting Eden's ideas of the exalted place of the Prime Minister in relation to the Cabinet, but the links between defence and overseas policy are obvious enough, and it is not surprising that Prime Ministers tend to take a particular interest in both.

81 *Cf.* R. H. S. Crossman, Introduction to Walter Bagehot's *The English Constitution*, Fontana paperback (1965 impression), p. 55.

82 Hugh Thomas, *The Suez Affair*, 1967, p. 159.

83 Anthony Nutting, *No End of a Lesson – The Story of Suez*, 1967.
84 Hugh Thomas, *op. cit.* p. 55.
85 *The Listener*, September 16, 1965, pp. 409–410.
86 *Ibid.* p. 410.
87 In a private interview with the present writer, July 1966.
88 Thomas, *op. cit.* p. 98.
89 Hugh Thomas, *op. cit.* p. 146.
90 See also Moran, *op. cit.* p. 710.
91 See article by Ronald Butt, "The Common Market and Conser—tive Party politics, 1961–2," in *Government and Opposition*, Vol. 2, No. 3, April–July 1967.
92 As one fairly recent Minister of Education put it to me: "There is a tendency to forget the limits on a Prime Minister's activities. Macmillan knew a lot about Housing – he had been Minister of Housing. But he did not know much (and it is not surprising) about state education." Emphasising that this was not a criticism of Macmillan "who was better informed generally than many Prime Ministers," he added: "Not only does the Prime Minister not know, but he has his own interests. Every Prime Minister since Baldwin has taken a great interest in foreign affairs – though independent actions by the Prime Minister in foreign affairs usually do not work."
93 Lord Butler of Saffron Walden, interview with Norman Hunt, *The Listener*, September 16, 1965, p. 408.
94 Reginald Bevins, *The Greasy Pole: a Personal Account of the Realities of British Politics*, 1965, p. 138.
95 *The Guardian*, February 1 and 2, 1966.
96 The publication of which produced from Mr. Marples the fatuous comment: "Still am against it. Look at the man's record. Then think if you want him appearing on the same stamp as the Queen." (*The Guardian*, February 2, 1966.)
97 Macmillan was perhaps most in sympathy with the policies of his last Chancellor, Reginald Maudling.
98 Brittan, *The Treasury Under the Tories, 1951–1964*, 1964, p. 219. Brittan's view is that "there is no sign that Macmillan ever tried to initiate anything himself on these lines before his Chancellor took up the idea, and it is Lloyd who must be given the credit for it." Sir Edward Boyle has, however, pointed out the element of over-simplification involved in such personal attribution of credit. In his words: "N.E.D.C. was the fruit of a number of things, not least the growing interest of the National Institute of Economic and Social Research in the work of the Commissariat in France. I would say the biggest stimulus to N.E.D.C. was the conference on the work of the Commissariat organized in April 1960 by the National Institute." (Proceedings of an R.I.P.A. Conference on "Who are the Policy Makers?" Published in *Public Administration*, Autumn 1965.)
99 Samuel Brittan, *op. cit.* p. 239.
100 Even the major economic statement of July 20 which by convention should have come from the Chancellor of the Exchequer was made by the Prime Minister.
101 *The Listener*, July 28, 1966, Butler-Harris conversation, p. 111.
102 R. T. McKenzie, *British Political Parties*, has in fact much valuable material on this

question, but more work might be done on the relevance of these relationships to prime ministerial power and the policy-making process.

103 Some rethinking of African policy had already occurred before the 1959 election but it became much more *overt* after. This was the period of Macmillan's African tour and his "Wind of Change" speech in Cape Town.

104 G. W. Jones, *op. cit.* p. 176.

105 On this point J. P. Mackintosh is more cautious than some of his disciples. There might appear to be an implied contrast with a later period in his comment on the late nineteenth century situation that "within the Cabinet, the Prime Minister could well be on the losing side in an argument" (*op. cit.* p. 303). But Mackintosh recognises that "in modern ministries policies advocated by the Premier have, on occasion, been modified or rejected." (*Ibid.* p. 384). A distinction is, perhaps, suggested by the contrast between "could well be" and "on occasion." Whether it is justified is more doubtful. Mackintosh himself gives *several* examples of Churchill being defeated within his Cabinet on matters of real consequence. (*Ibid.* p. 435.) Examples involving Eden (Suez cease-fire) and Macmillan (expansion *v.* deflation) have been suggested above.

106 Such is the diversity of view among those who use the term, "prime ministerial government," that I willingly concede that not all of them would necessarily accept all four of the above propositions. It should also be observed that there are scholars who hold that the present century has seen an increase in the Prime Minister's power who do not, however, believe that the development has been such as to merit the use of the new term, "prime ministerial government."

107 Mackintosh, taking a different view, argues that "the position and power of the prime Minister" have "not been due to the personality of any particular Premier or to any personal desires to arrogate power." (*Ibid.* p. 384.)

5

D. N. Chester

The British Parliament 1939–1966

Aus: Parliamentary Affairs, Bd. 19, London 1966, S. 417–445.
D. N. Chester ist seit 1954 Warden des Nuffield College in Oxford.

I. Events

One way of attempting to discover trends is by plotting a number of observations and linking them on a chart. This, however, can be done only when the observations can be measured. Nevertheless, I have listed the events and changes in the working of Parliament since around 1939 (excluding any special changes peculiar to the war years, e.g. secret sessions). They are not in order either of time or importance but events or observations with similar implications have been put near to each other. The reader is left to decide whether any pattern emerges.

1. In October, 1943, the Commons decides to rebuild its Chamber, destroyed by German bombers, on the same lines as the old. In the words of Winston Churchill, the Chamber "should not be big enough to contain all its Members at once without overcrowding, ... there should be no question of every Member having a separate seat reserved for him. ... If the House is big enough to contain all its Members nine-tenths of its Debates will be conducted in the depressing atmosphere of an almost empty or half empty Chamber. The essence of good House of Commons speaking is the conversational style, the facility for quick informal interruptions and interchanges ... (this) requires a fairly small space and there should be on great occasions a sense of crowd and urgency".[1] Thus there are still only 346 seats on the floor of the House and a further 91 in the side galleries for 630 members.

2. The Commons obtains full control over its premises. On 26th April, 1965, the control, use and occupation of the Palace of Westminster passed from the Queen to the two Houses. Before

then supreme control on behalf of the Queen rested with the Lord Great Chamberlain. While the House was sitting he delegated his powers to the Serjeant at Arms acting for Mr. Speaker. During the Recesses and weekends control reverted to the Lord Great Chamberlain and it was on these occasions that most of the difficulties arose. Control now is vested in Mr. Speaker, advised by the Select Committee on the House of Commons (Services) composed of the Leader of the House, the Chief Whips from the Government and Opposition, a former Conservative Leader of the House and 13 other members. The Lords control their own part of the building.[2] The ceremonial rooms still remain in the charge of the Lord Great Chamberlain.

3. Somewhat more office accommodation has recently been made available for Members by various small adjustments to the existing building and a small amount of new building. Personal desk space is now available for most Members who ask for it. But apart from Ministers and a few senior Members, no Member has an office to himself.[3]

4. The library, research and information services available to Members has been markedly increased since 1945. The Research Division of the Library now has a senior Staff of nine graduates, of whom three specialize in economic matters.

5. The "agenda papers" of the House, i.e. the Notice and the Order Papers, and the Vote, have been simplified and made clearer. In general a good deal of thought has been given to the "stationery" involved in the proceedings of the House. In 1965 specially printed forms were made available for Questions and Early Day Motions. Previously Members could use (and did) any odd bit of paper that came readiest to hand.

6. The Prime Minister is no longer Leader of the House. The last to hold both offices was Neville Chamberlain (1937–40).

7. The proportion of Members holding office in the Government has increased. The figures are as follows:[4]

	1900	1930	1950	1960	1966 (Feb.)
Number of M.P.'s holding Office⁺	33	50	68	65	88
Parliamentary Private Secretaries	9	26	27	36	28
Total number of M.P.'s involved	42	76	95	101	116
Size of House	670	615	625	630	630

⁺ Including Queens Household, Whips and Parliamentary Secretaries.

The number of Cabinet Ministers has changed little during the period. There has, however, been a big increase in the number of Parliamentary Secretaries and of Ministers of State (an office somewhat mid-way in status between a Parliamentary Secretary and the Ministerial head of a department). This increase is associated with the growing size of departments and the need to provide the Ministerial head with political assistance. Parliamentary Private Secretaries usually have little or no departmental duties and have greater freedom to express their personal views than other office holders.[5] It will be seen that in the Labour Administration of October 1964–March 1966 a third of the Parliamentary Labour Party held some kind of Government appointment. This point has to be borne in mind when considering what contribution Government back benchers can make, in terms of quality as well as numbers, to manning various committees.

8. Since October, 1964, the Opposition Chief Whip has become a paid public office "in view of the onerous duties in any modern parliament". He receives £3,750 plus £1,250 parliamentary allowance. The Leader of the Opposition now receives £4,500 plus £1,250.

9. The notion of a "shadow cabinet" has been increasingly formalized. In 1955 Mr. Attlee proposed that the Leader of the Party should formally designate Members of the Opposition Front Bench who should on most occasions be the Party's spokesman when a particular department or subject was under discussion. The Press often use the terms Shadow Chancellor, Shadow Minister of Health and so on. When Mr. Heath became Conservative Leader *The Times* opened a report headed "The Shadow Cabinet in Full" with the words: "Mr. Heath's list of 72 senior and junior front bench appointments . . ."[6] Herbert Morrison[7] criticized this development on three main grounds. First "the enormous patronage which as a whole is properly exercised by a Prime Minister in forming a Government is thereby duplicated . . .". Second, the selection will tie the hands of a new Prime Minister in choosing his Cabinet, and third, it introduces an undesirable rigidity in the arrangements for Front Bench speakers in major debates.

10. The extent of the Sovereign's discretion in the choice of Prime Minister has been further curtailed. When in January, 1957, Sir Anthony Eden resigned on the grounds of ill health, the Queen invited Mr. Harold Macmillan to be Prime Minister. It was thought in some quarters that Mr. R. A. Butler was the natural successor

but the Conservative Party held no meetings and did not overtly at least, express a group opinion. The Labour Party, however, announced that if a similar occasion arose during a Labour Administration the Queen ought not to make a choice until the Parliamentary Party had chosen its new Leader.

In July, 1965, Sir Alec Douglas-Home gave notice of his intention to resign from the Leadership of the Conservative Party. On this occasion it was not the responsibility of the Queen to choose the successor for the Party was out of office. Under rules introduced and agreed in February, 1965, the choice now lay with the Parliamentary Party by a method of voting devised to cover the possibility of no candidate getting an absolute majority at the first or second ballot.[8] The candidate so chosen has to be presented to a meeting of members of both Houses who take the Conservative Whip, of approved candidates and of the Executive of the National Union of Conservative and Unionist Associations. In theory it might reject the choice of the Parliamentary Party in which case the M.P.'s would have to ballot again or find some other solution. In effect, however, both the Conservative and Labour leaders are now chosen by their Parliamentary Parties. It is possible that the Conservatives may adopt the same attitude as the Parliamentary Labour Party towards the discretion constitutionally vested in the Sovereign should the Prime Minister die or retire when they are in power.

11. On 27th July, 1960, a Peer (Lord Home) was appointed Foreign Secretary. Some writers claimed this to be evidence of the decline in the power of the Commons and of the increased power of the Prime Minister and there were protests from the Opposition and from other quarters. Mr. Macmillan, however, at the same time appointed Mr. Edward Heath as Lord Privy Seal and responsible (subject, of course, to the Foreign Secretary) for a range of Foreign Office policy, particularly as regards negotiations for entry into the Common Market. The Foreign Secretary had been in the Lords in 1938–40 (Halifax) and in 1919–24 (Curzon). Home remained as Foreign Secretary until he succeeded Mr. Macmillan as Prime Minister in October 1963.

12. The powers of the Lords to oppose the Commons are reduced by the Parliament Act, 1949. The Parliament Act of 1911 provided that a Bill certified by the Speaker to be a Money Bill should become law within one month of being passed by the Commons and sent to the Lords whether or not the Lords had consented. Any other Bill (except a Bill to extend the duration of Parliament beyond

five years) could receive the Royal Assent despite its rejection by the Lords provided that it had been passed by the Commons in three successive Sessions and provided two years had elapsed between the Second Reading in the first Session and the Third Reading in the Third Session. The 1949 Act, which was actually passed by use of the provision in the 1911 Act for overriding the opposition of the Lords, reduced the three successive Sessions to two and the two years to one.

13. The Life Peerages Act, 1958, empowers the Queen to confer peerages for life, the holders of which can sit and vote in the Lords. It was seen as part of the reform of the Lords. When introducing the Bill in the Lords, Lord Home said the Conservatives still believed that the hereditary principle had a part to play but had willingly modified it to enable the Socialist point of view to be put more effectively. The first list of Life Peers published in July, 1958, contained 14 names of whom 6 were said to have been nominated by the Leader of the Opposition. By August 1966 129 Life Peerages had been conferred. In 1939 the House of Lords had 781 members, in 1960 the number had grown to 908 and has now passed the 1,000 mark, of whom some 90 are not in receipt of a writ of summons. The average attendance is about 150.

14. The Peerage Act, 1963, enables hereditary peers to renounce their titles and status for life. Existing peers were given six months in which to make up their mind whether or not to take advantage of the Act. Newly succeeding peers are given a year in which to decide, unless they are Members of Parliament, in which case only one month. The renunciated title remains dormant during the life of the holder but on his death may be resumed by his heir. This change was brought about by the courage, tenacity and skill of Mr. Anthony Wedgwood Benn after he had succeeded to his father's title. It was taken advantage of by Lord Home (now Sir Alec Douglas-Home) and Lord Hailsham (now Quintin Hogg) both of whom were contenders for the Conservative Party Leadership on the retirement of Harold Macmillan. But for the Act, Sir Alec Douglas-Home could hardly have become Prime Minister.

15. Since July 1957 peers have been able to claim a maximum of three guineas (4½ guineas since 16 October, 1964) per day for expenses incurred in attendance at the House, in addition to their travelling expenses. Prior to May 1946 they could not claim even their travelling expenses.

16. As from 1 April 1965 the Leader of the Opposition and the Chief Opposition Whip in the House of Lords have been paid a salary of £2,000 and £1,500 per annum respectively. The Leader of the Opposition in the House of Lords is defined as "the member of the House of Lords who for the time being is Leader in that House of that Party in opposition to Her Majesty's Government having the greatest numerical strength in the House of Commons (Ministerial Salaries and Members' Pensions Act, 1965, Section 2).

17. Members' salaries have been substantially increased. Originally fixed at £400 in 1911, the annual salary was raised to £600 in 1937 and to £1,000 in 1946. In 1954 there was added an allowance of £2 for every day, except Friday, on which the House sat. In 1957 the allowance was fixed at £750 per annum and a Member's salary became £1,750, i.e. £1,000 + £750. Though increases after 1945 failed to keep pace with the steady rise in the cost of living, there was always some opposition in the House to them and on occasion the issue got involved in acrimonious party politics. In December 1963 for the first time an outside Committee of three was appointed and reported a year later. Among the matters which the Committee had to consider was whether the salary should be regarded as recognition of full-time or part-time service. On this there was a marked difference of opinion amongst Members. A substantial number of replies to a questionnaire asking for their views on this point disclosed a firm belief that the House would suffer considerably in the quality of its work if it consisted entirely of full-time professional politicians and thus lost the benefit of the counsel of those Members actively engaged in the professions and other occupations. The Committee based their recommendation on the principle that the salary should be such as "to enable those Members who are without private means or the opportunity to earn income outside the House efficiently to discharge the duties of the service without undue financial worry and to live and to maintain themselves and their families at a modest but honourable level".[9] They therefore proposed a stipend of £3,250 a year which was accepted by the Government and the House and was put into operation from 16 October, 1964, the first day of the new Parliament. The same Committee dealt with the salaries of the Prime Minister and other Ministers, the Speaker, the Leader of the Opposition, etc., most of which had lagged a long way behind rising prices and standard of living. The salary of the Chancellor of the Exchequer, for example, had stayed at £5,000 since 1831. The Committee

proposed that Ministers' salaries should be substantially increased, the Prime Minister from £10,000 to £18,000 and the Chancellor of the Exchequer and other senior Ministers from £5,000 to £12,000, plus in all these cases a parliamentary allowance of £1,250 per annum. In view of the economic situation the Government decided to approve only half this increase,[10] which came into effect on 1 April 1965.

18. As from 16 October 1964 a new contributory Pensions Scheme has been introduced for Members. In return for a payment of £150 per annum any Member on ceasing to be a Member after 10 years' service will receive a pension calculated at the rate of £60 per annum for each year's service up to 15, and at £24 per annum for each year after 15, providing he is aged 65 – if not it will be paid when he reaches 65 (Ministerial Salaries and Members' Pensions Act, 1965, Part II). Whether this will encourage Members to retire earlier remains to be seen.

19. Though the Committee stage of the bulk of Government Bills, and always the Finance Bill, is taken in a Committee of the whole House, greater use is now made of small Standing Committees.

20. There has been a greater use of Committees for the purpose of enquiry and control. A Select Committee on Statutory Instruments was established in 1944 and on Nationalised Industries in 1955. The former has limited functions but the latter has ranged widely in what was thought to be a politically difficult field and has been noticeably successful. The Select Committee on Estimates, though existing before the war, is now a much more active and powerful body and its reports are beginning to attract attention. Recently it has been given power to employ advisers and assessors to assist on a particular enquiry, whereas previously it had to rely entirely on the staff of the Clerk of the House.

21. Early Day Motions have gained greatly in popularity. Any Member may give notice that he proposes to move a particular Motion and this appears on the Notice Paper under the heading "For an Early Day". Whether time is found to debate it depends on the Government or the "usual channels" and very few are in fact debated. The Whips do not, however, control the tabling of these Motions and on occasion, therefore, they are used by Back Benchers to elicit support for a particular policy. The promoter(s) of the Motion will try to get as many Members as possible to sign in order to demonstrate the strength of opinion in the House. Sometimes a Motion will attract signatures from all Parties. Sometimes

they are signed by a substantial number of Government supporters and are critical of and embarrassing to the Government, e.g. the notorious anti-American Motion signed by 120 Conservatives during the Suez crisis (November 1956). The use of the device is a good example of how Members will exploit new ways of expressing themselves as the more well-known ways come under control.[11]

22. Question Time has not kept pace with the demands made on it. The number of oral questions put down for answer has risen, but notwithstanding recent improvements the number answered on the floor of the House has fallen. As a result each Minister comes up for questioning not every day but sometimes only every three or four weeks, or at even longer intervals. The Prime Minister is now available for questioning on two days a week instead of four and only for a quarter of an hour on each occasion. The time devoted to Questions by the House is only a few minutes more than it was 60 years ago and less than it was at the beginning of the Century.

23. Some attempt has been made, by way of the Adjournment Motion each night and on the day before a Recess, to cater for those Back Benchers who wish to raise issues of their own choice. The right to choose the issue to be so debated depends on being successful in a ballot. This is some compensation for their loss of other opportunities.

24. Since 1965 a "greater measure of humanity"[12] has been introduced by the Whips in their pairing negotiations. This has been accepted as an alternative to a system of proxy voting for sick Members. This arrangement enabled Mr. Wilson to maintain his majority even when several of his paper majority of three or four, excluding Liberal support, were unable to attend the House. It reconciles a feeling that it is undignified for very sick Members to have to attend the House merely to record their vote with a dislike of introducing a general system of proxy voting.

25. The independent Member and the very small Party have disappeared from the scene. The Liberal Party, though small in terms of Members, attracts of course a substantial vote – over 3 million or 11.2 % in 1964, 2.3 million or 8.6 % in 1966. Whether the victory of the Plaid Cymru at Carmarthen in July 1966 was a straw in the wind or merely an exception remains to be seen.

26. There has probably been a steady increase in the number of professional, full-time or nearly full-time Members. I say probably because this trend is difficult to measure. A high proportion of Members have some other occupation, but a directorship, for

example, can range from almost a full-time job to a nominal attachment. No information is available about the amount of time individual Members spend in the House. Some Back Benchers clearly do not spend much time there – indeed, the only requirement is that they are present to vote when requested by the Whips. My impression, however, is that it has become increasingly difficult to have an occupation far from London and that the average Member now spends a higher proportion of his time on Parliamentary business than was customary in say, the 1930's.[13]

27. There is now much less drinking and it is very rare for any Member to show signs of intoxication.[14]

28. Members are now better behaved in the Chamber than they were 30 years ago. "In the last twenty years only two Members have been suspended ... for disorderly conduct; whereas in the twenty years between the wars it was a very peaceful Session in which only two Members were suspended for that reason".[15]

29. The authority of the Speaker in the Chamber is now less accepted without question. The Speaker derives his authority from the feeling of the House and therefore it must be presumed that the House does not greatly dislike procedural wrangles and the increasing tendency in the last 20 years for Members to raise points of order. Perhaps Members have been irritated by the strait jacket of Erskine May and by the few opportunities they have to express themselves. A succession of tolerant Speakers has also helped. There is hope that the situation will change under the new Speaker and indeed Question Time is already more productive.

30. "The issues now are more blurred. There is more bipartisanship ..."[16]

31. The appearance of Ministers and Members on television is a far-reaching change, the effects of which are still not fully evaluated. Whereas in the past Members were in the best position to assess the character and abilities of a Minister and so could make or break his career, the general public now have the chance to see him perform in straight talks, interviews and discussions. They can see how he behaves and judge his character from his appearance and his demeanour. They can decide whether or not they like him. Their impressions may be more superficial than those of Members and they may be judging him with rather different criteria in mind. But as in the end it is their votes that count Members must take account of the popular impression. It is also worth noticing that Ministers now spend much less time in the House than they did 40 or 50 years

ago and are to that extent less well-known to Members. The public also now have the opportunity to recognize and even appraise a number of Opposition leaders and Back Benchers who appear fairly regularly on television.

32. The public opinion poll is now an alternative measure to what Bagehot called the "expressive function" of the House, i.e. to express the mind of the English people on all matters which come before it.

33. On 21 April 1966 the State Opening of Parliament was televised. For the purpose of showing the arrival of Black Rod at the door of the House, his admittance, his summons of the faithful Commons and their procession to the House of Lords, the Chamber was brilliantly floodlit and conditions were hot and uncomfortable. Apparently the reason for the excessive brilliance was that Associate British Pathé, Ltd., were filming the proceedings in colour. The Leader of the House had to face strong criticism, partly because the House had not formally given its approval, partly because the proceedings were ceremonial and did not show the House at work, and partly because of the intolerable conditions produced.

34. On Friday, 19 November 1965, for the first time a notice was posted outside the St. Stephen's entrance to the House of Commons informing the public of the business to be taken in the following week.

II. Longer term trends

I have excluded from the above list the elements which have been operating over a much longer period, say since 1900. The most significant and general are:

1. There would appear to have been an increasing acceptance of the monolithic party. Differences of opinion are headlined by the press as a revolt or as a split in the party. Both the Government and the Opposition try to present a solid front. There is an unwillingness to engage in open discussion. Opportunities for criticism must not be given to the other side. The aim is to keep things out of politics unless one or other of the Front Benches, and both for preference, decide that the matter is in politics. Another possible way of stating this trend would be to say that it is a desire to keep things out of the press.

2. The Parliamentary time-table is now completely dominated by the "usual channels", i.e. the Leader of the House and the Government Chief Whip and their counterparts on the Opposition side. They are, of course, in touch with their respective supporters but in their arrangement of, for example, topics for debates they are primarily concerned with allowing expression to majority views in their parties.

3. It is now almost impossible for one or two Members to upset or modify the daily time-table. Certainty was the goal of the Balfour reforms of 1902, certainty that this or that item on the daily "agenda" would be reached at about the time stated. Any element which was not under Government control, e.g. the time available for answering questions, had either to have a time limit placed on it or else be put at the very end of public business. The aim of Balfour and of all those who have since represented the usual channels has been to see that Government business or Opposition business, i.e. the business agreed by the usual channels, has preference over any other business and occupies what Balfour once called the best hours of the day, i.e. roughly the hours before dinner. One of the last remnants of procedure to offend is the Ten Minute Rule. Under this Rule a Member can introduce a Bill at the end of Question Time on Tuesdays or Wednesdays, with a short speech not exceeding 10 minutes. A single speech of similar length can also be made in opposition and then a vote is taken. On two occasions Mr. Sydney Silverman used this device to introduce his Bill to abolish the death penalty. The Select Committee on Procedure of 1965, composed almost entirely of Back Benchers, proposed that the right should "for an experimental period" be exercisable at the end of the day's business. In the House this change was only narrowly carried by a vote of 128 to 118, notwithstanding a substantial number of Ministers voting for it. No action was taken to continue the 'experiment' in the first Session of the new Parliament.

It should be noticed that speeches and business after 10.0 p.m. are less likely to be reported in the press. This was one of the reasons why Balfour in 1902 wished to put Question Time at the end of the day's sitting. There is a general feeling in the House that some Members support "unusual" causes in order to gain personal publicity and one of the tests of sincerity therefore is whether they would support the same cause at an unpopular hour for the press. But this means, of course, that the cause itself gets little publicity. At one time the private Member had a variety of procedural devices at his disposal to force his views on the House. The chief one was the Motion for the Adjournment. The rules governing the moving of such a Motion (now controlled by Standing Order No. 9) by a private Member are now so tight that it is rare for it even to be accepted by the Chair, let alone carried. This and the previous trend are not a case of the Government and its supporters dictating to the rest of the House. The majority of Members of all parties accept, indeed welcome, the idea that the daily and weekly business should be arranged by their leaders to meet the general wishes of the Government and the Opposition and that one or two individuals should not be allowed to upset the time-table. Considering Members are interested in publicity they show a considerable suspicion of any Member (other, of course, than a Minister or recognized Opposition speaker) using the rules of the House to attract public attention. That is one reason, for example, why the House has preferred to limit the number of oral questions a Member can ask on any one day to two, rather than increase the time available.

4. I have a strong impression that the greatly praised Erskine May, or to give it its full title "A Treatise on the Law, Privileges, Proceedings and Usages of Parliament", is now beginning to act rather as a strait jacket. It is a good example of narrowing down from precedent to precedent. Each successive edition (the current edition is the 17th) adds to the record of rulings by earlier Speakers and these are generally regarded as binding on their successors, rather as top level judicial decisions are binding on lower courts. Judge made law, however, can be changed by Statute. The Standing Orders of the House, though modified from time to time, are in general terms and Speakers' rulings going back 60 to 80 or more years ago are still in use. A courageous Speaker would on occasion give a ruling more in keeping with current problems, but it is easier to stick to the book.

5. There has been a shift in interest from Imperial to local subjects, to use the terminology current at the beginning of the century. There are several reasons for this. The vast expansion in the Statute Book and in the powers of the central departments are a result of the growing preoccupation of Members with domestic matters and a continuing reason why the House must give more of its time to them. The growth of the Labour Party in the House has probably meant an increased interest in local matters. Some of this shift of interest is to be seen in the strength of the demand for "specia-

lized" committees.

6. There has been a vast increase in the number of organized interests. These are consulted by and they operate through Ministers and civil servants. To a much lesser extent, and then only by way of the individual Member, do they deal with the House. Committees of the House, for example, seldom hear evidence from such bodies. In so far as the principle of a Bill accords with general party policy and in so far as many of its details have been the subject of negotiation with the relevant interests, the scope for Parliamentary concern is to that extent inhibited.

7. No study is yet available of the impact of radio and television on the working of the House and on the roles it plays. My impression is that radio and television, combined with the growth of national newspapers, have intensified the attention given to the national governmental and parliamentary scene. In a unitary state there is no effective competition. The most remote rural parts of England are now in direct touch with happenings in London. Only politicians and a few students of politics can sustain, however, a continuous interest in political events. The mass of people need their attention stimulated. This is reflected in the treatment accorded by the mass media.

III. Non-events

As a tailpiece to this part of the paper I will add a list of things which might have but did not happen.

1. The House of Lords was not reformed (a few changes, mentioned earlier, were made).

2. Specialized[17] Committees, though proposed, have still not been accepted. The recent Select Committee on Procedure (4th Report 1964/5) recommended that a new Select Committee be set up, as a development of the present Estimates Committee, "to examine how the departments of state carry out their responsibilities and to consider their Estimates of Expenditure and Reports". The Procedure Committee thought that the object of its proposal was "to provide all Members with the means to carry out their responsibilities, rather than to elevate any Committees of the House to new positions of influence". The Government, however, rejected the proposal on the grounds that if the terms of reference of the Estimates Committee were so widened "the necessary detailed examination of

Government expenditure and administration is bound to give place to policy discussions" and the House would "lose a valuable part of the procedures on financial control".[18]

However, on 21 April, 1966, the Prime Minister said he believed "the time has now come when we might consider an experiment to extend this system (of committees) over a wider field of public administration". The Government were entering into discussion with the two Opposition Parties "on the suggestion of establishing one or two new Parliamentary Committees to concern themselves with administration in the sphere of certain Departments whose usual operations are not only of national concern but in many cases of intensely human concern". He referred to the Home Office and "our great social Departments". He even undertook that "Ministers, not necessarily in every case the senior Minister, because this is a valuable field in which junior Ministers can win their spurs, will make themselves available to these committees, whether as a Minister or as a witness will be a matter on which we shall want consultation".[19] A few days later he said that if the experiment succeeded "we might widen the idea to other committees and extend their period of existence for many years."[20]

3. A substantial volume of legislation, including the Finance Bill, is still taken in Committee of the Whole House.

4. There has been no marked change in length of Sessions. The average number of hours of sitting of the House during recent decennial periods are:[21]

1885–94	1,178
1895–1904	1,099
1905–14	1,177
1915–24	1,092
1925–34	1,156
1935–44	1,050
1945–54	1,316
1955–64	1,275

5. Morning sittings have not yet been introduced (but a limited proposal is contained in the First Report of the Select Committee on Procedure 1966/67).[22]

6. Mechanical voting has been rejected (Select Committee on Procedure 1959, p. xx).

7. Proxy voting has been avoided (See 24 on page 121).

8. Printing of speeches not delivered in the House has been rejected. (Select Committee on Procedure 1959, p. xxvii).
9. The televising of the proceedings of the House is still under consideration. A Select Committee on Broadcasting, etc., of Proceedings in the House of Commons issued a First Report in August 1966. The House of Lords have set up a separate Committee.

IV. The Status of Parliament

So much by way of background. The question is whether Parliament has declined or is declining. This is one of the most ambiguous, and one of the most traditional questions that a political scientist can be called upon to answer. There are really three distinct issues.

(i) Has Parliament declined in public opinion?
(ii) Is Parliament less powerful or less effective than it was?
(iii) Does Parliament do its job well?

The character of the answers to the first two questions depends on one's view of the past. Most of those who claim there has been a marked decline have a romantic view of the earlier period. They see it as a Golden Age, like the days of one's youth when the sun shone all day long in the summer. As no detailed studies yet exist of how Parliament worked in the 19th and early 20th Century or of how it was then regarded by public opinion, comparisons between past and present are usually comparisons between the generalized exposition found in earlier textbooks and a microscopic analysis of the current scene. Political institutions usually look grander in retrospect, for only the great men and the great occasions are remembered and the mass of trivia and petty controversy that engulfed them at the time are forgotten. It would, however, be quite easy to show that Parliament in the 1960's was much more effective than it was in the 1880's, or between 1900–1906 or in the 1930's. This would, however, perhaps be an overall view and one could argue a good deal about the meaning of the word effective. But many of those who complain that things are not what they were pick on one aspect of Parliamentary life. Thus it would be quite easy to show that the individual M.P. has very few opportunities now to assert himself in the House, whereas at least until the reforms of 1902 the daily time-table was to some extent at his mercy. But I doubt whether many would claim that the House would be more effective and rise in public esteem if it were now to work as it did in 1900 or 1890 when Question Time could be extended indefinitely and private Members' Motions moved at the sitting had precedence over major government legislation, so that the main business of the House was not reached until quite late in the evening.

Other critics talk nostalgically of the great orators and the great debates of the past as compared with the fare that is served in the Chamber to-day. This is usually a case of old men forgetting all except the highlights. Churchill in his evidence to the Select Committee of 1931/32 thought that the House had declined as "a grand forum of debate". Winterton on the other hand thought that though there were probably fewer Members who could fill the House, the general level of discussion was higher.

I do not see much point in trying to compare the past and the present in general terms, at least not until a lot more historical research has been undertaken. In any case, the real question is whether Parliament does a good job, and the job may be different at different periods, or at least require rather different methods of working. Let us therefore consider whether Parliament does its job effectively.

V. The Criticisms

The answer to this question can be approached in two ways. On the one hand one may start by stating the functions Parliament is required to perform and try to measure how effectively it has performed each in recent years. On the other, one may examine the strength of the criticisms of Parliament in recent writings safe in the assumption that every fault, however insignificant, will have been noticed in such a self-critical period. It will make for ease of presentation if I begin with the second approach.

Criticisms appear to fall into three groups.

(A) The House of Commons is now completely under the thumb of the Government;

(B) It is inefficient;

(C) It fails to attract, or to hold, able Members.

The first is the most general, and combined with the second is said to account for the third.

A. *The House and the Government*

The British have never thought it was the job of Parliament to govern, that is the job of the Government. As Gladstone once said to the House "Your business is not to govern the country, but ... to call to account those who govern it".[23] "The combination of responsible leadership by government with responsible criticism in Parliament is the essence of our Constitution" were L. S. Amery's words in 1947.[24] There is no real difference between the critics and the rest on this score. What the critics question is whether the House can any longer call the Government to account, whether its criticisms can now affect the Government's policy and administration – in other words whether the House has any longer any effective control over the Government. "One of the chief causes of the failure of the House of Commons to exercise an effective control over Government is the dictatorship wielded by the Cabinet..."[25] Writing before he was a Minister, Mr. R. H. S. Crossman implied that the Commons was now one of the dignified elements in the Constitution, along with the Monarchy and the House of Lords.[26]

The reasoning behind these statements is simple. General elections are now fought between highly organized Parties each with an agreed programme and with a leader who, should his Party be successful, will immediately become Prime Minister. In the House the two major Parties, controlled by the respective Whips, vote *en bloc* and the conclusion of any clash between Government and the Opposition is a foregone conclusion. Discussion in the House is therefore so much talk. Before deciding on the final shape of any proposals, Ministers consult outside interests and, having no control over such bodies, are more concerned with satisfying them than the House. In its most extreme form the critics or the "realists" see British government as a system in which a Prime Minister, assisted by the Civil Service and the Cabinet, governs the country with Parliament as the device for formalizing certain kinds of decisions, e.g. getting legislation on to the Statute Book.

When the criticism is examined in more detail it is found to be a mixture of rather different points. These can be considered in terms of four clashes.

(i) The Cabinet v. the rest.
(ii) The Cabinet, plus their supporters, v. the rest.
(iii) The Cabinet v. its supporters.
(iv) Front Benches v. the rest.

(i) The first can be quickly dismissed. Parliamentary government has never been conceived as meaning a Cabinet confronting the rest of the Commons. It implies a fairly cohesive body of "King's friends".

(ii) It also implies that the supporters of the Cabinet are in an absolute majority and because, on any system of voting, the majority will always beat the minority, there is nothing new or unsusual in the Cabinet getting its way. There are, however, three glosses to this last statement.

First, there is an implication that the majority will listen to the minority and take account of what it says. "There is no divine right of a mere numerical majority, of x : 2 + 1, any more than of kings."[27] Just when the majority are unreasonably ignoring the views of the minority is a matter of opinion. My impression is that this is not usually in the minds of those who allege Cabinet dictatorship.

Second, there is the size of the majority. Cabinets have governed with quite widely differing overall majorities. In the Parliament of 1931–35 the National government had a majority of 425. In 1945 Labour gained a majority of 146 over the rest, but in 1950 was returned with an overall majority of only 5. The overall majorities of the Conservative Party in recent elections have been 17 in 1951, 58 in 1955, and 100 in 1959. At the October, 1964, election Labour gained an overall majority of 4, which by the time of the dissolution in March 1966 was effectively down to 3. It is obvious that the House and the party system work differently with different sized majorities. It is noticeable that a good deal of the criticism of the ineffectiveness of the House has come from writers whose Party had been in a substantial minority for a number of years.[28] What they are really complaining of is that their opinions cannot prevail against majority opinion in the House.

Third, there is the situation in which the Government Party does not have an overall majority. This occurred in 1924 and 1929/31 and very nearly occurred in 1950 and 1964. Actually it is rare for a Government to be returned with an absolute majority of votes cast; only the Conservatives in 1931 and 1935 have done so since 1918. Ramsay Muir's answer to Cabinet dictatorship was proportional representation which he thought would probably prevent any Party having an overall majority. P.R. would almost certainly have given the Liberals a much larger number of seats in 1964 and so made some form of coalition government inevitable. On the assumption that a Government has less cohesion in a coalition than in a one-party majority, the House would to that extent be more effective and have greater influence, or rather both the Government and the

House would be weaker vis-a-vis minority groups.
(iii) The accusation of Cabinet dictatorship assumes that the parliamentary party will always vote for its leaders. But many commentators and critics appear to imply that the Party influences the Cabinet only when open revolt occurs. It would, however, be quite wrong to judge the working of the Parliamentary system by the number of times Members actually voted against their Party Leaders or openly abstained. The relations between the Government and its supporters are closer and more subtle than that. Collectively and individually Ministers cannot get far out of line with the views of their supporters in the House. The electoral campaign and Party manifestos, the basic attitudes of active Party members and the history of these attitudes, are as much part of the heritage of the Government as of their supporters and almost as compulsive on their actions. Even so, it is clear that there is a vast range of day-to-day decisions and a mass of detail in legislation which cannot by any stretch of imagination be said to be covered by generally agreed Party policy, or flow unquestionably from basic attitudes. In this area there is room for differences of opinion within the Party in power, which even if reflected in individual voting could hardly be held to threaten the basic unity of the Party.
But even on these small matters there is rarely any cross-voting. There are several reasons for this:
(a) There is, I think, an underlying presumption among Back Benchers that in matters of detail the Government is likely to be right. Ministers have an able and impartial Civil Service to advise them and have usually consulted and obtained the technical advice of the relevant interests. In contrast, Back Benchers have to find their own secretarial help, are provided with only very limited research and information facilities and if, as is mostly the case, they earn part of their living in other ways, have little or no spare time. Opposition Members have, of course, an incentive to find things wrong and criticize them in public and in the House, but even they tend to leave much of this to be organized by their leader and the Shadow Cabinet. A Government supporter has no such incentive and therefore requires to be considerably aroused before he opposes, let alone campaigns against, some item of Government activity.
(b) In apparent contradiction of the previous point it should perhaps be said that there is a general willingness on the part of Ministers to accommodate their Parliamentary critics. Their standing in the Cabinet and in the Party depends to a large extent on the opinion

they evoke in the House. The House will, of course, take account of their "image" in the country, but much more will depend on whether the Government's supporters think a particular Minister is doing a good job, his performance in the Chamber and his relations with them. The general attitude of Ministers is that if one can oblige a Member of one's Party (and for that matter any Member of the House) without giving too much away, one should do so. If one cannot, then one should refuse as gracefully and as persuasively as possible.

(c) Finally, there is the general dislike of giving public expression to differences of opinion within the Party. These are seized upon by the press and may receive a good deal of publicity. They may also be made much of by the Opposition. If the Government gives way, it is accused of being weak. If it uses the Whips to gain its way, it is accused of dictatorship. All this goes back to the basic attitude fostered by political leaders, the press and broadcasters, whereby the issue is seen in terms of a clash of two monolithic parties.

(iv) Quite often when individual Opposition Members are complaining of their inability to be an effective force in the House they are complaining more about their Front Bench than about the Treasury Front Bench. The subjects of debates, e.g. on Supply Days, are agreed by the usual channels. Unless he is successful in the ballot for the right to pick the subject to be discussed on the daily Motion for the Adjournment, the individual Member has little or no chance to raise issues on the floor of the House. There are now hardly any opportunities for forcing attention on the House. He must therefore wait until an opportunity occurs in a general debate or, more usual, rely on private approaches to the appropriate Minister or try to gain the support of his Front Bench.

B. *Efficiency*

Under the heading of inefficiency there are a variety of criticisms. Usually the procedure is said to be an out-of-date, "time wasting and archaic ritualism", "picturesque and antiquated ceremonialism" are the kind of emotive phrases used. The system of voting – tramping through the lobbies; the form in which some of the Motions are put; the amount of detail put in Bills and their handling in Committee of the whole House; these are some of the points made. Strangely enough, the longer Members are in the House the more they come to defend most of the procedure. When he gave evidence to the Select Committee on Procedure, the present Speaker,

Dr. Horace King, said he was a traditionalist and that traditions were part of the glory of the House. He also said, however, he would cut out the mumbo-jumbo. When asked in a television interview[29] what kind of mumbo-jumbo he had in mind, he said "Sometimes when the House wants to show displeasure with a Minister, we reduce the vote that we are giving to that Minister's department. My Deputy has to put that in a form in which a sum of £16,123,900 is moved and the amendment is to be £16,123,800. I think we could shorten that. There are little bits of formulae that we use that might conceivably be shortened".

Some Members feel much more strongly about this aspect of the life of the House. For example, on Thursday, 5 August, 1965, the last day before the Commons rose for the summer recess, Black Rod arrived at 4.0 p.m. to summon Members to attend the other Chamber to hear the Royal Commission read at length by the Reading Clerk, the titles of Bills (78 on this occasion) read out by the Clerk of the Crown and the Royal Assent (La Reyne le veult) pronounced in each case by the Clerk of the Parliaments. A score or so Members, however, continued to debate the issue then under discussion notwithstanding Mr. Speaker having left the Chair and therefore the proceedings being out of order.[30] Sir Geoffrey de Freitas protested that 20 minutes of the hour remaining before the recess should be used in this "ludicrous exercise" and suggested that a simpler and less time-consuming method be adopted for conveying the information.

A different interpretation is to be found in the terms of reference of the current Select Committee on Procedure: "to consider the Procedure in the Public Business of the House and to report what alterations, if any, are desirable for the more efficient despatch of such business ...". Here the aim is to increase productivity, e.g. to get more legislation through the House without increasing the length of the session. There is thus a search for labour-saving devices. Quite often, however, such devices involve shifting proceedings from the floor of the House into Committee. For example, the Select Committee recommended that the Second Reading of some Bills should be taken in a Committee specially set up for this purpose, the advantages being that the time saved on the floor might be used for other business and it would become possible for more Bills to be introduced. However, in so far as these Standing Committees were not to sit at the same time as the Chamber, and if the length of the daily sitting was not reduced, the effect would be to increase the claims on the time of Members and to intensify competition between attendance in the Chamber and attendance at Committee. It should be noticed that one of the main "improvements" proposed, i.e. the use of specialized committees, raises the same fundamental issue.

C. *Attracting Able Members*

The ability of Members varies tremendously. At one extreme are those who, judged by any standards, are men of great ability and who could have had distinguished professional, business, or academic careers. At the other extreme are those who have grown old in a safe Seat and who make little or no contribution other than obeying three-line Whips. The day-to-day job of the Back Bencher, however, can hardly be said to be exacting and require ability and intelligence well above average. No doubt the low financial reward, the awkward hours and the uncertainty deter a large part of the able adult population of the U.K. from becoming candidates, but there is never any shortage of contenders for any vacant nomination. The general impression is that the average ability of Members is higher now than it was 30 to 50 years ago.

The more difficult question, however, is whether the House is attracting sufficient outstanding men to provide two alternative Cabinets. Two critics[31] made a good deal of the departure of Geoffrey de Freitas, Hilary Marquand, Alfred Robens and Kenneth Younger from the Front Benches of the Parliamentary Labour Party as evidence that the House was losing its attraction. The main reason they left was, probably however, less dissatisfaction with the House of Commons than the realization that the Party was unlikely to be in power for at least another four or five years. It is the prospect of office that attracts and keeps able men in the House. The system assumes the pendulum will swing at reasonable intervals, but hope springs eternal in the eager politician's breast. I should have thought that there was no question that the ability of the present Labour Cabinet was as high as the often quoted Liberal Administration of 1906–16. Owing to the decline in the landed families which provided so many able Conservative Ministers and the fact that it is now almost impossible to have both a successful business or professional career and a leading role in the House, I suspect that the problem of obtaining sufficient first class Front Bench material may prove to be greater on the Conservative side than on the Labour side. But Front Benchers get plenty of chance to shine, even in the present arrangements in the House. Procedural changes are unlikely to make a great deal of difference to the attractiveness of the House to them.

VI. The Functioning of Parliament

Last, I turn to the job of Parliament and whether it still does it effectively. Bagehot[32] thought that the House had five functions which he defined as follows:
(1) "The main function of the House of Commons is... [as] an electoral Chamber; it is the assembly which chooses our president."
(2) "an expressive function... to express the mind of the English people on all matters which come before it."
(3) "the teaching function... to teach the nation what it does not know..."
(4) "an informing function... to lay... grievances... complaints, before the nation, which is the present sovereign."
(5) "the function of legislation..."
Looking at the functions in terms of the procedure and the use of the time of the House, Campion[33] listed four main functions:

(i) Representation of popular opinion.
(ii) The control of finance.
(iii) The formulation and contral of policy.
(iv) Legislation.

Campion did not mention the function of the House as an electoral Chamber, presumably because there is no formal provision in the procedure of the House for the exercise of the function, Party meetings not being part of the procedure. Legislation is included in both lists and Campion's first function no doubt covers numbers (2) and (4) in Bagehot's list. The control of finance and of policy cut across the classification, as Campion fully recognized, but are perhaps rather more tangible than Bagehot's approach – at least from the point of view of showing how the House uses its time.

The Electoral Function

In some ways the House is now more effective as an electoral Chamber than ever before. The pronouncement of the Labour Party as to how they would expect the Queen to act should their Leader die or retire when the Party was in power, and the new method of electing the Conservative Leader, have strengthened the role of the Parliamentary Parties. There is, of course, no control over the way Members vote for a leader. It is the free-est and most individual of the functions exercised by Members. Exercise of the power of dismissal is subject to the same restraints as other revolts in the House. Nevertheless, it was the Conservatives who got rid of their Prime Minister in May, 1940, and the resignation of Mr. Harold Macmillan, though ostensibly on health grounds, was undoubtedly hastened by feeling in the Party – as was Sir Alec Douglas-Home's resignation a year later.

Bagehot was writing 100 years ago and therefore, in view of current pronouncements about the power of the Prime Minister, it is worth quoting just what he said about relations between the Prime Minister and the House. "They guide him and he leads them ... He only goes where he believes they will go after him. But he has to take a lead; he must choose his direction, and begin the journey. Nor must he flinch. A good horse likes to feel that it is under worthy guidance ... The great leaders of Parliament have varied much, but they have all had a certain firmness. A great assembly is as soon spoiled by over-indulgence as a little child."[34] Picturesque language but not exactly a hundred years out-of-date.

The Legislative Function

The legislative Function is the next easiest function to discuss. Nowadays it is unusual in a normal session for a Government to fail to get passed into law the Bills it introduces. None is defeated, but lack of time may cause a few losses. About a third of the time of the House is spent in discussing the Government's legislative proposals. If the Finance Bill and Appropriation Bills are added, the proportion becomes about half. In contrast, only about 5–6 % of the time is available for Bills introduced by Private Members (including Government supporters).

Even though a Government measure is never defeated it may be quite radically amended. True the bulk of the amendments will have been formally sponsored by the Minister, for even in Committee and in respect of the details of a Bill Government defeat is rare. But discussion reveals both faults and the strength of the criticism, not all of which comes from non-Government supporters. The Finance Bill of 1965, which contained proposals for a Corporation Tax and a Capital Gains Tax and was a technical and complicated measure, attracted an unusual number of amendments. During the Committee and Report stages of the Bill over 1,100 amendments were put down and over 100 new clauses proposed. A good many of these were not discussed but there were nearly 250 Government amendments proposed in Committee and about 190 on Report. Twelve Opposition amendments were accepted as they stood and 30 or so were adopted in principle. Many of the "Government" amendments, however, particularly at the Report stage, were made in response to criticism in the House. Once the principle of a Bill has been accepted, and this is assured by the Government's majority, the tradition is for all to work to improve the draft. Of course, not all proposed amendments are innocent or without strong political content. Some are introduced by opponents to wreck or make the measure less workable and some raise issues almost as fundamental as the principal object of the Bill.

Outside interests cannot make direct representations to the Committee considering the Bill. They have therefore to get individual Members to move their amendments. A body such as the County Councils Association, representative of all the County Councils in England and Wales, will usually be able to find several Members to put its case to the House. Usually the Minister knows from other sources, or is told by the Member or the Association concerned, which interests are promoting which amendments and this no doubt has some influence on his receptiveness.

I do not think there has been much major criticism of the House as a body for discussing and passing legislation. Some would like to speed up the process and some would like to increase the resistance of the House and there are criticisms of detail about the procedure. The most serious criticism perhaps is that directed against the lack of expertise in and of expert advice available to the Standing Committees. This is a general point which I will leave for later.

The Informative Function

Strangely enough it is the effectiveness of the informative "function", the laying of grievances before the House, which has been seriously questioned in recent years. The argument runs as follows, Individual grievances (i.e. in contrast to the grievances of a large group) are normally taken up by the Member representing the person's constituency.[35] He has various channels open to him – letter to the Minister, unstarred or starred Question, Motion for the Adjournment, talking with the Minister, (or more likely the Parliamentary Secretary), etc. But his chances of raising the issue in the House are now very much less than they were. Question Time is so congested that the starred question may not come up to be answered by the

Minister for several weeks. If the Minister's reply to the main question and to the inevitable supplementary are unsatisfactory, almost the only other chance is to be successful in a ballot for the Adjournment Motion and this depends on the luck of the draw. If therefore the Minister refuses to do anything, the Member has to be exceptionally tough and convinced of his cause to pursue it further. Moreover, he has no direct access to Government files or information and the Civil Service rules against disclosure of information are quite tight.

Those who believe that the system is now weighted against the individual have recently been supporting the idea of an Ombudsman. In October 1965 the Labour Government published proposals for the establishment of a Parliamentary Commissioner for Administration. A Bill to give effect to the proposals was introduced in February 1966 and was reintroduced in the new House in July 1966. The Government proposes that the Parliamentary Commissioner should be an independent officer, appointed by the Crown and dismissable only by a parliamentary motion. He will investigate a complaint of personal injustice against Government Departments submitted to him by a Member on behalf of the complainant.[36] The Commissioner will not normally pursue matters which are within the competence of the courts or of an administrative tribunal, nor will he look into personnel issues or those which are purely commercial relationships of departments with customers or suppliers. The significant feature of this proposal in comparison with the arrangements in some countries is that this "Ombudsman" will reinforce the role of the M.P., not eliminate it. In the words of the White Paper "we do not want to create any new institution which would erode the functions of Members of Parliament... nor to replace remedies which the British Constitution already provides".[37]

The new arrangement when it becomes law will give Members a new tool of investigation, for the Commissioner will have power to compel production of documents including departmental minutes and to take evidence under oath, if necessary. It will also provide a new weapon of publicity. Should the Commissioner find justifiable grounds for the complaint and the department refuses to put it right, he may report the matter to Parliament. A Select Committee will probably be set up to deal with his reports. There will still be quite a number of grievances that can only be handled by the traditional procedures, e.g. policy decisions and the exercise of departmental discretion in which there is no question of a fault in administration. On the whole, however, the power of the individual Member should be considerably strengthened.

The Control of Expenditure

The control of expenditure is probably less effectively done than formerly. Control over the total amount has been affected by two changes. At one time total expenditure was closely related to total income and Mr. Micawber's dictum was accepted by everybody. But fiscal policy is now related to economic policy and not directly to expenditure. The issue turns not on whether the "budget" has balanced, but whether the estimated surplus or deficit is of the right order of magnitude, an order probably not measurable to within £50–£100 million. This change has coincided with a changed attitude to expenditure. Few believe in retrenchment or even restraint. Moreover steady inflation has made it more difficult to judge. Increases due to rising prices and wages must be accepted if the quality of service is to be maintained, but how much of any proposed increased expenditure is due to this feature and how much to waste or to improved services is difficult to assess.

Control of the amounts proposed to be spent on individual items, e.g. health or defence or education, is affected by the general attitude. But the House has not for a long time been particularly effective in its control of individual estimates. Debates in Committee of Supply, the traditional method of discussing departmental estimates, are now almost entirely devoted to general issues of policy. The Select Committee on Estimates, now much more active and better staffed, uses individual estimates largely as a peg on which to hang an examination of some general issue, e.g. recruitment to the Civil Service. It can, of course, be argued with some justification that discussions of general issues are more profitable for financial control than immersion in detail – a debate on Defence, including for example a discussion of Britain's role East of Suez, is a more profitable way of controlling the large sums spent on the Armed Forces than a discussion of this or that military device. Even so, this is but another way of admitting that the House no longer concerns itself with the details of the Estimates. The proposal mentioned earlier to widen the terms of reference of the Estimates Committee is a further straw in the wind. The Public Accounts Committee, which is concerned with audited expenditure is still an important and effective body.

The Expressive Function

Finally, we come to the expressive function – called by Campion the representation of popular opinion (Bagehot would not have so qualified opinion). This is a function which runs right through everything else – from the choice of a party leader to voting on an amendment to a Bill. Three reasons are used to show that this function is less significant or less well performed than previously. They are:

(1) The growth of other forms of expression. As indicated already, interest groups deal direct with civil servants and to a less extent with Ministers on a wide range of matter. Public opinion polls provide a guide to popular opinion on major current topics and on the popularity of the Parties and their leaders. Radio, television and the mass national press provide a forum for the expression of opinion and the discussion of current issues, a forum which in the case of television comes vividly into the voter's home. Finally, some major developments in policy emerge from the reports of Royal Commissions and similar committees on which Members are seldom asked to service.

(2) Party discipline inhibits the public expression of opinion contrary to the accepted views of the Member's Party or makes its expression less effective because the Member's vote will not be cast in support of it.

(3) The functions fo Government are now so wide-ranging and demand such a great deal of knowledge for their understanding that the ordinary Member is less and less a match for Ministers supported by the vastly increased Civil Service.

There is something in each of these and together they add up to the obvious conclusion that the House now operates in very different conditions from those prevailing 30 to 50 years ago. But that is not to say that the expressive function of the House is no longer needed or is no longer effective. One important element in the British system is usually forgotten or minimized in discussions of this issue. As Mr. R. A. Butler said in 1958 "there is probably no Executive in the world, ... which is more constantly in touch with the legislature than the British Government is with the British House of Commons".[38] The Prime Minister and senior members of the Cabinet may not be reached every day at Question Time but they are still open to be questioned in the House, the Prime Minister twice a week. A Minister is unlikely to be successful if he is unpopular in the country, but he is even less likely to be successful if he is unpopular in the House, particularly with his own Party. An interest group may operate through the Civil Service if the policy it advocates is acceptable to the Minister, but it is still dependent on the issue being taken up by a Member, either behind the scenes or in the House should the other approach fail. The perseverance of a very back bench Member can still achieve important results as witness the overthrow of a Government's agricultural land policy and the Minister of Agriculture in the Crichel Down case. The House is by no means intimidated by the opinion polls, witness its attitude to the abolition of the death sentence.

The basic fact is that Ministers are usually Members. They have usually had a period on the back benches, or at any rate spent a number of years in Opposition. The House is a small community in which reputations are made and unmade in the Smoking Room and corridors as well as in the Chamber. In the end everything comes down to this. The whips may on occasion perform miracles and overcome tough opposition in their Party, but they cannot afford to ignore opinion in the Party, at least not for long. Mr. Wilson on Vietnam and Mr. Callaghan on public expenditure may have to pay regard to American opinion and opinion generally in the country, but they still must deal with opinion in the Parliamentary Party.

In recent years the critics have focused their attention mainly on improving the expressive, and for that matter the teaching function, by advocating changes that would increase the information and services available to Members. This has been the main aim of the Study of Parliament Group, a group composed partly of academics and partly of staff of the House.[39]

There are many views that Members can still express very effectively. There are some which come from deep-seated feelings, e.g. re the nationalisation of the steel industry. There are some which come from first-hand experience, e.g. a farmer M.P. on some aspect of agricultural policy. There are others for which the information is provided by a constituent or an interest group. Finally, there is the Member's postbag and "surgery" which gives him some indication of current discontents. In some quarters these are felt to be sufficient to enable the Member to play his role adequately. The critics, however, say that administration and policy are now too complex for Members to have to rely only on these "personal" sources of information. Members so ill-armed are no match against Ministers backed by the whole resources of the Civil Service. Moreover,

Members do not have ready access to the information and expertise available in the departments. There is a very strong tradition of official secrecy. Unstarred Questions are quite a good way of obtaining answers on specific points, e.g. how many economists are employed by the Department of Economic Affairs, but are not an effective means of finding out, for example, how the department's regional machinery is working. It must be remembered that unlike in English local government in which the chief officials are the servants of the Council, civil servants owe their allegiance to the Crown, i.e. to the Government, and not to Parliament.

It is for these and other reasons that 'specialist' committees have recently been strongly advocated. The Select Committee on Nationalised Industries, the establishment of which was strongly opposed by Mr. Herbert Morrison and other leading Members of the House, has been a considerable success. It has provided Members with a great deal of information without involving a clash between the Committee and the Government. The Select Committee on the Estimates has also worked in the same way. The Government has, however, refused to widen the terms of reference of the Estimates Committee to enable it to consider the work of departments generally. The intention of the proposal was that the Estimates Committee would establish sub-committees to deal with the main aspects of administration – social services, economic affairs and so on – and that these would in time become accepted as the Committees of the House concerned with these fields.[40]

It should be noticed that the advocates of this development are concerned with investigation rather than with control – with administration rather than general policy. Like the present Estimates Committee the new committees would examine civil servants not Ministers and therefore issues of policy and political controversy would be ruled out.

Opposition to proposals of this kind draw on three main arguments. First, there is the fear that Ministerial responsibility to the House may be blurred. The tradition of the British system is that Ministers do not attend Select Committees, such as the Estimates Committee, because the Committees are concerned not with Government policy but with the details of administration. For this reason the Committees work in a non-political manner in which on the whole Party differences are muted. The Front Benches fear, however, that a widening of the terms of reference combined with concentration of each sub-committee on a particular field of government activity, would in time involve the committees in policy issues. This would mean either that Ministers would have to attend, or else Members of the committees would be free to act very differently there from the way they could act in the Chamber.

Second, there is the fear that a considerable increase in the use of committees would be at the expense of debate and effectiveness in the Chamber. Members can only be in one place at a time and already have heavy claims on their time.

"Every new committee which is established means a further reduction in the number of hon. Members sitting in the House." Moreover, "all the topics of debate in this House would be hashed and re-hashed before they ever got to the House...". Finally, "The cosier the committee, the more likely it will be that we shall have bipartisan politics." These quotations are from Michael Foot's vigorous onslaught[41] on the idea of specialist committees. He was concerned "to restore this Chamber as the central forum of debate in the country". His main solution was the televising of Parliament.

Third, there is the fear that the committees would in time come to make heavy demands on the time of senior civil servants and their departments, for quite apart from attendance there would be the preparation of numerous memoranda. Moreover, the Civil Service would be almost completely at the mercy of the committees, becoming their servants as it were instead of servants only of the Minister.

It will be seen that even in the limited form proposed the specialized committee raises fundamental issues in the working of the British parliamentary system. There is, however, one current principle which the proposers apparently do not wish to upset. One might be forgiven for thinking that the purpose of providing Members with information and expertise would be to give them more effective control over the Administration, and that this would imply less subjection to the Whips. But so far as I can judge, Professor Crick (and no doubt others who support the use of specialized committees) does not envisage that the change would result in Members of the Party in power voting against their Government. So presumably the assumption is that the increased effectiveness will come from Ministers finding it more difficult to withstand "better informed" criticism. The critics are still very British – they believe in strong government and in the receptiveness of the Executive to informed criticism. But apparently only the electorate, not their representatives in the House, have the right to defeat a Government, even on matters of comparatively minor importance.

One is left wondering whether set debates in the Chamber and diligent work in committee can be really significant unless Members' votes are affected by them – if only occasionally.

Anmerkungen

1 H.C. Deb. 28 October, 1943. Vol. 393. Col. 405.

2 The steam for heating the Commons is generated under the Lords but the air conditioning plant for the whole building is under the control of the Commons. The Palace of Westminster is held on a long lease from the Queen. On the control of the House, see the Debate of 2 November, 1965. H.C. Deb. Vol. 718, Cols. 878–957.

3 In July 1966 there were 134 allocated writing places for private Members in rooms in the precinct, 18 Members were on the waiting list and 13 Members with desks outside the precinct wished to move in. H.C. Deb. Vol. 731. Col. 1456.

4 The figures for 1900–60 are from D. E. Butler and J. Freeman. British Political Facts 1900–60, p. 44.

5 In May 1949 five Parliamentary Private Secretaries voted against the Government in a division on the Government of Ireland Bill. Four of them were dismissed following a letter from the Prime Minister (Mr. Attlee) to the Ministers concerned, and the fifth saved himself from the same fate only by prior resignation. See *The Parliamentary Private Secretary – a danger to the free functioning of Parliament?* by R. K. Alderman and J. A. Cross, *Political Studies,* Vol. XIV, No. 2, 1966.

6 *The Times,* 6 October, 1965. Mr. Heath now calls it the "leaders' committee", *The Times,* 20 April, 1966.

7 *Government and Parliament,* 3rd Edition, 1964, pp. 359–62.

8 Previously the choice was made by a method of informal consultation.

9 Committee on the Remuneration of Ministers and Members of Parliament 1964, Cmnd. 2516, p. 11. The Chairman was also Chairman of the National Incomes Commission, the predecessor of the Prices and Incomes Board.

10 H.C. Deb. 16 November 1964, Vol. 702, Cols. 36–45.

11 See Backbench Opinion in the House of Commons, 1955–59 by S. E. Finer, H. Berrington and D. J. Bartholomew (1961).

12 Select Committee on Procedure, 1964/5, Fifth Report. Voting Arrangements for Sick Members. The Committee recorded their view that there now seemed no alternative to proxy voting for the seriously ill "unless the usual channels can agree upon an alternative acceptable method".

13 "The House of Commons concerns itself with too many little matters that should and could be the concern of lesser bodies. . . . The effect of this is to render it impossible for those who have great responsibility outside the House to stand for Parliament." (Mr. Clement Davies, *The Times,* 8 January, 1958.)

14 P. G. Richards, Honourable Members (1964), Second Edition, p. 90, quoting Mr.

Fenner Brockway. From time to time allegations are made about drunkenness in the House. In February 1965, for example, Mr. P. Duffy, the Labour Member for Colne Valley, alleged drunkenness among Conservatives in the House, but subsequently apologized to the Committee on Privileges.

15 Sir Edward Fellowes (a former Clerk of the House) in *Political Quarterly*, July–September 1965, p. 261.

16 E. Shinwell, H.C. Deb., 2 November, 1965, Vol. 718, Col. 916.

17 I use 'specialized' in preference to 'specialist' (after consultation with Professor Bernard Crick) to meet an American critic who said that 'specialist' implied that the members of the Committee would be chosen for their particular expertise.

18 H.C. Deb., 27 October, 1965, Vol. 718, Col. 183.

19 H.C. Deb. Vol. 727, Cols. 75–80.

20 H.C. Deb. Vol. 727, Cols. 537–8.

21 Select Committee on Procedure 1959, p. 194, for the period 1885–1954.

22 Mr. Silverman's Bill for the Abolition of the Death Penalty was taken in the mornings because a Government motion to refer it to Standing Committee was defeated.

23 Quoted Crick, *The Reform of Parliament*, p. 45.

24 *Thoughts on the Constitution* (1947), p. 32.

25 Ramsey Muir, *How Britain is Governed* (Third Edition 1933), p. 197.

26 Introduction to Bagehot's *English Constitution*, Fontana Library Edition (1963), p. 54.

27 Amery, p. 45; also quoting Burke as saying that our Constitution "is something more than a problem in arithmetic".

28 e.g. Muir, Hollis, and some of the Left Wing criticism made towards the end of a long period of Conservative rule.

29 *The Listener*, 6 January, 1966, p. 5.

30 The event was not therefore recorded in *Hansard*. This report is from the *Daily Telegraph*, 6 August, 1965.

31 *What's wrong with Parliament?* by Andrew Hill and Anthony Whichelow. (Penguin Special 1964), p. 10.

32 *English Constitution*, Chapter IV.

33 Select Committee on Procedure 1946, Third Report, pp. xxii, et seq.

34 Fontana Library Edition (1963), p. 151.

35 Except where the remedy of an appeal to a administrative tribunal is available.

36 He will have discretion to refuse to pursue a case where he thinks there are insufficient grounds for the complaint or where he does not regard it within his scope.

37 Cmnd. 2767, para. 4.

38 H.C. Deb. 31 July 1958, Col. 1621.

39 See *Reforming the Commons* by Members of the Study of Parliament Group. P.E.P. October 1965.

40 The Estimates Committee now has sub-committees on Technological and Scientific Affairs, on Economic Affairs, on Social Affairs, on Defence and Overseas Affairs and on Building and Natural Resources but its terms of reference remain unchanged.

41 H.C. Deb. 27 October 1965, Vol. 718, Cols. 206–211. "Only some academic university professor could consider the present system of committees and conclude that the cure is more committees." See, however, the very interesting contribution of W. Hamilton in the same debate.

6

Geoffrey Marshall & Graeme C. Moodie

Ministerial Responsibility and the Crown

Aus: Some Problems of the Constitution, Hutchinson University Library, 4. Auflage, London 1967, S. 41–57.

Das Buch erschien zuerst 1959.

G. Marshall ist Fellow am Queen's College, Oxford.
G. C. Moodie ist Professor für Politikwissenschaft an der Universität von York.

1. *Conventional responsibility*

In law, Ministers are like other royal servants. They are appointed by the Monarch, may be dismissed by the Monarch, and are thus presumably responsible to the Monarch for their conduct. But this is true only in law. Constitutionally the relationship between Monarch and Ministers is regulated by the conventional doctrine of ministerial responsibility. By this phrase is meant (briefly) that Ministers are responsible *for* the general conduct of government, including the exercise of many powers legally vested in the Monarch; and that they are responsible *to* Parliament immediately, and ultimately, through Parliament and parties, to the electorate. When the British system of government is described as one of responsible government, it is to the doctrine of ministerial responsibility that reference is primarily being made. Given its fundamental place in the modern constitution, it is all the more noteworthy that there should exist uncertainty as to its precise extent and application. In this and the following chapters some of the uncertainties will be explored, beginning here with that aspect which concerns the relations between Ministers and the Monarch.

About the ordinary everyday constitutional powers of the Monarch there is no dispute: the Queen exercises her formidable legal powers only upon the advice of a responsible Minister or Ministers, and may not reject the advice they give. Politically she must be impartial in public, and discreet in private. She may attempt to influence the conduct of government, but the decisions are taken by Her Majesty's Government, severally or collectively. In our constitutional monarchy, as in others in Europe, the basic principle is that normally the Monarch does not govern, but must subordinate herself, in her political activities, to those who do, her official advisers. By this separation of legal and conventional responsibility it has been possible to maintain intact the legal structure of hereditary Monarchy within a democratic form of government. Only thus could the Monarchy have survived into an age when hereditary status no longer carried with it the authority to rule, and when the powerful sections of the community insisted that the government be responsible to them. This demand could not be met by the Monarchy: being hereditary and not elective it could not easily become politically accountable to the governed, while the doctrine that *rex non potest peccare* stood in the way of any developing alternative of legal accountability. The Monarchy had no real option, therefore, but progressively to relinquish its governmental powers. (These comments, it should be added, are intended to be analytical rather than historical in character, and to indicate logical rather than historic connections. The actual development of the so modern doctrine of ministerial responsibility was much more involved and much less purposive than these comments would suggest.)

The word 'responsible' has several meanings in the constitutional context, which must be noted. The difference between legal and conventional responsibility is rarely overlooked. Within the second of these categories, however, a further distinction may be made between mere accountability, as it may be called, and moral responsibility (culpability). To say that someone is responsible (in the sense of accountable) may sometimes be to say that he is the proper person to be visited with the constitutional consequences of an action, or that he is the person under whose authority the action was taken. On the other hand to say that he is responsible (in the second sense) may be to imply that he is either the actual agent, or the person morally deserving blame or praise for the action.

'Culpability' might be reserved for the second of these notions and 'accountability' for the first were it not that 'culpability' suggests blame exclusively. As it happens, however, questions of responsibility tend to be raised and constitutional disputes tend to be prompted by actions of which people in fact *dis*approve. 'Accountability' is open to a different kind of objection when applied, for example, to certain actions of the Monarch. The word implies the existence of some constitutional means of holding a person to account, of making him render account. Ministers are ultimately accountable in that they may be forced to resign or fail to be re-elected; but the very essence of the Monarch's position is that there exists no comparable constitutional machinery.

In so far as the penalties exacted of the accountable person tend to vary with the degree of his culpability, there is a tendency for the two types of responsibility to coincide, or for those concerned to seek the means of bringing them together. It is possible, indeed, to see the development of ministerial responsibility as an example of this process, with Ministers seeking to become culpable as well as in part accountable for royal acts of government, and succeeding when once the party system has provided them with an alternative basis for their power and position. There is a point beyond which men will not shield others, and after which they will insist that they be responsible (accountable) only for their own actions.

2. *The personal prerogatives*

Today the powers of the Crown (the prerogatives) have largely been transferred to elected Ministers who are responsible in both senses for their exercise. But not entirely so: there continue to exist personal prerogatives for which, under certain circumstances, the Monarch is said by some writers to be personally responsible. These powers include certain relatively minor ones, like the conferment of some Honours or, less minor, the appointment of the Queen's Private Secretary, as well as major ones pertaining to the selection of a Prime Minister, the dissolution of Parliament, the dismissal of a government, and the refusal of the Royal Assent to a bill passed by Parliament. Only the major ones have given rise to serious constitutional problems. We will therefore confine our attention to them. The Monarch's powers in relation to the dissolution of Parliament, the dismissal of Ministers, and the giving of assent to bills may conveniently be treated separately from the selection of a Prime Minister, which involves a different kind of 'exception' to the doctrine of ministerial responsibility. The selection of a Prime Minister cannot properly be subject to the normal machinery for ministerial responsibility, as we shall see. In this respect it is unique among the Monarch's powers. The other powers under consideration can be, and are usually, subject to that machinery. The problem about them is to decide whether there exist any circumstances under which the Monarch may constitutionally use her discretion in exercising the powers of dismissal, dissolution, or assent.

3. *Dissolution, dismissal, and assent*

In 1913 a section of the Unionist Party urged the King to 'veto' the Home Rule Bill. Had the King done so, it would have been the first use of this prerogative since the reign of Queen Anne, whereas instances of the others can be cited from the nineteenth century. Partly for this reason, not even an ardent Unionist like Dicey seemed prepared to countenance this proposal. But he did lend support to the view that the King was entitled to insist upon the holding of an early dissolution (even at the cost of forcing the resignation of the Liberal Government) in order to test public opinion. As he pointed out in a letter to *The Times*, this would or could accomplish all that was claimed for the 'veto'.[1] Any refusal to give Royal Assent to a measure passed by Parliament would in fact inevitably raise questions about the prerogatives of dissolution and dismissal.

Walter Bagehot, in his *English Constitution*, argued strongly that it was undesirable, for the sake of good government, that the Monarch should be vested with these powers.[2] His arguments have not prevented the continuation of controversy. Nor, apparently, have authority or precedent provided conclusive evidence about the rules which regulate the use of these crucial powers. It is significant, for example, that substantially similar ground was covered by the correspondents on this subject in *The Times* in September 1913, and in April 1950. Roughly speaking there are two lines of argument, the divergence between which is, at first sight, remarkably small. There appears to be universal agreement that the Monarch may never use these powers arbitrarily and entirely on his own responsibility: some Ministers must be prepared to advise and then defend the Monarch's action. But whereas one view implies that a Monarch may actively seek Ministers who are prepared to give the desired advice, the other insists that a Monarch is restricted to accepting the advice of whichever Ministers are in office at the time (or, in other words, that these are not personal prerogatives at all). Neither of these positions is entirely free from objection. Before discussing them, however, it would be useful to look briefly at the precedents to which reference is sometimes made.

In the United Kingdom no Monarch has refused a dissolution when requested by a Prime Minister, or forced one against advice; nor has a government been dismissed (unless one counts Peel's resignation over the 'bedchamber question' in 1839) since Queen Victoria came to the throne. Examples from earlier periods are numerous, but it is doubtful how far they can properly be regarded as precedents for the very changed circumstances of today. For more recent precedents one must turn to other parts of the Commonwealth with similar constitutions. The Governor-General of Canada in 1926 and the Governor-General of South Africa in 1939, wielding the powers of the Crown, refused a dissolution to the then Prime Minister. In each case, therefore, he had no option but to resign. In each case an alternative Government was available – the Canadian one lasting only a few days before being forced itself to request a dissolution (which was granted), and the South African one maintaining a majority until after the war had been won. In each case, too, the Governor-General became the target of criticism coming mainly from supporters of the government which had, in effect, been dismissed. Even were it universally agreed that the Governors-General had acted constitutionally, which it is not, one could not safely conclude that the same judgment would apply to similar action by a Monarch in the United Kingdom (or elsewhere). It is not certain, for one thing, that precisely the same rules must always apply in the United Kingdom as in the other Commonwealth countries whose constitutions derive from it. More important, it is not certain that the same rules apply to a Governor-General as to the Sovereign in person. Admittedly the powers of a Governor-General are officially the same as those of the Monarch in the United Kingdom but, in the absence of any clear formulation of the latter, it is not easy precisely to enumerate those powers. It cannot be disputed that in 1926 and 1939 the Governors-General exercised powers which had once belonged to the Monarch. Furthermore, had these actions been taken by the Monarch personally, and been accepted as constitutional at the time, it could not be disputed that they were instances of powers properly belonging to Governors-General. This is to say that what the Queen may do, her representatives may do also, in the absence of any legal provision to the contrary. But it does not necessarily follow that what is done by them may constitutionally be done by the Queen. The essential point to remember is that a Governor-General is, nowadays, appointed for a limited term on the advice of the Commonwealth government concerned, and thereafter acts on the advice of Commonwealth Ministers, and not on the advice or instruction either of Ministers or of the Monarch in the United Kingdom. It follows that his involvement in controversy concerns himself alone, and not necessarily the place of the Crown. The temporary and appointive nature of his office, moreover, means that the real or apparent partisanship of any one incumbent need imperil nothing more than his own tenure. Neither of these statements can safely be made about the Monarch personally. It must be concluded, therefore, that these precedents provide no clearer guidance than do the opinions of constitutional authorities.

Amongst these opinions what might be called the 'older' doctrine (in the sense of having been advocated for the longer time, and not necessarily in the sense of being old-fashioned or out of date) was put clearly by Sir William Anson in his letter to *The Times* (10 September 1913) in which he said that 'if the King should determine, in the interests of the people, to take a course which his Ministers disapprove, he must either convert his Ministers to his point of view, or, before taking action, must find other Ministers who agree with him'. Mr. Asquith in 1923, and Mr. Churchill in 1944, expressed similar views about the right to *refuse* a request for a dissolution, and other authorities could also be quoted to the same effect.[3] Despite the existence of many *prima facie* precedents which might seem to support this argument, important grounds of principle have been advanced against it by proponents of the 'newer' doctrine, labelled the 'automatic' doctrine by Lord Hugh Cecil in his contribution to *The Times* correspondence of 1913. Leaving aside the vital question of how the King shall determine what is 'in the interests of the people', the essential objection to an exercise of the power to refuse or insist upon a dissolution is the difficulty thereafter of keeping the Monarch out of politics, particularly under a two-party system, however strenuous the efforts of his new Ministers to shoulder the responsibility. The other party, and possibly a majority of the electorate, would still hold the Monarch culpable – and rightly so. *The Times'* leading article of 8 September 1913 put the objection thus: 'A dissolution of Parliament by an exercise of the Royal Prerogative, *proprio motu regis,* might be followed by a vindication at the polls of those very Ministers whose advice had been set aside', thereby producing a situation where the Monarch is in open disagreement with his people. Even if this did not happen, the fact is that *before-*

hand there is no certainty that it will not. More is required to protect the Monarch's position than the probability of an electoral majority in support of his policy. As Lord Chorley has put it: 'It is very important that in such circumstances the King should be bound by a clear and simple rule which there can be no mistaking, and this is exactly what the convention that he must accept the advice of his Prime Minister provides.'[4] The 'old' rule satisfies this requirement, of course, in the sense that it is capable of a clear and simple formulation. On the other hand, it does not prescribe any one simple line of action to be followed by the Monarch. In order to discover whether alternative advice is obtainable the Monarch may become involved in complicated and protracted negotiations with political leaders. To distinguish justifiable consultation from improper intrigue may then prove very difficult. To this extent the 'old' rule is probably not sufficiently clear and simple.

Two other objections may be quoted. Mr. Roy Jenkins pointed out in 1950 that if Mr. Attlee were refused a dissolution, Mr. Churchill (as the only alternative Prime Minister) would have to be granted one, 'and the Crown would be placed in the intolerable and dangerous position of granting to a minority Prime Minister what it had recently refused to a majority Prime Minister'.[5] The King would thus necessarily have appeared to favour one of the two major political parties. The other objection was put forward by Professor J. H. Morgan in the earlier *Times* correspondence. 'The right of dissolution,' he wrote, 'regarded as a ministerial right, owes its existence to a general recognition of the Sovereign's immunity from responsibility for its exercise; until that immunity was achieved any dissolution was a source of grave anxiety to the Sovereign as carrying with it the implication that not only was the Ministry defeated, but the Crown compromised or, to use the language of Queen Victoria in the early days of her reign, "affronted".' Here one can see not only a convincing argument against the 'old' theory, but also the reason why it should perhaps be superseded. In present times the Monarch is expected to refrain from political intervention to an extent unknown a century and more ago. What was accepted as legitimate political influence then is not so accepted now when a greater emphasis is placed on such conceptions as 'the sovereignty of the people'. Whether in fact people would vote for or against a government which was believed to possess royal support, it is now generally felt to be undesirable that this be an issue at all. Governments and parties should be supported or opposed on their merits and their record, and not on their acceptability to the Monarch. Only if a dissolution is felt to be the decision of the Prime Minister, not of the Monarch, can an election be freed from the essentially irrelevant question of royal preferences. And only thus may the Monarch satisfy the constitutional requirement that she be, in fact and appearance, politically impartial.

These considerations seem conclusive. There appears to be no issue which could justify the exercise of the Royal Prerogative of dissolution. Similar arguments apply against the dismissal of a government. But does it follow that one must accept a complete 'automatic' theory? There is one situation in which such a theory should not probably be acted upon. If a Prime Minister has been defeated at a general election and then requests another immediate dissolution, the Monarch would surely be entitled, if not obliged, to refuse the request, always assuming that an alternative government could be formed without another election. The doctrine of ministerial responsibility is designed not only to safeguard the Monarchy from political involvement, but also to ensure that the power to govern is wielded by those who have the authority to govern. This authority can hardly be claimed by a Prime Minister who has been clearly rejected by the electors in favour of another man or party. For the Monarch to refuse him a second immediate dissolution would therefore be to uphold the authority of the electorate against an attempt to undermine the whole constitutional system. Of course, if the electoral verdict is confused, in the sense that no other government can be formed either, then on either theory the Monarch ought to accede to the request and allow the electorate the opportunity to make a fresh decision. Even if the electoral verdict is clear the Monarch may still prefer to leave it to the electorate to penalise the Prime Minister who has challenged that verdict. The essential point is that to grant or withhold a dissolution would probably, under the circumstances envisaged, be a matter for the Monarch's discretion. The principle seems to be clear, although it is possible to imagine a situation in which its application would not be. It is difficult, for example, to decide in advance whether the rule applies on the basis of upholding the authority of the electorate when a Prime Minister, who has lost his parliamentary majority, has yet obtained (say) 60 per cent of the votes cast; or when the request for a second dissolution is made not within a few days of Parliament's assembly but, possibly because of a small shift in parliamentary allegiance, after one or even two months.

A major source of difficulty and confusion is that the behaviour constitutionally demanded of the Monarch may differ according to the number and nature of the political parties with which she is confronted. At least some of the gap between proponents of the 'old' and 'new' doctrines of ministerial responsibility may be explained by the fact that the 'new' one pertains most clearly to our modern two-party system, while the 'old' draws largely upon experience of a time when parties were more numerous or less coherent, and pertains rather to a minority government's relations with the Crown. To dismiss the Government, or dissolve Parliament against its wishes, may be considered undesirable in any circumstances, but it may be that it is only under a disciplined two-party system that the right to *refuse* a dissolution should be as restricted as we have suggested. Whether the problem here is one of the content of the relevant rules, or of their application, is a matter for debate. The party system is also an important, and complicating, factor in relation to the other personal prerogatives to be discussed here.

4. *Selection of a Prime Minister*

The most frequently invoked of the so-called personal prerogatives is the selection of a Prime Minister. It has already been noted that the constitutional problem here is to discover and state what rules apply, given that no Minister can be responsible in the ordinary way for the Monarch's decision. On this last point there is general agreement. Clearly there could be no 'automatic' theory which made the advice of the outgoing Prime Minister or Cabinet mandatory as to the person who should be invited to form a new government. The objections to this procedure are threefold. It must be remembered, firstly, that ministerial responsibility involves the principle that a Minister be accountable or answerable to Parliament for his actions, the ultimate sanction being the loss of his office. But in the instance given, this sanction would not apply: since he was retiring from office in any case, the possibility of losing the confidence of Parliament or electorate would hold no terrors for him. He would be culpable but not fully accountable, the very disjunction of responsibilities which the system of ministerial responsibility is designed normally to prevent. The second objection is that a defeated Prime Minister, as distinct from one who voluntarily resigns in favour of another member of his own party, is clearly without the parliamentary authority to give mandatory advice. The third is that for a retiring Prime Minister to have the right to nominate his successor is to grant him a potentially important power without the assurance that it would not be used in a highly partisan or even capricious way. This is most obvious with reference to a two-party system. One has only to imagine what might have happened had a mischievous Conservative selected Mr. Bevan in 1945, or an impish Labour Leader chosen Mr. Butler in 1951, to see how dangerous the power could be. The point of these examples, it should be said, is not that Mr. Bevan and Mr. Butler would necessarily have been worse Prime Ministers than the men actually selected, but that their selection (assuming that they would have accepted office) would have imposed a possibly fatal strain upon the unity of their parties at the time. It may be argued that no person likely to become Prime Minister would ever behave in so untrustworthy a fashion, but of this there can be no certainty. It is in fact generally accepted that the Monarch is not bound to accept ministerial advice in her selection of a Prime Minister. For the use of this power she is and must be culpable. But it is sometimes argued that she is not constitutionally accountable, and that the responsibility (in this sense) lies with the incoming Prime Minister. This was the view of Professor Berriedale Keith, who argued that a Prime Minister could decline the invitation to form a government,

> 'and he ought so to decline if constitutional propriety under the British system does not mark out his appointment as right and proper on the part of the sovereign. When, therefore, he accepts office, he assumes therewith the duty of defending the formation of the new ministry,'[6]

including, it seems, the circumstances of the fall of his predecessor in so far as this involved the Monarch. Keith here quotes with approval the statement made by Peel when he became Prime Minister in 1834 after Melbourne's apparent dismissal by the King: 'I am, by my acceptance of office, responsible for the removal of the late Government.'[7] Clearly a Prime Minister is solely responsible (in both senses) for accepting the invitation to assume power, just as the Monarch alone is culpable for issuing the invitation in the first place, or for dismissing the previous Government. The doctrine that the Prime Minister and not the Monarch should be accountable for the latter is a pure fiction[8] which, today, is most unlikely to divert attention and criticism (if any there be) away from the Monarch. The doctrine did not have this protective effect in 1931 when the King was criticised, rightly or wrongly, for his part in the selection of Mr. Ramsay MacDonald to head the National Government of that year, nor was it offered as a defence of George V by those most directly concerned.

To say that ministerial responsibility does not apply to the selection of a Prime Minister is not, however, to claim that the Monarch has complete discretion subject to no constitutional rules. It is generally agreed that other rules do operate, although their precise nature is debatable. A further distinction might be drawn here between substantive and procedural rules. Instances of the former are that a Monarch should not publicly appear to favour one political party or policy, or that the powers of the Crown should (very broadly speaking) be used only to further the aims of, or at least in such a way as to secure acceptance by, a parliamentary majority. The trouble about rules of this sort is that, crucial and fundamental though they may be, they provide canons of judgment, once the deed is done, rather than unambiguous guides to action by a Monarch seeking to behave constitutionally. How is the Monarch to decide what will appear partisan, or what will be acceptable to the majority? How can she avoid mistakes which will lead to criticism and, possibly, her unwilling involvement in political controversy? It is to answer this type of question that procedural rules may be required, though the distinction is of course only one of degree. The supreme but not the only example of such a rule is the principle of ministerial responsibility. Generally speaking the Monarch will be fulfilling the substantive rules mentioned, or (which is sufficient) will be accepted as so doing, if she acts in the way advised by her Ministers, i.e. follows a prescribed procedure in using her legal powers. It is the lack of precision about the procedural rules relevant to the selection of a Prime Minister which has given rise to uncertainty in this sphere.

Accepted procedural rules appear to be that the person selected must have the support of a majority in the House of Commons (if need be, after a new general election), and that the Monarch must 'secure the strongest Government in the minimum time'[9] while still observing the need for public impartiality. Most frequently, under the two-party system, all these requirements are met easily by sending for the Leader of the Opposition or of the majority party, as the case may be, upon the fall of a government – as happened, for example, in 1945 and 1951. Here the facts are such as to allow of no other choice. There is one situation, however, in which the Monarch may be called upon to exercise a degree of discretion, even when there are only two major parties: when the ruling party has no officially designated leader.[10]

5. *The example of 1957*

This situation arises when a Prime Minister dies in office or resigns for personal reasons, that is to say, when a vacancy occurs which is not accompanied by any change in the position of the parties. Even then, there may sometimes be no room for choice, as when Sir Anthony Eden succeeded Sir Winston Churchill. But when Sir Anthony retired in his turn in 1957, the Queen was not presented with any one obvious successor. Under such circumstances it is normally assumed that, although the Monarch will probably seek advice in order to discover what persons would be acceptable to the party in power, yet for the final choice she alone is morally and constitutionally responsible. It is clear, however, that an unwise or ill-advised Monarch might conceivably act in a manner which could be construed as partial, in that it appeared to reflect a royal preference for one particular group within the party. It is true, and important, that a party in a majority is able to reject any selection of which it does not approve – if it is prepared to undergo the internal conflict this would probably entail. A royal 'mistake' is not final; but it could still harm the Monarch's own reputation. To prevent this there must exist rules capable of serving as effective guides to action. Such a rule seems to be implicit in the facts, even although it cannot yet be asserted definitely to have been accepted as such. In 1957, on Sir Anthony Eden's resignation, the Queen apparently sought and acted upon the advice of Sir Winston Churchill[11] and Lord Salisbury, both elder statesmen of the Conservative Party who had themselves no personal ambitions at stake, and who appeared to have the confidence of their own party. At the same time the Labour Party took the opportunity of outlining the procedure it wished to be adopted in the selection of a Labour Prime Minister under comparable conditions. It declared that the Monarch should make no selection until a new Leader had been elected by the Parliamentary Labour Party in the same way as a Leader is chosen when the Party is in opposition. The Labour Party, thus, has given notice that it would not be prepared to accept a Leader chosen for it by the Monarch. The Conservatives, on the other hand, appear still to accept the traditional method of selection. It is to be doubted, however, whether they would do so if the Monarch in fact exercised a wide personal discretion without seeking the advice of Conservative elders. In effect the Conservative Party accepts what the Labour Party insisted upon in 1957: that similar selection procedures be followed whether the Party is in or out of office. For in the selection of its Leader in the

House of Commons when in opposition the Conservatives appear usually to rely upon similar informal methods of 'sounding opinion' and recommendation by the senior members of the Party.[12] In both situations the choice may be said to emerge from the feelings of the group, but in the one case it is ratified by the Monarch at once, while in the other it is not ratified until next the Party wins a general election. Both parties, therefore, seem concerned to limit or even abolish the Monarch's culpability in this situation, and to insist upon a new procedural rule of what might be called 'party responsibility'. Such a 'rule' would not conflict with authority and precedent which require, essentially, only that the person selected be acceptable to the party in question. What it would do is extend the requirement to include methods of selection which would virtually guarantee that the 'proper' choice is made for each party. To acknowledge this rule would thus have the double advantage of eliminating any appearance of royal partiality in selecting a Prime Minister on these occasions, and of ensuring that the parties obtain the leaders they want by the methods they want.

Reluctance to accept this conclusion may stem from a desire to have precisely the same rules applied to the rather different circumstances obtaining when there are three or more parties to be reckoned with. Under these conditions different procedural rules will probably be required to achieve the same substantial ends. It would clearly, for example, have been of little practical value to a President of the Fourth French Republic merely to have told him 'to send for the Leader of the Opposition' or even 'of the largest party not supporting the previous government'. And in fact a different set of (non-legal) guiding rules developed.[13]

The essential point is that if it is necessary to form a coalition government (as it normally was in the Fourth Republic) there may arise a situation in which the Monarch is or seems called upon to exercise a significant degree of personal discretion with little guidance as to the best way to perform her constitutional duties.

6. *The example of 1931*

Coalition governments in Britain are not as rare as is sometimes thought. Six times in this century governments have been formed, either on a multi-party basis or by a single minority party with the support of another (in 1915, 1916, 1924, 1929, 1931, and 1940), although the first of these should perhaps not be counted in that it was formed without any immediately preceding resignation. So far as can be judged from the published accounts, however, in all cases except that of 1931 the Monarch in fact had no significant discretion, the decision having been made for him by negotiation and agreement among the parties. It has even been argued that the one exception should not properly be so regarded.[14] The formation of the National Government of 1931 has, however, long been thought by both its defenders and critics to have been in some degree the result of the King's discretionary decision. The ensuing controversy raised a constitutional problem of some interest.

That King George V acted within the established rules is no longer seriously in dispute. On the other hand this has not saved him from criticism. Mr. MacDonald's acceptance of office as Prime Minister of the new National Government was denounced by the overwhelming majority of his own party, which refused to support the new administration. Given the belief that the King had had some choice and influence in the matter, it is not surprising that doubts should have been cast upon the wisdom or impartiality of his decision. Mr. Bassett has argued,[15] as have others, that such criticism is purely partisan, and that the King acted solely in the national interest. No grounds exist for thinking that the King had any other concern than to further the national interest, but opinions will often differ as to what the national interest demands. When such differences exist, then to embrace any one view of the national interest must necessarily seem less than fully impartial. When, moreover, that view is shared by some of the major political parties but not by all (as happened in 1931), then to accept it will necessarily be partisan, in the literal sense, whatever the intrinsic wisdom of the view. To defend as well as to attack action taken in furtherance of the view will also be partisan. The argument does not, therefore, necessarily avoid the need to question the adequacy of the existing rules as a defence of the Monarch's detached status.

If a constitutional problem exists here, and not everyone would agree that it does, it relates to the possibility of devising more effective methods whereby to keep the Monarch free from political controversy. To devise a mandatory procedure providing for the consultation of political parties would be difficult and probably not generally acceptable.[16] Another procedural 'rule' has, however, played a large part in the arguments about MacDonald's selection. The King's choice has been widely defended because it was agreed to and finally advised by the Leader or Acting-Leader of each of the there major political parties, even although MacDonald's initial reluctance had evidently to be overcome by persuasion on the part of his new colleagues and the King. But though this fact may be relevant to an assessment of the wisdom of the King's action, it would seem, by the canons of constitutional behaviour then generally recognised, to be irrelevant to the discussion of its constitutional propriety. It may be, however, that monarchs, in their efforts to remain above party politics and to avoid involvement in political controversy, have adopted the practice of seeking and acting upon the advice of the official party Leaders in the selection of coalition Prime Ministers, just as they appear to act upon the advice of party spokesmen in other circumstances.

7. *The example of 1963*

The selection of Mr Macmillan's successor presented more difficulties than did his own selection in 1957. Essentially this was because the Conservative Party was more deeply divided about a larger number of 'contestants' and because there was no suitable elder statesman available to give authoritative advice to the Monarch. All sections of the Party seemed to agree only that the real decision must be taken by and within the Party itself. Certainly all factions behaved as if the Party's preference was conclusive, and Sir Alec Douglas-Home seems in fact to have been chosen by the Party, albeit under the skilful guidance of his predecessor. But the uncertainties about the appropriate innerparty machinery still left room for doubt about the actual and desirable role of the Monarch. It may be, therefore, that the events of October 1963 will speed the acceptance of 'party responsibility' as the proper procedural rule. Alternatively, the example of 1963 may be influential primarily because it revived an older procedure for dealing with situations where it is difficult to identify the next Prime Minister. On future similar occasions the Monarch may again emphasise party responsibility by, initially, only inviting someone to form an administration and not appointing him until his success is assured.

8. *Mr Heath's selection as Conservative Leader, 1965*

After the Conservative Party was sent into opposition by the general election of 1964 it examined its own procedure for selecting a Leader and, early in 1965, adopted an elaborate system of election. The procedure was soon tested when Sir Alec Douglas-Home resigned. Mr Edward Heath was thereupon elected to succed him after a decorous contest. It seems that the Conservative Party, like the Labour

Party, will insist upon electing its own Leader by the same method even should the need arise when it is in office. There is thus, apparently, no possibility that the Monarch will exercise a genuine choice in the appointment of future Prime Ministers of one-party governments nor, by implication, of coalition governments. In both cases 'party responsibility' seems likely to provide the operative procedural rule – at least for as long as the present two major parties continue to dominate British politics. The logic of the situation as we have described it seems thus to have led to the expected conclusion.

Anmerkungen

1 15 September 1913. This and other contributions to the controversy are quoted in Jennings, *Cabinet Government*, App. III.

2 W. Bagehot, *The English Constitution* (1867), ch. VII.

3 See Lord Simon's letter to *The Times*, 24 April 1950. None now argue that the Crown may *force* a dissolution.

4 *The Times*, 26 April 1950.

5 Ibid.

6 A. B. Keith, *The British Cabinet System* (2nd ed. by N. H. Gibbs, 1952), p. 277.

7 Op. cit., p. 273.

8 Sir Ivor Jennings, *Cabinet Government* (3rd ed.), p. 449.

9 Ibid., pp. 20–58.

10 The likelihood that room will be left for the exercise of discretion by the Monarch has been greatly reduced since the following pages were first written, both existing major political parties having established their own procedures for choosing their leaders, as is shown below.

11 In a speech at Woodford in 1959 Sir Winston Churchill said, 'I recommended Mr. Macmillan and was most delighted to see it was acted upon.' (*The Times*, 7 January 1959.)

12 R. T. McKenzie, *British Political Parties*.

13 P. Williams, 'Crisis in France: A Political Institution', VII *Cambridge Journal* 1 (1953), pp. 36–50.

14 R. Bassett, *1931: Political Crisis* (1958).

15 Op. cit.

16 Cf. G. C. Moodie, *The Monarch and the Selection of a Prime Minister: A Reexamination of the Crisis of 1931* (5 Political Studies, 1, 1957), and the criticisms advanced in Mr. Bassett's *1931: Political Crisis*, at pp. 370–5.

7

R. T. McKenzie

British Political Parties

Aus: British Political Parties. The Distribution of Power within the Conservative and Labour Parties. Mercury Books Nr. 32, London 1964, S. 635–649.

Das Buch erschien zuerst 1955.

R. T. McKenzie, einer der bekanntesten Fernsehkommentatoren des Landes für Fragen der politischen Parteien, lehrt Politikwissenschaft an der London School of Economics.

The distribution of power within British political parties is primarily a function of cabinet government and the British parliamentary system. So long as the parties accept this system of government effective decision-making authority will reside with the leadership groups thrown up by the parliamentary parties (of whom much the most important individual is the party leader); and they will exercise this authority so long as they retain the confidence of their respective parliamentary parties. The views of their organized supporters outside Parliament must inevitably be taken into account by the party leadership because of the importance of the rôle these supporters play in selecting candidates, raising funds, and promoting the cause of the party during elections. But, whatever the rôle granted in theory to the extra-parliamentary wings of the parties, in practice final authority rests in both parties with the parliamentary party and its leadership. In this fundamental respect the distribution of power within the two major parties is the same.

As was shown in Chapter I, both major parties have consistently exaggerated the differences between their party organizations with a view to proving that their own is "democratic" and that of their opponents is not. The Labour Party customarily argues that the Conservative Leader rules his party with the iron hand of an autocrat; that he is not subject to the effective control either of his followers in Parliament or of the mass organization of the party outside Parliament. Labour spokesmen claim that, in contrast, their own party is fully democratic because their party leaders are subject to annual re-election (at least when the party is in opposition) and both the Leader and the parliamentary party, they claim, are ultimately responsible to the annual conference of the party. The Conservatives habitually reply that the Labour Party in Parliament is in fact subject to the control of a tight-knit clique of party managers at the party head office and of a group of trade union oligarchs; these party "bosses", the Conservatives charge, manipulate the affairs of the party in their own interest and are in no way responsible to the electorate. The Conservative spokesmen draw a sharp contrast between this state of affairs and the position in their own party, where the parliamentary Leader (who is subject to the control of the electorate) is assigned full responsibility for the affairs of the party, although (the Conservatives add) he gives due weight to the views of his party followers both inside and outside Parliament.

All of these descriptions of the power structures of the rival parties, proffered by the parties themselves, are fundamentally misleading. The Conservative statement of the position within their own party is perhaps the least misleading of the four views summarized above. (Although, as was shown in Chapter III, the Conservative Leader plays nothing like the almost dictatorial rôle Conservative literature would seem to suggest.) But the Conservative view of the Labour Party and the Labour Party's own picture both of itself and of its opponents are highly misleading.

Some part of the confusion about the power structure of the parties arises, as was noted in Chapter I, from a careless use of terms and a failure to distinguish between several autonomous organizations which are loosely associated together for common political purposes. Two parliamentary parties face each other in the House of Commons: they are correctly called "the Conservative Party" and "the Parliamentary Labour Party". Each is an autonomous organization which is aided for electoral purposes by a mass organization of its supporters: the Conservatives by "The National Union of Conservative and Unionist Associations", the Parliamentary Labour Party by a body properly known as "The Labour Party". At the regional and national level each of the mass organizations is sustained by a professional staff, the Conservative Central Office and the Labour Party head office. The mass organizations are best understood as voluntary associations of the politically-active members of the population who are prepared to work for the return to office of one or other of the parliamentary parties. Each mass organization represents a reservoir of largely voluntary and unpaid labour of the sort which is indispensable in the era of the mass electorate. All other functions of the mass organization are, and must remain, subsidiary to their primary task as vote-getting agencies. They can and do exact a certain price for their labour; they expect to be, and are, listened to by their leaders. Like Bagehot's constitutional monarch, the annual party conference has the right to be consulted, the right to encourage, and the right to warn. But this is not to say that the members of the mass organization have the right, under the British parliamentary system, to control or direct the actions of their parliamentary leaders.

The evolution of the British political parties in the era of the mass electorate has witnessed two striking developments, both of which reflect the ascendancy and the primacy of Parliament. Until well into the nineteenth century the Conservative Party was no more than a grouping of a few hundred Members of Parliament and Peers who were associated together for sustaining (whenever it proved feasible) a Conservative cabinet. They had neither a professional staff of any size nor a mass organization of voluntary supporters in the country; nor did they need them. They were able to rely for the most part on the allegiance and authority of the squirearchy and the generous financial contributions of a section of the business community to provide the very considerable financial resources which were required to win elections in the days of widespread political corruption. Two developments forced the Conservative Party to transform itself. The first was the rapid expansion of the electorate, especially in 1867 and afterwards; and the second, the drastic tightening of the electoral laws against corruption. Even if the Conservatives had not themselves become aware that these developments would force a transformation of the party, the initiative of the Liberals under Joseph Chamberlain would certainly have forced them to do so. In any event, a combination of pressures forced the Conservative Party to devise a mass organization of voluntary supporters to sustain the Conservative cause and to secure votes at elections. Disraeli and Lord Randolph Churchill provided a new statement of Toryism which succeeded in attracting a wider range of popular support, and a number of hardworking party managers did the job of building the National Union as the co-ordinating agency of Conservative activity in the country.

It was by no means certain (when Ostrogorski* wrote at the end of the century) that the National Union or the Central Office (or both) might not manage ultimately to become the controlling influence in the affairs of the Conservative Party. Parliament might, as Ostrogorski feared, ultimately be supplanted by the caucus. But this has not happened. Effective control of the affairs of the Conservative Party remains in the hands of the Leader thrown up by the parliamentary party and those he chooses as his associates; they retain their authority als long as they retain the support of their followers in Parliament. The National Union remains what it was declared to be in its earliest beginnings, a "handmaid" to the party in Parliament, although, as befits a more democratic age, it has fairly frequently talked to its masters in a way that no Victorian domestic servant would ever have dared to do. The Conservative Party has been transformed since the mid-nineteenth century; it now has a large popular organization which labours on its behalf between and during elections; but the working of the parliamentary party has been remarkably little affected.

A combination of factors has helped to ensure the autonomy of the Conservative parliamentary party. The first has been the sharp awareness of the dangers of extra-parliamentary control on the part of the leaders of the party. The party had existed in Parliament long before it found it necessary to call its mass organization into being. Its leaders, familiar with the rules and conventions of cabinet government, were instinctively aware of the dangers of allowing the extra-parliamentary party to claim a decisive voice in the affairs of the party. Moreover their authority has been reinforced by the fact that the party has been so frequently and continuously in office during the modern period. (In the 77 years since 1886 the Conservatives have been in opposition for only 21 years.) While the Leader of any party is Prime Minister, and his principal colleagues constitute a cabinet, there can be no debate as to where, in principle, final authority in the party lies. In practice, the party's activists outside Parliament may on occasion become so bitterly hostile to policies of the parliamentary leadership that they can play a considerable part either in changing those policies or in overthrowing the existing Leadership. (This was certainly the case in 1922 when Austen Chamberlain, then Conservative Leader in the Commons and a member of the Lloyd George coalition, failed in his attempt to carry

* Vgl. M. Ostrogorski: Democracy and the Organization of Political Parties, 2 Bde., London 1902.

the Conservatives into a permanent alliance with the Lloyd George Liberals.) But, in general, party Leaders in office (whether Conservative, Liberal or Labour) have little to fear from their activists outside Parliament.

In addition, the traditional Conservative concepts of leadership and discipline have tended to discourage (although not to eliminate) the possibilities of rebellion. In all normal circumstances revolt against their leaders is furthest from the minds of even the most militant Conservative party workers. Subtle considerations of social deference towards their leading parliamentarians (especially when they are the Queen's ministers, as they tend to be for so much of the time) reinforce the party's own view that it is the prime duty of "followers" to sustain rather than to attempt to dominate their leaders. Except in comparatively rare circumstances, therefore, the Conservative extra-parliamentary organization does no more, so far as policy-making is concerned, than to fulfil its appointed rôle within the party organization: that is to offer advice (which may or may not be acted upon) to the party's parliamentary leaders.

This should not be taken to mean that the National Union has played a wholly insignificant part in the affairs of the Party. It loomed very large indeed in the great controversies over Tariff Reform before the First World War; it had to be taken seriously into account during the struggle over the Irish Treaty in 1921 and during the downfall of the Coalition in 1922. Baldwin was frequently in trouble with his followers outside Parliament and had to pay close attention to their views during the period of the General Strike and during the great debates on the future of India in the early 1930s.

Since 1945 the National Union appears to have had an explicit influence on party policy only on rare occasions. (As it did for example in the matter of the 300,000 houses issue, discussed on p. 197 above.) This may have been one consequence of the post-war "democratization" of the party undertaken by Lord Woolton. The annual conference is manifestly more representative of rank-and-file Conservative support in the country than ever before; right-wing ideological dogmatism has been much less in evidence than it was, for example, in Baldwin's day. But, in addition, for the twelve years after 1951 the party leaders constituted the government of the country and this in itself assured their absolute ascendancy within the party assemblies.

The transformation of the Labour Party in the half-century of its existence has been in one sense diamentrically different from that of the Conservatives, although the end product is in certain important respects strikingly similar. While the Conservative Party in Parliament created a mass organization to serve its purposes, Labour began as a movement in the country which created a parliamentary party to give the working class a voice in the House of Commons. A gathering representing some hundreds of thousands of organized trade unionists and a few thousand members of socialist societies decided in 1900 to co-operate together for this purpose. They soon found it necessary to instruct their representatives in Parliament to form themselves into what amounted to a parliamentary party. This body began increasingly to resemble the other great parliamentary parties as it came to rival them in size and strength. By the time the Parliamentary Labour Party had taken office in 1924 its transformation was almost complete. By accepting all the conventions with respect to the office of Prime Minister and of Cabinet government it ensured that effective power within the party would be concentrated in the hands of the leadership of the PLP. When the party has been in power this proposition has been self-evident and largely unchallenged. Each of the two governments formed by MacDonald and by Attlee wielded not one whit less authority than other governments in comparable circumstances; nor were they in any sense subject to external direction by the party outside Parliament. Indeed, if abothe Lur Party had been as continuously in office as the Conservatives have been, it is highly likely that the issue of external control of the Parliamentary Party would be as nearly dead in the Labour Party as it is with the Conservatives.

But even with Labour so continuously in opposition the autonomy of the PLP and the authority of its leaders has been demonstrated beyond question. From Keir Hardie to Gaitskell the Leaders have repeatedly refused to accept external direction. They have taken the view expounded by Morgan Phillips, the former Secretary of the Party, which was quoted in the account of the unilateralist dispute in Chapter X: "... the Parliamentary Party could not maintain its position in the country if it could be demonstrated that it was at any time or in any way subject to dictation from an outside body which, however representative of the Party, could not be regarded as representative of the country."[1] And it was particularly significant that, on the day of his election as Leader in 1963, Harold Wilson stated that he did not consider himself bound by the Labour Party conference resolution demanding withdrawal of the American Polaris base from

Britain because that resolution had not been accepted by the Parliamentary Labour Party.

The Labour Party's devices for ensuring the ascendancy of the Parliamentary Party and its leaders (analysed in Chapters VI–VIII above) are infinitely more complex than those which obtain in the Conservative Party. But basically they have depended on the existence of a bond of confidence between the parliamentary leaders and a sufficient number of leading trade unionists to command preponderant support for the policies of the party leadership at the party conference. During most of Labour's history it has been overwhelmingly clear that the initiative in the main areas of policy-making (with the possible exception of industrial relations) has lain with the parliamentary leaders rather than with their trade union allies; the latter appear tacitly at least to have recognized that the leaders of the PLP, as a potential cabinet or "Shadow Government", cannot appear, even in opposition, to be reduced to the rôle of political spokesmen for the trade union movement or for the Labour Party conference, with its dominant trade union movement or for the Labour Party conference, with its dominant trade union block vote. It was also shown in Chapter VIII that, in all normal circumstances, Labour's parliamentary leaders (who, like their Conservative opposite numbers, will take into account the currents of opinion within all sections of the party in the course of determining their policies) are likely to be sustained by majority support within the PLP and the NEC, and in *both* the trade union and the constituency sections of the mass organization. Except on the rarest occasions in the history of the party it has been a Centre-Right majority in the PLP which has carried the day against a Left minority within each of the constituent elements of the party.

The left-wing activists in the constituencies have been repeatedly disillusioned on discovering that the party's rhetoric about "inner-party democracy" bears so little relation to its practice. R. H. S. Crossman, one of the recent heroes of the activists, has summarized the situation, as the militants tend to see it, with cruel precision:

"... since it could not afford, like its opponents, to maintain a large army of paid party workers, the Labour Party required militants – politically conscious socialists to do the work of organizing the constituencies. But since these militants tended to be 'extremists', a constitution was needed which maintained their enthusiasm by apparently creating a full party democracy while excluding them from effective power. Hence the concession in principle of sovereign powers to the delegates at the Annual Conference, and the removal in practice of most of this sovereignty through the trade union block vote on the one hand, and the complete independence of the Parliamentary Labour Party on the other."[2]

The only occasion when the party's policy-decision mechanisms broke down completely was in 1960–61 when, on a major issue of policy, the party leadership was unable to win preponderant trade union support in the conference (although at Scarborough in 1960 two-thirds of the constituency delegates supported the parliamentary leadership). And in this profoundly important test case a sufficient number of the dissident unions subsequently reversed themselves in the following year to ensure that the next party conference would fall in line again with the Parliamentary Party. Thereafter the autonomy of the PLP could hardly any longer be in dispute. But what was in dispute was whether the party could continue to cling to a policy-decision process which conveyed the *public* impression that Labour's parliamentary leaders (and therefore the alternative government) were repeatedly on the point of destruction at the hands of their more militant "supporters". In fact, of course, Gaitskell emerged from the struggle of 1960–61 a more powerful figure in his party than all but a very few Leaders of any of the main parties in this century. And this helped enormously to enhance his personal standing as a prospective Prime Minister. But the opinion polls and other evidence strongly suggest that the Labour party has suffered grave electoral damage as a consequence of its bitter public quarrels. Yet, incredibly enough, the party has made no move even to re-examine its decision-making processes in almost half a century.

Friction between parliamentary parties and their supporters outside Parliament is no doubt inevitable; the parliamentarians, in determining their policies, must take many factors into account and, whatever weight they may give to the views of their active supporters on particular issues, they cannot allow themselves to be reduced to the rôle of spokesmen of the active minority who control their extra-parliamentary organizations. The Labour party endowed itself with a party constitution which raised this danger in sharpest form. Yet the leadership group of the PLP, while paying lip-service to the theory of inner-party democracy, has repeatedly and consistently refused to accept direction from its extra-parliamentary supporters. Setting aside the party myths and the inter-party propaganda it is clear that the primary function of the mass organizations of the Conservative and Labour parties is to sustain two competing teams of parliamentary leaders between whom the electorate as a whole may periodically choose. When the electorate has made its choice, the leaders of the successful team don the garments of authority which are provided under the Cabinet system and they retain this authority so long as they retain the confidence of their followers in Parliament (and, of course, of the electorate). Their followers outside Parliament become little more than a highly organized pressure group with a special channel of communication directly to the Leader, the Cabinet and the parliamentary party. Any disposition to take advantage of this special relationship is normally more than neutralized by feelings of pride and loyalty to their leaders and by an anxiety not to embarrass them in the execution of their duties or to provide aid and comfort to the rival team, who are eagerly preparing to overthrow them at the forthcoming election. Most governments at one time or another find it advisable to make concessions on some issue of policy to the clearly expressed views of their followers outside Parliament. But they make such concessions much more frequently to their followers *in* Parliament, on whose day-to-day support in the division lobbies the government depends, than they do to their followers in the country whose allegiance is tested normally only at five-yearly intervals. While the parliamentary party is in opposition it tends to listen more readily to the voices of its supporters in the country; but even while in opposition no major parliamentary party in the modern period has allowed itself to be relegated to the rôle of spokesman or servant of its mass organization.

Ostrogorski's fears notwithstanding, the institution of Parliament has survived almost unimpaired into the age of mass electorates and of mass parties. One of the few significant developments has been the decline of the independent Member of Parliament (although this has been a much less spectacular process than some have maintained)[3] and in addition, the diminishing freedom of action accorded to the independently-minded members of both of the great parties. As each parliamentary party has developed a vast, cumbersome, but highly organized appendage outside Parliament, the flexibility of parliamentary parties has undoubtedly declined. The parliamentary leaders can be virtually certain that the withdrawal of the whip by the parliamentary party, if it is followed by expulsion from the mass organization, will result in the political death of the apostate concerned. In this respect it may be argued that the growth of the mass party has greatly increased the rigidity of party relationships in the House of Commons.

In such circumstances it would appear to be more than ever important that minority groups within each of the great parties should be given reasonable scope for expression of their views and for an opportunity to convert their fellow party members both in the House of Commons and in the mass party outside to their own point of view. Admittedly no party can tolerate a fully organized "party within a party"; this was shown conclusively by Labours's experience during the period 1929–31 (discussed in Chapter VII) which culminated in the break with the ILP. It is largely because of this experience that the Labour Party has viewed all attempts to organize minority opinion within the party as an intolerable threat to its own survival. There are clearly defined limits beyond which organized minorities cannot be permitted to go if the parent party is to function as a coherent contender for office. But the Labour Party appears to lean towards a dangerously rigorous conception of party discipline which sometimes appears to resemble the Communist conception of democratic centralism. If both major parties become too grimly intolerant of honest differences of opinion among their followers on major matters of policy then there are real grounds for concern in a period in which the prospects for minor parties and independent candidates are so poor. The danger has been more evident in the case of the Labour Party; but in another form it is no less real in the case of the Conservatives. They have found it less necessary to rely on rigid codes of discipline; this may be in part a reflection of the fact that ideological disputes culminating in threatened party splits are rare. But, as was shown in Chapter X, the Conservatives have tolerated a type of constituency discipline applied to certain of their M.P.s which has been almost as harsh in its effects as the disciplinary codes imposed by the PLP. If the two great parties together are to dominate the whole political life of the community, then it is essential that every encouragement should be given to the expression of honest political differences within each. These differences become a source of concern only if they threaten the ability of a party to form and sustain a government. Short of this, intra-party differences must be welcomed as an indispensable means of preventing the sort of intellectual sclerosis which appears at times to threaten the two great parties of this country.

Apart from these particular sources of concern, one must face the more fundamental question as to whether the present system of party organization in Great Britain deserves the label "democratic". Because the party leaders in parliament do not hold themselves directly responsible to the members of the party outside Parliament it is sometimes alleged that this proves that both great parties are "undemocratic". Or, as some would argue, it provides a triumphant vindication of the "iron law of oligarchy" associated with the name of Robert Michels.[4] Certainly the analysis in Parts I and II of this study has shown that there is ample evidence of the working of what Michels calls the "technical" and „psychological" factors which tend to ensure the emergence of, and the retention of power by, a small group of leaders in each party. But evidence has also been provided (it is perhaps more extensive in the history of the Conservative Party than in the Labour Party) of revolts against the party leaders which have culminated in their overthrow. The "law of oligarchy" is certainly not an "iron" law. Parties are usually content to be led; but this is largely because there is no other way in which they can operate. This does not mean, however, that party leadership groups can ignore with impunity the moods and aspirations of their followers; they must carry their followers (and above all their followers in their parliamentary party) with them. And to do so, they have to take into account at every stage the clearly defined currents of opinion within their party. Blind appeals to loyalty (either to the person of the Leader or to the party itself) are frequently resorted to, and often they achieve their purpose. But they are rarely successful in bridging a real gulf when one does develop between the leaders and their followers.

Another factor must be taken into account in assessing the relevance of Michels' theories. Largely no doubt as a result of his own continental background, Michels appeared to assume that a "democratic" political party ought ideally to be under the direction and control of its mass membership. Michels suggested that this relationship never proves feasible in practice because of the operation of his law of oligarchy. But in the British context there is another reason of greater importance: the conventions of the parliamentary system (which have been accepted by all parties, including the Labour Party) require that Members of Parliament, and therefore parliamentary parties also, must hold themselves responsible solely to the electorate and not to the mass organization of their supporters outside Parliament. In other words, a crude application of Michels' theories would ignore what might be termed the division of labour within British political parties. It would ignore the fact that the primary function of the mass organizations is to sustain competing teams of potential leaders in the House of Commons in order that the electorate as a whole may choose between them. All other functions (involving attempts by the mass organizations to influence the formulation of policy and the emergence of leaders within the parliamentary parties) are, and must remain, subsidiary. The mass organizations may be permitted to play some part in these respects; but if they attempted to arrogate to themselves a determining influence with respect to policy or leadership they would be cutting across the chain of responsibility from Cabinet, to Parliament, to electorate, which is fundamental to the theory of the British parliamentary system.

But Michels apart, many of the other criticisms of the alleged undemocratic nature of party organization reflect a persistent belief in what might be termed the classical conception of the democratic process. In a penetrating analysis of the shortcomings of this classical conception, Joseph Schumpeter has shown how little relation it bears to the democratic process as it has evolved in Britain and most other political democracies.[5] In the late eighteenth century it was assumed that the democratic process would ensure the triumph of the common good by permitting the people themselves to decide issues through the election of representatives who assembled to carry out "the people's will". The electorate, is was assumed, might be called on to pronounce on certain major issues (perhaps by means of referenda); all other issues would be decided by a committee (Parliament) elected by the whole adult population. The function of the members of this committee would be to voice, reflect or represent the will of the electorate. Lip-service is still paid to this classical conception of democracy even by many who are aware of the extent to which it has proved unworkable. The study of the psychology of political processes has revealed the importance of the extra-rational and the irrational elements in social behaviour. The parallel development of the arts of political propaganda has enabled political leaders to exploit the irrational element in human behaviour and to manufacture what is often a purely synthetic "general will"; so much so that some are prepared to argue, with Schumpeter, that the will of the people is the product and not the motive power of the political process.

It has also become increasingly evident that the classical theory attributed to the electorate an altogether unrealistic degree of initiative; it came near to ignoring completely the importance of leadership in the political process. It is no doubt more realistic to argue that the essence of the democratic process is that it should provide a free competition for political leadership. The essential rôle of the electorate is not to reach decisions on specific issues of policy but to decide which of two or more competing teams of potential leaders shall make the decisions. The democratic process ensures that there will be a periodic opportunity for the electorate to review the record of the decision-makers who currently hold office; and, if the electorate wishes, it may replace them with an alternative team. The competing teams usually offer broad declarations of policy respecting their long-range goals; they may also promise to introduce specific items of legislation; or alternatively they may, like the National Government formed in 1931, ask only for a "Doctor's Mandate" to do whatever they may subsequently decide to be necessary in the national interest. In the formulation of electoral programmes the mass party usually plays some part, although in both the Conservative and Labour Parties final decisions in this regard rest with the parliamentary leaders. These leaders are bound to be concerned mainly with their own conception of the national interest and with the competing demands of various interest groups which may or may not be adequately reflected within their party organizations. But one thing is certain: initiative in the formulation of policy cannot possibly come primarily from the several millions of party supporters or from the electorate as a whole. The active party workers must devote themselves primarily to sustaining the teams of candidates for leadership between whom the electorate may choose (although the interest group system enables those elements in the electorate who wish to do so to press their views and demands on the team that secures office).

The mass organizations of the Conservative and Labour Parties have, of course, additional functions which have been examined in some detail in the course of this study. They serve as a two-way channel of communication between the leaders of the parliamentary parties and their supporters in the country; when the parliamentary party is in office its mass organization plays a vital rôle in explaining and defending the work of the government and in keeping it informed of currents of opinion in the country. A further function of the mass political organizations is to provide a means whereby the politically active individuals in the community can play some part, however limited, in influencing both the formulation of party policy and the emergence of party leaders. And for those citizens who seek to play a more influential part in the political life of the community, participation in the mass organizations provides an excellent preliminary training for parliamentary candidature and eventual entry into Parliament.

Seen from the viewpoint of society as a whole, mass political parties of the kind that have emerged in Britain fulfil an invaluable set of functions. By exposing the electorate to a cross-fire of political argument and debate they stimulate public interest in the essential business of "attending to the arrangements of society". The mass parties also fulfil an important integrating function. They are one of the main channels trough which interest groups and both organized and unorganized bodies of opinion can bring their views to the attention of parliamentarians. The parliamentary leaders in turn must weigh and evaluate the views that are conveyed through these and other channels. Inevitably these views are taken into account in the formulation of parliamentary policy.[6] Lord Bryce saw American parties as "brokers" whose primary business it was to serve various interests and to reconcile them. In the much more homogeneous society of Britain the mass parties are inevitably less preoccupied with this task; they do nevertheless play an important rôle in integrating the diverse and sometimes conflicting interests and opinions in the community. But this study has been concerned not with the broad social function of parties but with their internal structure and the distribution of power within each. And no emphasis on the auxiliary functions of the mass organizations outside Parliament can be allowed to obscure the basic proposition that the mass parties are primarily the servants of their respective parliamentary parties; that their principal function is to sustain teams of parliamentary leaders between whom the electorate is periodically invited to choose.

If this is a fair description of the realities of the democratic process then it should be evident that the two major British political parties are well suited to play an appropriate rôle in this process. They have managed to avoid most of the serious pitfalls into which party organizations in many other countries have fallen. The ideological conflict between the parties is not so great as to threaten the survival of the democratic process itself; yet it is great enough to ensure that the members of the mass organizations of the two main parties will work willingly for the victory of their cause without seeking illicit material rewards for their efforts. The autonomy of the two great parliamentary parties is almost completely unimpaired, although each of them has devised a system of consulation with its mass organization which ensures that the latter will not be so exasperated with its impotence as to refuse to fulfil its function as a vote-getting agency. Each major party has organized a professional machine which works alongside the mass organization and ensures the latter's efficiency without appearing too obviously to dominate it. Neither of these machines has in any way threatened to become the real centre of power within its respective party organization. Both great parties have tapped large-scale financial resources without becoming completely beholden to those who provide the funds; neither party in office has sacrificed its conception of the national interest in order to serve the purposes of those sections of the community which finance its operations.

Reference has been made throughout this study to serious shortcomings in each of the major party organizations; there is plenty of scope for the reformer in both the Conservative and Labour Parties. There may also be scope for those who seek to modify or to transform other aspects of British parliamentary democracy. But an extensive review of the working of British party organizations inspires neither alarm nor gloom; sixty years after Ostrogorski wrote there appears to be no reason to conclude that events have justified his pessimistic expectation that the parliamentary system was unlikely to survive the emergence of the mass party. It might be argued, indeed, that the parliamentary system gives every appearance of outliving the age of the mass party; there is much evidence to support the view that the traditional electoral activities of the mass party, including the conduct of public meetings, canvassing and the rest, are now of declining importance in influencing the outcome of elections. It seems likely that the really effective electioneering of the future will rely increasingly on the newer mass media of radio and, above all, of television. Perhaps in retrospect it will be evident that the mass party saw its heyday during the period when the extension of the franchise had created a mass electorate, but there was as yet no effective means of reaching the voters in their own homes. But meanwhile, there can be no doubt that despite the many new problems it created, the mass party did not fulfil the gloomy expectations of its early chroniclers. Perhaps the most apt conclusion for this study can be borrowed from Lord Bryce's foreword (written in 1902) to the first edition of Ostrogorski's *Democracy and the Organization of Political Parties*. Bryce had praised Ostrogorski's work very highly, but he questioned his preoccupation with "the pathology of party government". Bryce concluded: "In England, happily for England, the party organizations have not ceased to be controlled by men occupying a position which makes them amenable to public opinion, nor have they as yet departed far from those traditions in which the strength of English free government lies." Bryce's observation is equally valid to-day.

Anmerkungen

1 Phillips, M., *Constitution of the Labour Party*, London, 1960, p. 4.

2 Crossman, R. H. S., in his Introduction to the Fontana edition of Bagehot, W., *The English Constitution* (1963). To trace the gyrations in Crossman's own position, see McKenzie, R. T., *British Political Parties*, p. 626.

3 See Butler, D. E., *The Electoral System in Britain, 1918–1951*, pp. 153 ff.

4 See Chapter I.

5 Schumpeter, J. A., *Capitalism, Socialism and Democracy*, London, 1952, pp. 250 ff.

6 For a fuller statement of the present writer's views on the rôle of interest groups in the political system see McKenzie, R. T., "Parties, Pressure Groups and the British Political Process", *The Political Quarterly*, Jan.-Mar., 1958, pp. 5–16.

8

Peter G. J. Pulzer

Voting Behaviour

Aus: Political Representation and Elections in Britain. 2. Auflage, London 1968, S. 93–126.

Das Buch erschien zuerst 1967.
Peter G. J. Pulzer ist Lecturer der Politikwissenschaft an der Universität Oxford.

Although an election is a ritual which involves much beside the making of choices, it is also a choice; indeed, some languages have only one word for the two processes. What we think about the merits of making political choices by means of elections depends on what we think of our fellow-citizens' capacity for making choices.
Most nineteenth-century advocacy of an extended franchise rested on the asumption that voters are capable of choosing rationally, though even the most advanced liberal theorists, like James and John Stuart Mill, admitted that the least educated were least equipped to do so. At the beginning of this century Lord Bryce stipulated a more modest requirement, the 'average man',
'The man of broad common sense, mixing on equal terms with his neighbours, forming a fair unprejudiced judgment on every question, not viewy or pedantic like the man of learning, nor arrogant like the man of wealth, but seeing things in a practical, businesslike, and withal kindly spirit, pursuing happiness in his own way, and willing that everyone else should do so. Such average men make the bulk of the people, and are pretty sure to go right, because the publicity secured to the expression of opinion by speech and in print will supply them with ample materials for judging what is best for all ... He may have limited knowledge and no initiative, yet he may be able to form ... a shrewd judgment of men ... What he lacks in knowledge he often makes up for by a sympathetic comprehension of the attitude of his fellow-men.'[1]

The foundations of such assumptions have been pretty thoroughly undermined by the progress of two modern disciplines, psychology and sociology. As a result we know much more about why people hold the political views that they do, though the implications for representational theory are by no means clear-cut.

Before we ask *why*, it is best to ask *how*. The raw material of voting behaviour is in the voting figures (See Table on page 184). At the parliamentary level, these shifts in voting have led to great variations in representation. But then, the British electoral system is notorious for exaggerating the effects of such shifts. The chief impression which the voting figures convey is one of stability, not volatility. Figure 1 shows that since the war neither of the major parties has gained less than 39,7% of the total vote or more than 49,3%. (For the sake of simplicity Northern Ireland and the university constituencies are excluded throughout this chapter.) The contrast with the United States is striking (Figures 1, 2). Only once, in 1945, has the gap between the two main parties in Britain exceeded 7%. The movement from election to election has also been small. This movement is normally measured in terms of 'net swing', which can be calculated in a variety of ways.[2] The most widely used[a] and most easily comprehensible, although also the crudest, is to average the percentage gain by one major party and percentage loss by the other, e.g.

$$\text{Example 1} \begin{cases} \text{Party A: } + 5\,\% \text{ of all votes cast} \\ \text{Party B: } - 5\,\% \text{ of all votes cast} \\ \text{Party Z: } \pm 0\,\% \text{ of all votes cast} \end{cases}$$

$$\text{Swing} = 5\,\%$$

$$\text{Example 2} \begin{cases} \text{Party A: } + 2\,\% \text{ of all votes cast} \\ \text{Party B: } - 7\,\% \text{ of all votes cast} \\ \text{Party Z: } + 5\,\% \text{ of all votes cast} \end{cases}$$

$$\text{Swing} = \frac{2 + 7}{2} = 4^1/_2\,\%$$

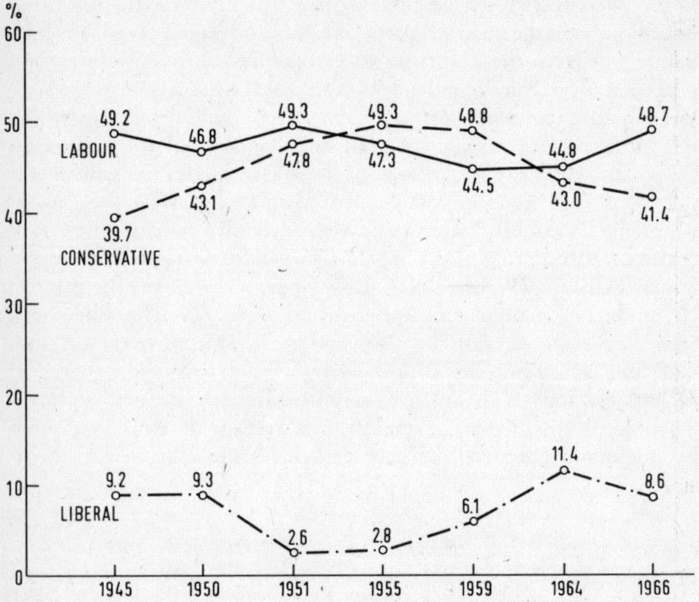

Figure 1: Percentage of total vote by Party, 1945–66 (Great Britain only)

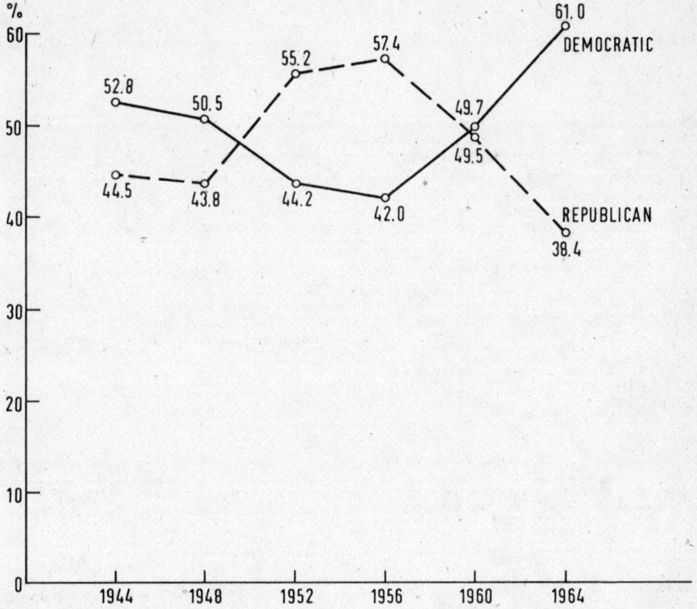

Figure 2: Percentage of total vote by Presidential candidates in USA, 1944–64

VOTES CAST IN BRITISH GENERAL ELECTIONS, 1945–1966

	Electorate	Conservative		Labour		Liberal		Other		Turn-out
		votes	%	votes	%	votes	%	votes	%	%
1945 +	32,836,419	9,577,667	39·8	11,632,891	48·3	2,197,101	9·1	674,703	2·8	73·3
1950	34,269,770	12,502,567	43·5	13,266,592	46·1	2,621,548	9·1	381,964	1·3	84·0
1951	34,645,573	13,717,538	48·0	13,948,605	48·8	730,556	2·5	198,969	0·7	82·5
1955	34,858,263	13,311,936	49·7	12,404,970	46·4	722,405	2·7	321,182	0·2	76·8
1959	35,397,080	13,749,830	49·4	12,215,538	43·8	1,638,571	5·9	275,304	1·0	78·8
1964	35,892,572	12,001,396	43·4	12,205,814	44·1	3,092,878	11·2	348,914	1·3	77·0
1966	35,966,975	11,418,413	41·9	13,056,951	47·9	2,327,470	8·5	456,909	1·7	75·8

+ Voting figures adjusted to allow for double-member constituencies in which electors had two votes each, and to omit university seats.

SEATS WON IN BRITISH GENERAL ELECTIONS, 1945–1966

	Total	Conservative	Labour	Liberal	Others	Overall Majority
1945	240	213	393	12	22	Lab. 146
1950	625	298	315	9	3	Lab. 5
1951	625	321	295	6	3	Con. 17
1955	630	345	277	6	2	Con. 60
1959	630	365	258	6	1	Con. 100
1964	630	303	317	9	1	Lab. 4
1966	630	253	363	12	2	Lab. 97

On this calculation, the purpose of which is to isolate that section or the electorate which seems to have changed its mind, the swing at postwar elections has been

1950 2·9% to Con.
1951 1·1% to Con.
1955 1·8% to Con.
1959 1·1% to Con.
1964 3·1% to Lab.
1966 2·7% to Lab.

In 1951, 1955, 1966 over half the constituencies had a swing which was within 1% of the national average, though in 1959 and 1964 the divergence was rather greater. This consistency is in keeping with the social and ideological homogeneity which have already been noted. Its development has accompanied – both as cause and as consequence – the rise of the modern disciplined political party, but it has become overwhelmingly true of British politics only since the establishment of the Labour-Tory duel. Up to the First World War changes determined by local conditions and going against the tide were common. In January, 1910, when the Conservatives gained 128 seats, Liberals and their Labour allies were still able to gain thirteen seats that they had failed to capture in the landslide of 1906. The second election of that year, in December, led to virtually the same overall result,[b] but fifty-six seats changed hands.[3] Since the war the greatest number of seats to change hands against the tide was six (in 1959); in 1950, 1951 and 1966 there were none at all. 1959 was also the only post-war election in which more than one-sixth of the seats showed swings in the opposite direction from the general trend. Only since the war have both major parties attempted to cover the entire country. 1950 was the first election in which all constituencies outside Northern Ireland were contested, with Labour candidates in every seat (except the Speaker's) in England, Scotland and Wales. It was not until 1964 that the Conservatives followed suit. The elimination of the Independent MP is also a post-war phenomenon. As late as 1945 territorial constituencies returned two Communists, one ILP and seven Independents against the opposition of the major parties. Of the Independents, four were party rebels, the other three 'genuine' non-party men. Except for the ILP members who had joined the Labour Party they were all defeated in 1950. Since then no Independent or minor party candidate has been elected, or come anywhere near it, at a general election, but one Welsh Nationalist has been successful at a by-election.

It is, no doubt, possible to exaggerate the firmness of British party loyalties. Not only opinion polls but by-elections and municipal elections show that the limits within which opinion can move are quite wide. Between 1959 and 1964 Gallup recorded a maximum Conservative lead of 13% in October, 1960, just after the Scarborough conference, and a maximum Labour lead of 20% in June, 1963, just after Mr. Profumo's resignation.[4] National Opinion Poll, the other main polling organization, showed the following maximum fluctuations:[5]

	Conservative	Labour	Liberal
	%	%	%
August, 1960	50	39	11
March, 1962	29	33	38
June, 1963	33	52	15

Opinion polls, though accurate enough as guides to the direction in which opinion is moving, are not so accurate that any one sample can be taken literally. The extreme points in the parties' popularity came immediately after spectacular events – Labour's defence split, the Orpington by-election, the Profumo affair – and receded fairly quickly. At the same time, it is evident that the number of *potentially* volatile voters is much greater than those who appear to have actually changed their minds at an election.

If party loyalty is as strong as the election figures suggest, then it is clear that most electors are not, as rationalist utopians once thought, in a state of perpetual choice. On the contrary, most political allegiance seems to be a matter of habit, and it is here that the psychologists' and sociologists' explanations become relevant. What determines these habits of allegiance? Family influence, class, region, religion, sex and age all play their part, though these categories do not fall into watertight compartments. Easily the most important of all is class. Class is the basis of British party politics; all else is embellishment and detail.

Class and Party

Until the middle of the nineteenth century 'connection' and local influence were as powerful as any other factors in determining party loyalty, the more so as the parties themselves had neither easily recognizable policies nor coherent internal organization. Over the last hundred years, however, class and party have increasingly coincided. Especially since the Second Reform Act 1867, the further one went down the social scale, the more likely one was to find support for the party of the left (Liberal until 1914, Labour thereafter). This is more easily established for the years before the ballot than after. An examination of the poll books, in which every voter's preference was recorded shows the following results for two typical constituencies.

Rochdale, 1857[6]

	Liberal	Conservative
Drink interest	28	118
Capitalists	34	54
Craftsmen	133	95
Retailers	167	102
Professional & dependants	88	106
Others	36	54
	480	527

Cambridge, 1868[7]

	Liberal	Conservative
Craftsmen	809	393
Labourers	289	123
Servants	90	235

How is class measured? Occupation and income are the most obvious criteria and to a large extent they overlap, but occupation is the more reliable of the two. The simplest course is to divide society into 'middle' and 'working' class (or manual and non-manual). The great majority of people, when asked to place themselves socially, use one of these two categories (or some fairly obvious equivalent, such as 'professional' or 'labouring') rather than any of the more refined sub-divisions that a social scientist would prefer. But simplicity is sometimes achieved at the expense of over-simplification: a division of society into two is not as easy as Marx and Engels once imagined it to be.[c] To use only two classes involves arbitrary decisions about the dividing line. This may not matter much if one simply wants to demonstrate that in general party goes with class, or to plot long-term developments in the relationship. But it becomes

a serious obstacle if one wants to identify sub-groups, such as working-class Conservatives and middleclass Socialists. For this reason social investigators tend to use more elaborate scales. The first of these is an adaptation of the one used by the Registrar-General since 1911,[8] with a sub-division in the largest and most heterogeneous of the five clases, C (Routine white-collar and skilled manual). This scale is used by the Institute of Practitioners in Advertising and most market research organizations, and by NOP (National Opinion Polls).
The Gallup Poll uses a slightly different scale:

<table>
<tr><th>NOP</th><th colspan="2">IPA</th><th colspan="2">GALLUP</th></tr>
<tr><td rowspan="2">12 % AB</td><td>A</td><td>Higher managerial, administrative or professional</td><td>Average + / well-to-do</td><td>6 %</td></tr>
<tr><td>B</td><td>Intermediate managerial, administrative or professional</td><td rowspan="2">Average/upper middle and middle class</td><td rowspan="2">22 %</td></tr>
<tr><td>22 % C1</td><td>C1</td><td>Supervisory, clerical; junior managerial, administrative or professional</td></tr>
<tr><td>37 % C2</td><td>C2</td><td>Skilled manual workers</td><td rowspan="2">Average-/lower middle and working class</td><td rowspan="2">61 %</td></tr>
<tr><td rowspan="2">29 % DE</td><td>D</td><td>Semi-skilled and unskilled manual workers</td></tr>
<tr><td>E</td><td>State pensioners, casual workers</td><td>Very poor</td><td>11 %</td></tr>
</table>

The third is the Hall-Jones scale which uses seven categories:

1. Professional and high administrative, e.g. surgeon, chartered accountant;
2. Managerial and executive, e.g. personnel manager, primary school headmaster;
3. Higher-grade inspectional, supervisory and other non-manual, e.g. police inspector, farm bailiff;
4. Lower-grade inspectional, supervisory and other non-manual, e.g. insurance agent, costing clerk, tobacconist;
5. Skilled manual and routine non-manual, e.g. compositor, drapery shop assistant;

6. Semi-skilled manual, e.g. assembly worker, butcher's shop assistant;
7. Unskilled manual.

This has the advantage of combining 'objective' with 'subjective' assessment, since Hall and Caradog-Jones conducted a survey to discover the status which various occupations enjoy.[d]

The most recent attempt to locate as exactly as possible the elusive dividing line between 'middle' and 'working' class has been made by Butler and Stokes who, using the market-research / registrar-general classification, found that class C1 (lower non-manual) straddled this line, both in the self-assessment of those who belonged to it and in objectively observable habits. At the top this class (telegraph operators, qualified local authority officers, secretaries and typists with subordinates, draughtsmen) 60% classed themselves as 'middle'; as many as 20% took a quality newspaper *(The Times, Guardian or Daily Telegraph)*. At the bottom of the class (shop assistants, policemen, transport inspectors, lodging housekeepers) only 32% classed themselves as 'middle' and only 5% read a quality newspaper.[11] As Figure 3 shows, the drop in self-assessed status between C1a and C1b is greater than that between any other two classes, though the sharpest break in political support occurs between C1b and C2. Whether this marginal category is attributed to the broader 'middle' or 'working' classes makes a great difference to the correlation between social status and party affiliation. If it counts as middle (as is usually done, since its members are non-manual) then the two parties show degrees of class support which are almost mirror-images.

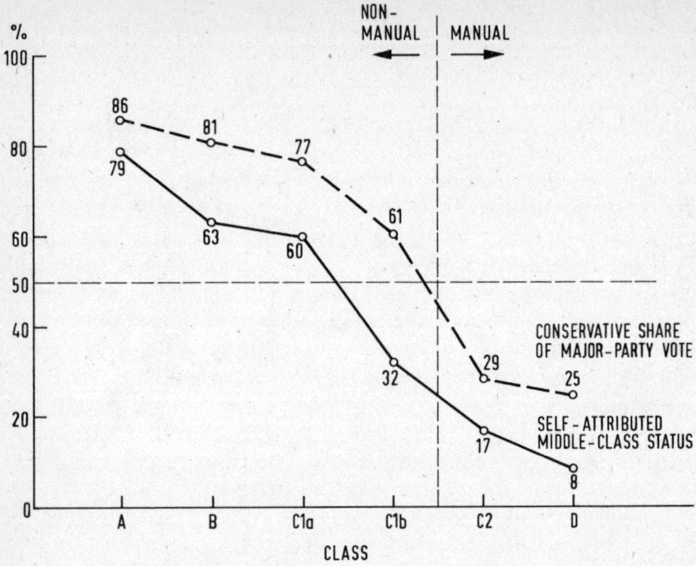

Figure 3: Self-attributed middle-class status and Party preference by classes (Summer, 1963).

Party support by class, counting C1b as 'middle' (Summer 1963)

	Middle	Working
Conservative	77 %	27 %
Labour	23 %	73 %

If, on the other hand, it is consigned to the working class, as most of its members seem to think it should be, the imbalance in class support becomes considerable:[12]

Party support by class, counting C1b as 'working' (Summer 1963)

	Middle	Working
Conservative	80 %	32 %
Labour	20 %	68 %

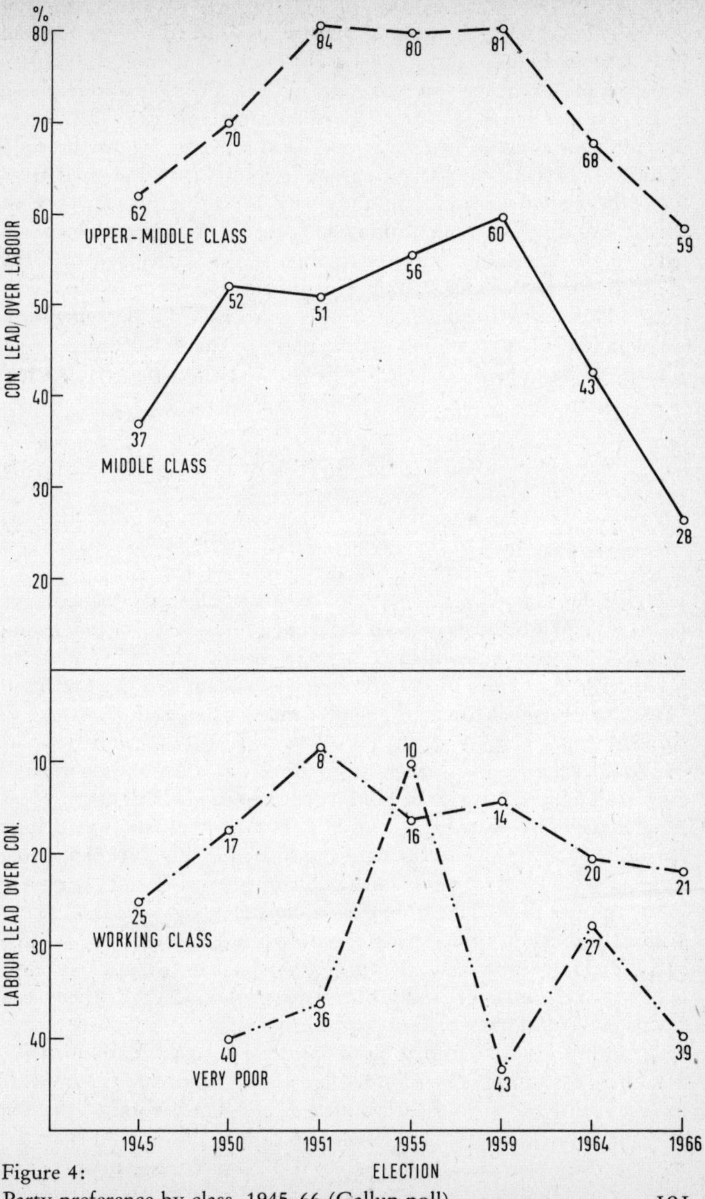

Figure 4:
Party preference by class, 1945–66 (Gallup poll)

These details apart, the general picture, reinforced by the opinion poll data in Figures 4 and 5, is a familiar one. People in manual occupations – however defined – are, in the majority, Labour; those who are not are, in the majority, Conservative. This 'obvious' observation requires two qualifications. Class is by no means the only plausible criterion for party cleavage in a modern state; it is true, however, that British party politics are more highly class-bound than those in most other countries. A recent comparison between four Anglo-Saxon democracies (Britain, USA, Canada, Australia) showed that of the four Britain had the highest[e] index of class voting.[13] This index is constructed by subtracting the percentage of non-manual workers voting for the party of the Left from the percentage of manual workers who do so, thus revealing the gap between the classes, e.g.

	% voting for Left party
Manual:	75
Non-manual:	25
Index of class voting:	+ 50

A high index may therefore be achieved when most manual workers vote Left and most non-manual workers do not. A lower index may result *either* from many manual workers voting Right (e.g. Western Germany),[14] *or* from many non-manual workers voting Left (e.g. Norway);[15] an even lower or negative index when both happen (e.g. Canada).[16]

This makes the second qualification important. Class voting in Britain may be high, but it is by no means as high as it might be. Most people, asked to locate the centre of class-consciousness in Britain would probably point to the working class; and this is correct in that class-consciousness among workers is more explicit and overt than in the middle class[f]. The middle class, however, shows much greater political cohesion. In post-war elections the Labour Party has not succeeded in getting more than 20–25% of the non-manual vote or 10–15% of the business and professional classes. On the other hand at least a third of the working class consistently votes Conservative. Put another way, if (according to the 1961 Census) two-thirds of working population are employed in manual occupations, approximately onehalf of the Conservative vote regularly comes from the working class, but only about one-sixth of the Labour vote from the middle class (Figure 6). Indeed 'pure' class voting, or anything approaching it, would put an end to the British party system. The Conservative Party has survived the democratization of the country by its ability to gain votes of the poor. For that reason, the 'Tory working man' has been subjected to more study than the other politically deviant group, the middle-class Socialist. While some middle-class sympathy may be important to the Labour Party in providing it with leadership and local organization, and perhaps also in confirming its claim to speak for workers 'by hand or by brain', it does not have the statistical significance that working-class support has for the Conservatives.

What is the basis of working-class Toryism? The most important ingredient is social deference, though this may take many forms. In the nineteenth century Tory Democrats like Disraeli and Lord Randolph Churchill appealed to workers on the grounds that the Tories, unlike money-grubbing Liberal mill-owners, were true aristocrats and above the class-struggle. Factory hands who would not dream of voting for Mr. Gradgrind could therefore confidently follow the Duke of Omnium. This appeal evoked, and still evokes, a response:

'The Conservatives have had more experience over the centuries. It's in the blood for them, running the country. There's more family background in the Conservatives, more of the aristocratic families, more heritage.

'They're gentlemen born. I think they're made for that sort of job.'[17]

Coupled with it is a respect for education, remembering that education is at least as much social training as intellectual qualification: 'The Conservatives are better suited to running the country. They're better educated – I think there is nothing better than to hear a public school man speak English.'[18] But equally there is respect for money and business success – as indeed there was in the nineteenth century when a great many working men were willing to follow the lead of their local Liberal or Radical employers. Today money as well as birth is associated with Conservatism: 'The Conservatives do represent big business and I think that makes them the more efficient party. Running the country is, after all, just the biggest business of them all.'[19] To some extent the snobbish attitudes implied by this deference are reflected in the Tory worker's views of himself. Conservative manual workers are more likely to attribute middle-class status to themselves than Labour manual workers.[20] But deference

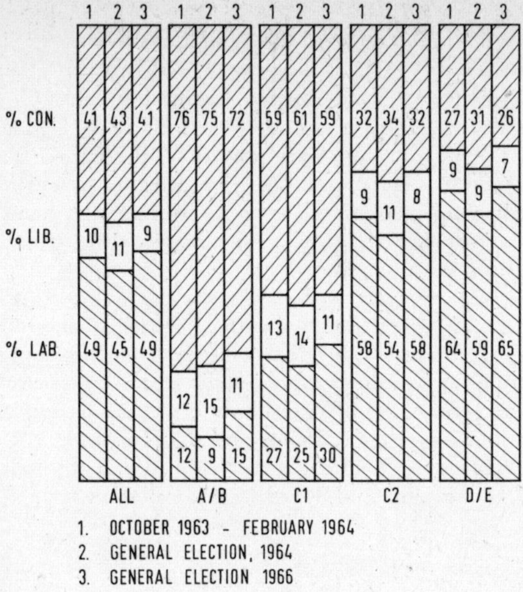

Figure 5: Party preference by class, 1963–66 (N.O.P.)

implies just as strongly a desire to maintain the established distance between classes, to acknowledge the superiority of 'gentlemen born'.

Deference alone, however, can hardly account for the whole of working-class women are more right-wing than working-class men, gory, whom McKenzie and Silver call 'secular' Conservatives[21] – predominantly younger voters who happen to approve of private enterprise, value consumer affluence or view trade unions unfavourably. They are less committed emotionally to leadership from the upper classes and take a more hard-headed and pragmatic view of Conservative capacity to govern. The fact that over the last twenty years the Conservatives have emerged relatively weaker in the older industrial areas (North of England, Scotland, Wales) than in the areas of more recent expansion (Midlands, South)[g] suggests that the secular element may be gaining over the traditionally deferential.

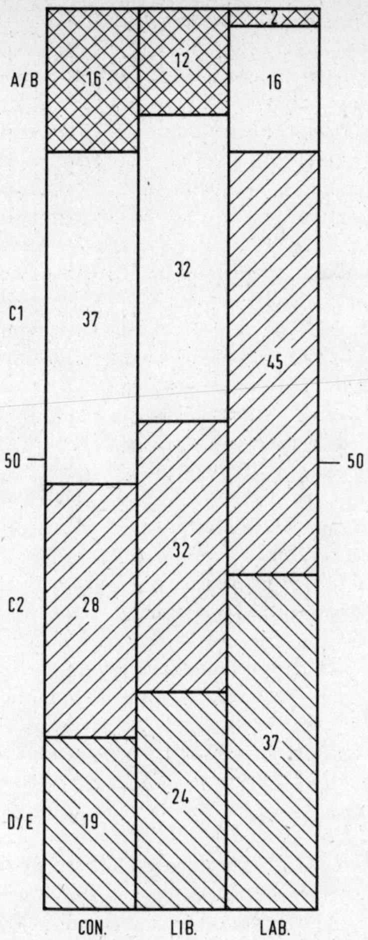

Figure 6: Sources of support for Parties, by class (N.O.P. 1964)

so much the most important conditioner of political allegiance that it becomes difficult to disentangle it from others. There is overwhelming evidence that women are more conservatively inclined than men,[22] as in most other countries.[23] Men have given Labour a majority at every election since the war; women only in 1945 and 1966. If men only had voted, it is improbable that Dr. Adenauer would ever have become Federal Chancellor of Western Germany, or that General de Gaulle would have been re-elected to the Presidency in 1965. Sex is the one factor which indubitably counter-balances class trends: working-class women are more right-wing than working-class men, middle-class women are more right-wing than middle class men. In certain Continental European states religion, especially Catholicism, plays an important part in making women more right-wing. In Britain, where this factor is less influential, the 'sex gap' is correspondingly smaller.

Age, too, correlates fairly closely with party preference, youth being more left-wing than middle age or old age.[24] Yet problems of causality arise. It may or may not be true that the older we get, the more conservative we become; in any case it has yet to be proved that this results in vote-switching on a large scale. It is also probably true that the older we get the higher we may rise in the social scale, though the opposite may also happen, and here some conscious switching of allegiance may well take place. At the same time the middle classes (who are known to be more conservative) have a higher expectation of life than the working classes, and women (who are also known to be more conservative) than men. Is the conservatism of the elderly a function of their age alone, or is it also a function of their class and sex?

The same difficulty confronts us over the influence of religion. There are valid historical reasons for associating the Church of England with Toryism, and Dissent (and Catholicism) with the Left. The Church of England is, after all, the Established Church; the alliance, at the national level, of Church and King, and at the local level of squire and parson, was bound to give it a Tory flavour. Macaulay called the Church of England 'the Tory party at prayer'. Dissenters, not merely because they were, until 1827, second-class citizens, but also because of the more democratic structure of their churches and the causes dear to the Nonconformist conscience, were drawn to Liberalism. Religious affiliation could indeed infect quite a strong ideological content into political loyalty. Mr. A. J. P. Taylor, himself of Nonconformist orgigins, is quite confident of this:

'I doubt whether anyone with an Anglican background can become a true Radical. George Lansbury came nearest to it. Yet there was always a subtle dividing line between him and the rebels round him. Gladstone tried hard, but he could never rid himself of the belief that a duke or a bishop had more political sense than Cobden or John Stuart Mill. The rule still applies in the Labour Party. Its leaders with an Anglican education seek radical ideas, but they lack radical instincts ... Religious dissent is the only safe background for a radical.'[25]

At the same time religion can fairly easily be equated with class and occupation. Here are lists of the most strongly dissenting English counties (a) in the 1850's (b) in the 1890's.[26]

1850's	1890's
Bedford	Bedford
Cheshire	
Cornwall	Cornwall
	Cumberland
Derby	Derby
Durham	Durham
Huntingdon	
	Isle of Ely
Lancashire	
Leicester	
Lincoln	
Monmouth	Monmouth
Northumberland	
	Nottingham
Stafford	Stafford
	Warwick
Yorkshire	Yorkshire (N & W ridings only)

Except for the 'Cromwellian' counties of Eastern England, these represent the country's principal mining and industrial areas. In political representation they were overwhelmingly Liberal. The outstanding change between the middle and the end of the century took place in Lancashire, where there was not only a successful Anglican counterreformation but a marked swing to the Conservatives: between 1865 and 1906 the Liberals only once gained a majority of seats there.

One of the reasons for this swing to Church and Toryism was the influx of Irish immigration. The fact that from the beginning of the nineteenth century onwards most Catholics in Britain were either Irish labourers or their descendants naturally coloured Catholic politics. The Tories were the party of the Protestant ascendancy in Ireland, the Liberals the party of Home Rule. Catholics in Britain belonged overwhelmingly to the poorest classes. The question therefore is: does the predominantly left-wing affiliation of Nonconformists and Catholics simply reflect their social composition, or is there an independent, additional denominational factor? For the nineteenth century the evidence is incomplete. Almost all Dissenters active in politics were Liberals or Radicals and many of the leaders of Radicalism – Bright, Chamberlain, Lloyd George – were Dissenters. This may mean no more than that militant Dissent was overwhelmingly committed to Liberalism, though the example of Lancashire suggests that there was some correlation between denomination and party, transcending class. But it is worth remembering that even at the height of the Victorian religious revival, the urban masses remained largely untouched by religious observance, let alone sectarian disputes.[27] For the present day survey data are even more tenuous. It seems reasonably certain that the Liberals continue to enjoy disproportionately high support from Nonconformists,[28] but there is nothing to suggest that Labour, nationally, benefits from any residual dissenting radicalism (which has in any case declined in this century). In the areas of heaviest Irish immigration round Liverpool and Glasgow, sectarian feeling has tendend to dominate politics and not only politics, as any spectator at a Celtic-Rangers match may observe. Here the Conservatives have emerged as the 'Orange' party, supported by Protestants of all classes. In Scotland generally, and in Glasgow particularly, working-class Catholics are much more strongly pro-Labour than working-class Protestants, and middle-class Catholics almost as strongly pro-Labour as Catholic workers.[29] Of Liverpool one American observer has remarked that it is the only English city he visited in which 'religious imprecations' heavily outnumbered the wall-slogans of CND and Fascists combined.[30] However, the exceptionally heavy swing to Labour on Clydeside and Merseyside over the past ten years suggests that even here sectarianism in politics is a declining force. For other parts of the country there are some indications to support the general impression that Catholics vote Labour more heavily[h] than their class structure would indicate,[31] but local samples are usually too small to be really reliable. The most interesting example of denominational politics which has been discovered in recent years is in Glossop, Derbyshire, *where among manual workers only,* members of the various churches voted as follows in 1951:[32]

	% Con.	% Lib.	% Lab.	% did not vote
Active Anglicans	55	5	29	12
Inactive Anglicans	43	5	36	15
Nonconformist	25	16	44	15
Roman Catholic	20	4	54	21
No religion	20	—	40	40

But Glossop is an old-established cotton town with highly traditional community ties; it may be more illustrative of popular, and largely out-of-date, stereotypes than of present-day reality.

There are similar difficulties in trying to isolate regional influences on voting behaviour. Scotland, Wales, East Anglia or Durham certainly have their distinctive voting characteristics. But is it really possible to distinguish the politics of coal, agriculture or shipbuilding from the sentments of a region? In general, not. Durham is what it is because of coal, Clydeside because of ships, the Highlands because of crofting. But some regions are more distinctive than others. Distance from London or anti-English nationalism can play a part; so can religion, the only other factor capable of neutralizing the influence of class. This emerges most clearly in what is often referred to as the 'Celtic fringe' – Scotland, Wales and Cornwall. Its Anglican and monarchist connections have made the Tory Party predominantly English. It has failed to gain a majority of English seats in only four of the twenty-two elections since 1885: in 1906, 1929, 1945 and 1966, the years of its worst defeats. In Scotland, on the other hand, it has gained a majority of seats only five times, in 1900 (the first time ever), 1924, 1931, 1935 and 1955. In Wales the Tories have been in a minority since 1857; since 1885 they have only four times exceeded a quarter of the seats (1895, 1924, 1931, 1935); once, in 1906, they held none at all.

Wales, therefore, presents the clearest examples of political regionalism in Britain. Its nationalism is radical and based on the chapel. Until 1918 this radicalism was expressed through the Liberal Party and found its greatest expression in David Lloyd George. The major constitutional grievance of Welsh Dissent was removed with the disestablishment of the Church in 1920. But the populist radicalism survived unweakened; Labour inherited its legacy not merely in the Depression, but in the rural areas also. Since the war the Liberals have lost five of their six remaining rural seats, all to the benefit of Labour. Only in Wales does Labour consistently hold non-industrial constituencies, such as Anglesey, Merioneth and Pembroke. Only in Wales do the Conservatives lose deposits not merely in the Rhondda, but in Carmarthen and Merioneth. Outside the coastal resorts, the border counties and the Cardiff area Conservatism is still regarded, as it was sixty years ago, as foreign, even hostile to the interests and aspirations of Wales.

Popular radicalism was a much less important ingredient of Scottish Liberalism than of Welsh. Until well into the nineteenth century its leaders and parliamentary representatives were overwhelmingly aristocratic;[38] their social outlook was correspondingly more conservative. The hegemony of Scottish Liberalism came to an end in 1885 under the dual impact of the Third Reform Act (which emancipated the crofters) and the Irish Home Rule controversy. Significantly, the Conservatives in Scotland were until 1965 officially known as Unionists (i.e. favouring union with Ireland). But separatist feeling has kept Scottish Conservatism weak. Most of Labour's strength is derived from the industrial belt of Central Scotland, but of the remaining nineteen Border or Highland constituencies outside this belt the Conservatives held only eleven in 1966; five went to Liberals, three to Labour. As in Wales, the Liberal Party is associated with aspirations to self-government and is to that extent a rival to the self-confessedly nationalist parties. The association is, however, of long standing: it dates from the beginnings of the Church disestablishment controversies in the mid-nineteenth century and Liberal espousal of Irish Home Rule.

Regional political issues in Scotland and Wales are dominated by national sentiment. They do not solely arise, as they tend to in England, out of the problems of particular industries – for instance, the decline of heavy industry in the North-East in the early 1960's. The special rôle of the Liberal Party in expressing this Celtic discontent means that in rural Scotland and Wales there is three-party rather than two-party competition. The only area of England of which this is true is the South-West. Here, too, remoteness from London may be a factor; more relevant, probably, are the survival of a nineteenth-century social structure, the strength of Nonconformity, especially among farm-workers and small farmers, and the sparsity of large-scale industry. The four counties in which the contest is waged fairly equally between the three parties are Cornwall (the most strongly Celtic and dissenting of them) Devon, Dorset and Hereford.

Regional tradition may influence the long-term relative popularity of the parties in a given area; local community ties are much more important in shaping the individual's allegiances. Again, this is easiest to demonstrate for class-consciousness: the trend, not surprisingly, is to conform with the predominant character of the neighbourhood. The Newcastle-under-Lyme study showed that in the most heavily industrialized wards the proportion of manual workers who vote Labour is above the constituency's average, while in the farming and commuting areas it is below the average. It also emerged that only in the heavily working-class wards does Labour get appreciable support from non-manual workers.[34] The pressure of environment can influence not only party allegiance but the intensity with which it is felt. In 1950, when class-feeling ran more strongly than it does today, the group of seats with the highest median turn-out were those where Labour had majorities of over 40%. There were forty-eight such seats, thirty-three of them coal-mining, indicating 'a unique sense of working-class solidarity which has to be demonstrated at the polls'.[53]

The class basis of politics explains one of the minor curiosities of the British electoral system, namely a flaw in the 'cube law'. The cube law states that if the parties' votes are in the proportions of A:B, their seats in parliament will be in the proportions of $A^3 : B^3$. Put differently, it means that a swing of 1% will cause between fifteen and twenty seats to change hands. Post-war elections have borne out the general validity of this law.

Swing and Seat changes, 1945–1966

	Swing	Net gain in seats	Seats per 1 % swing
1945–50	2·9	81	28⁺
1950–51	1·1	23	21
1951–55	1·8	24	13⁺
1955–59	1·1	21	19
1959–64	3·1	59	19
1964–66	2·7	46	17

es that there was a redistribution of seats.

However, on four occasions since the war (1950, 1951, 1955, 1959) there appeared a bias in the system in favour of the Conservatives of about $1^1/_2$% – that is, to secure the same number of seats as the Conservatives, Labour would need about $1^1/_2$% (or 500,000 votes) more than the Conservatives. The reason for this lies in the uneven distribution of Labour support: Labour voters are mainly industrial workers and industry, especially heavy industry, tends to be concentrated in compact areas. Labour therefore 'wastes' more votes than the Conservatives. In 1951, when Labour won more votes, but fewer seats, than the Conservatives, thirty-seven out of forty-eight majorities over 20,000 were in Labour seats. In 1964 and 1966 this 'bias' disappeared. It might be tempting to attribute this to migration. The average electorate of Labour-held seats in 1966 was several thousands smaller than in Conservative-held seats. There is, however, no convincing evidence that Labour gained more seats *through migration alone* (i.e. through New Town or council estate development) than it lost (i.e. through middle-class commuter development). The main reason appears to be an above average drop in the turn-out in safe Labour seats. All that has happened is that Labour is under-polling about 1-$1^1/_2$% of its potential support.

Party Choice

If it is true that social characteristics determine most people's party allegiance, what has happened to the concept of an election as choice? No two elections produce identical results. *Some* choice, therefore, does take place. Sociology in the main explains the reasons for longterm loyalty; psychology is more useful in explaining why some people change. Both emphasize the non-rational elements involved in political choice. A pioneer in this field was Graham Wallas, who in 1908 launched the much-abused term 'political image':

'The origin of a political party may be due to a deliberate intellectual process. It may be formed, as Burke said, by "a body of men united for promoting by their joint endeavours the national interest upon some particular principle in which they are all agreed". But when a party has once come into existence its fortunes depend upon facts of human nature of which deliberate thought is only one. It is primarily a name, which, like other names, calls up when it is heard or seen an "image" that shades imperceptibly into the voluntary realization of its meaning. As in other cases, emotional reactions can be set up by the name and its automatic mental associations. It is the business of the party managers to secure that these automatic associations shall be as clear as possible, shall be shared by as large a number as possible, and shall call up as many and as strong emotions as possible.'[36]

One important variable is missing from this catalogue, however. The association needs not to be not only clear, widespread and strong, it must also be favourable. This is the most difficult one to guarantee, for the same image may stand the party in good stead one year and harm it in another. This applies, in particular, to a party's class image. The most important difference between Labour and Conservative supporters in their 'images' of the parties is that Labour people tend to see parties in terms of class interest or general aims ('for the working class', 'for the rich', 'for the man in the street'), while Conservatives do so in terms of issues or competence ('against nationalization', 'for individual freedom', 'having a clear policy').[37] This leaves wide open the question of how potent this image is under differing circumstances. The 'cloth-cap' image may well have helped Labour in 1945 or 1950; it was probably a liability by 1959, when memories of unemployment had faded and consumer affluence had eroded proletarian solidarity. The 'grouse-moor' image may well have helped the Conservatives in tapping the reserves of deference for most of this century; but in 1964 or 1966, when administrative failure and the leadership squabble had tarnished it, it became, temporarily at any rate, a vote-loser.

'Image' is also used, rather confusingly, to describe transient aspects of parties and political leaders which influence the mood of the moment. We may read that one man's 'television image' is unfavourable, perhaps because he has not mastered the techniques of the medium; or that a party's 'image' is one of disunity or lack of policies. Such factors change from one year to the next. They may well help to explain why people change their opinions, but they are not what Graham Wallas had in mind. His 'images' consisted of long-term attributes; their purpose is to establish a permanent brand-loyalty 'in the dim and shadowy region of emotional association'.[38] Image, as conceived by Wallas, is therefore more useful in explaining political loyalty than political change. There is, indeed, a good deal of evidence, both from this country and the United States, that many habitual supporters are either ignorant of their parties' programmes or in substantial disagreement with them. In one Bristol survey Conservative, Liberal and Labour voters scored respectively 60, 58 and 53% in attributing policy statements to the main parties: even completely random answers would have scored 50%.[39] Perception of issues is one matter, slavish adhesion to the party line is another. Party preference tends, after all, to be a relative rather than an absolute matter. It is sufficient to agree with a majority of the partys stands on major issues, especially since some policy statements are themselves the outcome of bitter controversy within the party – one thinks of nationalization or defence in the Labour Party, decolonization or crime and punishment among Conservatives. Moreover, issues are not of equal importance. One person may be more concerned with the abolition of health service prescription charges, another with Rhodesia. Even so, the degree to which party policy is accepted is remarkably low and it tends to be lower among Labour than Conservative supporters. In Greenwich, for instance, the largest group of supporters within each party agreed with only 40–60% of official policies; 7% of Conservatives and 21% of Labour supporters were actually more in agreement with their opponents than with their own party.[40] Similarly the assessment of party leaders is not necessarily translated into electoral preference. In 1966, 55% thought that Mr. Wilson would make the better Prime Minister and 30% that Mr. Heath would.[41] But this 25% lead became a lead of only 6% in votes cast. All in all, the permanent image seems to be a more potent factor than changing issues or successive party leaders. It may even be more potent than rationally considered self-interest. After all, it by no means follows that the same party is at every election the best for the working (or middle) class, as most electors seem to think. There is a lot to be said for Professor Alford's view that it is 'class-based traditionalism', not ruthlessly evaluated economic interest, that is the chief motivator.[42]

Who, then, *does* change his mind? Is there such a creature as the 'floating voter'? It would probably be better if the term had never been invented. In the first place it must be remembered that the electorate itself is constantly changing. Every year approximately 600,000 adults die and 750,000 adolescents come of age. This alone could gradually affect the political balance in the country. But the word also suggets that the electorate can be conveniently divided into two categories, on the one hand the faithful supporter of the big battalions, on the other, earnest individuals seeking after truth. All survey evidence suggests the contrary: that there is a relatively small core of 'thick-and-thin men', shading off, through weak and conditional party-support into neutrality (or apathy). One survey, taken less than a fortnight before the 1966 General Election, illustrates this:[43]

How strongly would you say you support the Conservative/Labour/Liberal Party?

Very strongly	38%
quite strongly	36%
not very strongly	20%
not at all strongly	6%

How much do you personally care which party wins the General Election?

Very much	40%
quite a lot	32%
not very much	22%
not at all	3%

These figures are very similar to those recently found in other countries:

Intensity of Party Identification in USA, Norway, and W. Germany (in per cent)[44]

	USA 1956	Norway 1957	W. Germany 1961
Strong identifiers	36	25	25
Weak identifiers	37	34	46
Independents (identification rejected)	23	25	5
Unpolitical (question not understood)	4	9	19
Not ascertained	—	7	5
	100	100	100

In fact, we can identify no fewer than four types of non-constant electors –

1. those whose involvement with the party of their choice is low and who therefore hesitate between voting and abstention;
2. those who experiment with alternative allegiances but generally return to the party of their first choice at election time;

3. those who support a minor party but may be deprived of a candidate of their highest preference;
4. those who experience a genuine conversion and transfer their allegiance.

These four types between them amount to a substantial minority among the electorate; and the total is certainly greater the number who 'float' in any one election. The contrast between the violent fluctuations of opinion polls and the relatively small swing at general elections illustrate how much more numerous the potential waverers are than the actual changers. Constituency surveys agree that anything up to a quarter of electors have not firmly made up their minds at the beginning of an election campaign.[45] Of course, the 'swing' figure is misleadingly small. A 'net swing of 5% from Conservative to Labour conceals reverse changes from Labour to Conservatives, changes to and from both parties involving the Liberals, as well as changes from abstention to voting and *vice versa*. Even so, the fact that most waverers in the end revert to their former loyalties[46] is significant, and confirms the existence of a gap between waverers and actual changers.

Those who decide late and hesitatingly how they should vote could be, and in traditional liberal mythology are, the independent-minded, rational élite. Modern evidence, however, points overwhelmingly in the opposite direction. In both Britain and America it has emerged that 'waverers' are *on average* less well informed on current affairs, less exposed to the political items in the newspapers or on radio or TV, less likely to read election literature or attend meetings, less likely to discuss politics with friends or members of their family.[47] The pressures on them to participate in politics are either weaker than for most other people, or they are contradictory. Electors subject to 'cross-pressures', e.g. whose family votes differently from most of their friends or who are uncertain of their social status, have particular difficulty in making up their minds. The statistical evidence can deal in averages only. Some of those who hesitate before voting almost certainly do live up to the liberal ideal of the rational citizen. But the majority do not.

Local Issues, Personalities and Band-Waggons

So far it has been assumed that all political choice in Britain is between parties. The stability of party loyalties and the uniformity of the swing show that this is indeed so. But local issues do arise and there are frequent attempts to exploit them. It is remarkable how seldom this works. Economic grievances are an obvious example of a potential local issue. In 1959 parts of Lancashire and of Scotland swung to Labour against the national trend, presumably because of the depressed state of the cotton industry and shipbuilding, perhaps also because of a general feeling that these areas were not sharing in the growing affluence of the country. Conversely in 1964 the swing to Labour in the West Midlands was below average, presumably because the prosperity of that region gave less reason for discontent with the Conservative Party. Regional deviations of this kind can be explained in terms of spontaneous reaction by voters. Little or no persuasion is needed by candidates or party leaders to bring them about. Moreover, the state of the economy looms so largely in most people's thinking about politics that it can hardly be isolated as a separate issue.

Education and immigration are more promising as genuine local issues. In 1964 there was a below-average swing to Labour in the Bristol area and this was attributed to local opposition to the Labour council's comprehensive scheme; at any rate, Conservative candidates emphasized their sympathy with the opponents. Immigration was a more obvious, though by no means uniform, cause of deviant results in 1964. Swings to the right in Smethwick, Southall and Eton & Slough were obviously connected with resentment at coloured immigration, but other constituencies with equally heavy influxes (e.g. Brixton, Bradford E.) seemed less worried.[48] Anti-immigrant Independents in three constituencies secured between $7^1/_2$ and 10%, much the same as Sir Oswald Mosley had gained in 1959 in N. Kensington on a similar platform. But the rôle of the candidate is not the only factor. Mr. Griffiths, who gained Smethwick from Labour, emphasized the issue; Sir Anthony Meyer, who gained Eton & Slough, admittedly on a much lower swing, did not. Local issues, it is evident, can influence individual results, but their impact is limited. Much more influential in encouraging or discouraging a propensity to swing is the social environment. Mining seats, where the class lines are more sharply drawn than anywhere else, have shown the lowest swings in either direction since the war. Predominantly rural seats, with their stable social relationships, have the next-lowest swings. As urbanization increases so does volatility, both in changes of opinion and in variations of turn-out.[49] The large cities show the greatest propensity to change, and the lowest turn-out of

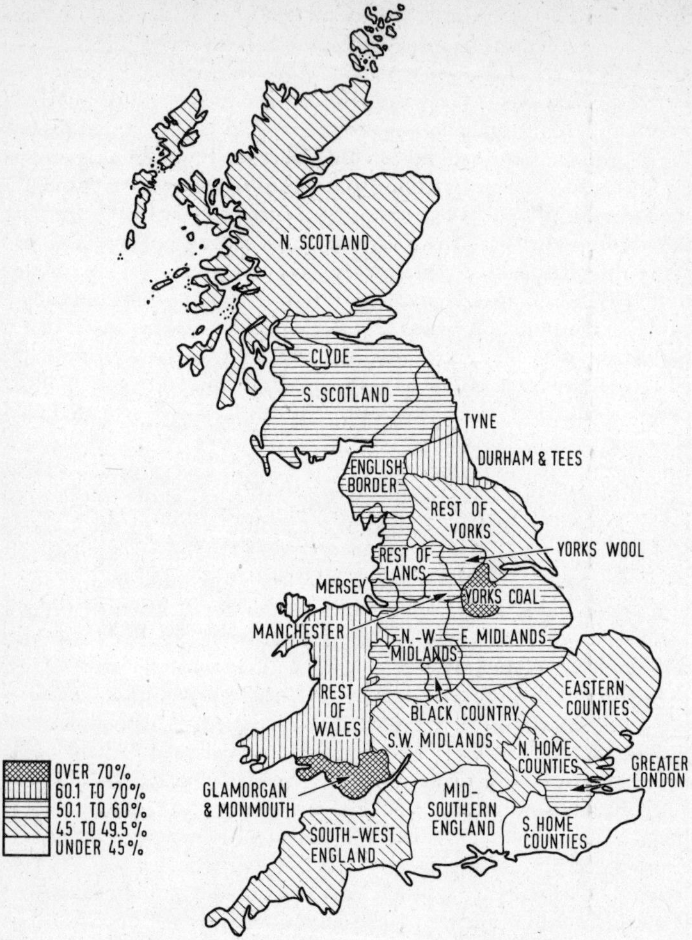

Figure 7: Labour Party's share of major Party vote, 1966, by regions (as defined by *The Economist*)

Figure 8: Change in Labour Party's share of major Party vote 1945–66, by regions (as defined by *The Economist*)

all. Urbanization may, therefore, affect our calculations of regional swings. Consistently low swings in East Anglia or the South-West are best attributed to the rural character of these areas; high swings in London or the North-West to their industrial character. Such factors cannot, however, account for longterm shifts in the political allegiance of different areas. Figure 8 shows that since 1945 the North and the older industrial areas have become markedly more favourable to Labour, the rest of the country (except Inner London) to the Conservatives.

Marginality also affects voting behaviour. Marginal seats did indeed show swings slightly above the average in 1964 and 1966, but there is no general tendency for them to contain a greater number of volatile electors. On the other hand, marginality has, since 1955 at any rate, helped to raise turn-out and to depress support for Liberal candidates.[50] This last point is important for any discussion of the function of parties in the British system, and the possible effects of electoral reform. We might expect the 'wasted vote' argument to weigh least in a marginal constituency, for two reasons. Marginal seats have, by definition, a more balanced social composition than safe ones (which are heavily middle-class or heavily working-class), and the Liberal party has the most evenly spread social following (see Figure 6). Moreover a marginal seat offers the best opportunity for victory on a minority vote. Where the parties are evenly balanced a mere 35% may suffice to win a three-cornered fight. In fact, Liberals do exceptionally badly in marginal seats; we have already observed that the greatest Liberal successes have been in seats where the minority major party has no hope of success. In Britain political success depends on the ability to form a strong government, and the elector in a marginal constituency is well placed to bestow or deny such success.

One further conclusion follows, namely that Liberal intervention has less effect on the outcome of a general election than is sometimes thought. Comparison between different types of contests enables us to calculate how Liberals would vote if they had no candidate of their own:[51]

1. In no election did the Liberals take more than 60% of their vote from one of the major parties.
2. Liberal voters are representative of the national trend. When the country is swinging right their votes are, in the majority, potentially Conservative (1950, 1951, 1955, less so in 1959); when the country

is swinging left, their votes are, in the majority, potentially Labour (1945, 1964, uncertain in 1966).
3. In safe seats Liberal votes are drawn heavily from the minority party, in marginal seats much more evenly from both major parties, though with some regional variations.
Granted this, and the low Liberal vote in marginal seats, Liberals have had an important effect only twice since 1929. Had they contested no marginal seats in 1950, it is probable that the Conservatives would have become the strongest party, but without an absolute majority (instead of a Labour majority of five). Had they contested no marginal seats in 1964, Labour would probably have had a majority of ten, possible sixteen, instead of only four.[52]
If local issues count for little, what about the personality of the candidate? The *obiter dictum* of an anonymous election agent that 'no candidate is worth 500 votes'[53] has become part of British election mythology. Even if it were true it would not reduce the candidate to insignificance. In 1964 twenty-five seats were won by majorities of less than 500. Few personal characteristics of the candidate have any measurable impact on electors. Women fare no worse than men. Jews and Roman Catholics – with very few exceptions – fare no worse than Protestants. Those who stand on the Right of the Conservative Party or the Left of the Labour Party do no better and no worse than those who toe the line. There is, however, strong evidence that at least two types of candidates do have a personal effect. The first consists of minor-party challengers. There is little doubt that most of the Liberals, members of other small parties and Independents who have succeeded in entering parliament since the war have done so, in part at least, on the strength of their personalities. The same applies to exceptionally good performances, especially at by-elections, which fell short of victory. Candidates of major parties can achieve less in this respect. All they can do is to build up a personal following on the basis of conscientious constituency service. This unquestionably does pay off, though there are pitfalls in calculating its exact extent. Different swings in seats defended by incumbents and newcomers could be due to regional bias or constituency-type bias (an excess of suburban over rural seats in the sample). Even taking this into account, it is evident that 'familiar' MPs may at the height of their popularity be worth extra swing of $1^1/_2$ to $3^1/_2$% to their party. This is an average: the exceptionally popular MP will be worth even more than that. There are two caveats, however. Very long-serving MPs may outstay their welcome

and begin losing votes for their party. If, however, the MP concerned, like a wise prima donna, retires at the right moment, some of his increment stays with the party: his successor will suffer some loss of support, but not as much as a strict party average would indicate.[55]

The different behaviour of electors in marginal and safe seats, both in their decision whether to vote at all and in the support they give to minor parties, is evidence of increasing sophistication – a growing tendency to join in the social scientists' game of standing back and watching individuals reacting towards each other. There was, for instance, much greater interest in opinion polls in 1964 and 1966, if only because more organizations than ever before were making national and local predictions. All social science depends on the assumption that it is possible to make valid generalizations about human behaviour. All sampling techniques depend on the assumption that if a carefully chosen small percentage of individuals are studied, valid conclusions can be drawn about the whole of society. Opinion polls, and the publicity that surrounds them at election time, are subject to two criticisms. The first is that they are unreliable. This charge may be justly levelled at the majority of inexperienced organizations which dabble in this difficult exercise. Of the 54 individual constituency surveys conducted during the 1966 election eight had an error of more than 10% in their prediction of the final majority.[56] But the major polling businesses have been steadily improving their performance and they are unlikely ever again to commit mistakes like the notorious forecast of President Truman's defeat in 1948. The best records in 1966 were those of NOP and Research Services, using the random method, and Gallup, using the quota method[i].

Accuracy of eve-of poll forecasts, 1966[57]

	Actual result (GB only) %	NOP %	Gallup Quota %	Research Services %
Labour	48·7	50·6	49½	49·7
Conservative	41·4	41·6	41½	41·6
Liberal	8·6	7·4	8	7·4
Labour Lead	7·3	9·0	8·0	8·1
Error		1·7	0·7	0·8

A second criticism is that publication of the polls influences the outcome. People like to be on the winning side; the polls oblige by showing them which way the band-wagon is rolling. There is, however, no evidence that this is what happens, at any rate at General Elections. If the band-wagon effect had operated in 1966, Labour's lead should have increased in the course of the campaign, instead of decreasing as it in fact did. No doubt consistent prophecies of defeat depress the losing side who then anxiously search for scapegoats. No doubt a foregone conclusion robs a contest of much of its suspense and excitement. But to ban the publication of opinion polls – as has been suggested – would be a quite unjustified act of paternalism and would diminish even further the elector's right of free access to information.

Polls and sampling techniques are among the methods which have enabled us to know much more than even a generation ago how people vote, what conditions their allegiances, why they change their minds. There remains one further, vital, question: how relevant is the whole electoral process to government of a modern industrial state?

Anmerkungen

a e. g. in the Nuffield College election studies, *The Times Guide to the House of Commons, The Economist* and by both broadcasting networks.

b	Conservative	Liberal	Labour	Irish
January, 1910	273	275	40	82
December, 1910	272	272	42	84

c 'Our epoch, the epoch of the bourgeoisie, possesses ... this distinctive feature: it has simplified the class antagonisms. Society is more and more splitting up into two great hostile camps, into two great classes directly facing each other – bourgeoisie and proletariat.' (*Communist Manifesto*, 1848).

d The reliability of this scale has been disputed. See D. V. Glass (ed.) *Social Mobility in Britain*, ch. 2, and M. Young & P. Willmott, 'Social Grading by Manual Workers,' *British Journal of Sociology*, VII (December, 1956).

e But there is some evidence that it is as high in New Zealand as in Britain. (Chapman, Jackson & Mitchell, *New Zealand Politics in Action*, pp. 175–6.)

f See below p. 201.

g See Figure 8 below p. 209.

h Professor Alford's discussion of the possible influence on Catholic voters of the Church's conservatism seems hardly relevant to Britain (*Party and Society*, pp. 139–41). Its connection with monarchical absolutism disappeared too long ago, and its link with the aristocracy is too tenuous, for this to count for very much. The same applies to the 'anti-Socialist political tendencies of the Church' (*ibid.*, p. 140). These are rooted in the experience of continental Europe, and arise out of the anticlerical, rationalist and revolutionary character of the Liberal and Marxist movements. When a Catholic hierarchy was re-established in England after a lapse of 400 years, its first major intervention in social policy was in favour of the dock strikers in 1889.

i The quota method requires the interviewer to collect interviews from persons he selects, provided their numbers are typical of the nation as a whole in age, sex and occupation. The random method requires him to interview respondents whose names have been randomly selected from the electoral register, leaving him no discretion. The eve-of-poll Gallup forecast, as published in *The Daily Telegraph* (March 31, 1966) was a combination of the quota survey and a less accurate random survey, giving a Labour lead of 11% – error: 3·7%.

1 Bryce, Viscount: *Modern Democracies* (London, 1921), pp. 168–9.
2 See Steed, M. in: Butler & King: *British General Election of 1964*, pp. 337–8; Berrington, H. B.: The General Election of 1964 in *Journal of the Royal Statistical Society*, Series A, CXXVIII (1965), pp. 17–21; Rasmussen, J. S.: The Disutility of the Swing Concept in British Psephology, *Parliamentary Affairs* XVIII (Autumn, 1965).
3 Jenkins, R.: *Mr. Balfour's Poodle. An Account of the Struggle Between the House of Lords and the Government of Mr. Asquith* (London, 1954), pp. 202–8.
4 *Gallup Political Index* (monthly).
5 Figures kindly supplied by NOP.
6 Vincent, J. R.: *The Formation of the Liberal Party, 1857–1868* (London, 1966), p. 17.
7 *Ibid.*, p. 81.
8 Stevenson, T. H. C.: The Vital Statistics of Wealth and Poverty, *Journal of the Royal Statistical Society* XCI (1928), esp. pp. 211–2.
9 Durant, H.: Voting Behaviour in Britain, 1945–64. In: Rose, R. (ed.) *Studies in British Politics. A Reader in Political Sociology* (London, 1966), p. 124. Supplementary information kindly supplied by Social Surveys (Gallup Poll) Ltd.
10 Hall, J. & Caradog Jones, D.: Social Grading of Occupations, *British Journal of Sociology* I (March, 1950), pp. 33-4, 40.
11 Kahan, M., Butler, . E. & Stokes, D. E.: On the Analytical Division of Social Class, British Journal of Sociology XVII (June, 1966), p. 128.
12 *Ibid.*, pp. 128–9.
13 Alford, R. R.: *Party and Society. The Anglo-American Democracies* (London, 1964), pp. 101–3.
14 Zölnhofer, W.: Parteiidentifizierung in der Bundesrepublik und den Vereinigten Staaten. In: Scheuch, E. K. & Wildemann, R. (eds.): *Zur Soziologie der Wahl. Kölner Zeitschrift für Soziologie und Sozialpsychologie.* Sonderheft 9 (1965), p. 1953.
15 Rokkan, S. & Campbell, A.: Citizen Participation in Political Life: Norway and the United States, *International Social Science Journal* XII (1960), p. 94.
16 Alford, *op. cit.*, p. 252.
17 Samuel, R.: The Deference Voter, *New Left Review* I (January, 1960), p. II.
18 *Ibid., loc. cit.*
19 *Ibid.*, p. 12.
20 Runciman, W. G.: *Relative Deprivation and Social Justice*, ch. IX; also Mark, Benney & Pear: *How People Vote*, p. 188; Bealey, Blondel & McCann, *Constituency Politics. A Study of Newcastle-under-Lyme* (London, 1965), p. 176.
21 McKenzie, R. T. & Silver, A.: Conservatism, Industrialism & the Working-Class Tory in England, *Transactions of the Fifth World Congress of Sociology* (1962); reprinted in Rose, R. (ed.), *Studies in British Politics*, p. 28.

22 Durant, H. in: Rose, *op. cit.*, p. 125; Butler & King, *British General Election of 1966*, p. 264.
23 Lipset, S. M.: *Political Man* (London, 1960), p. 247.
24 Durant, H., *loc. cit.*
25 Taylor, A. J. P.: The Thing, *The Twentieth Century*, October, 1957, p. 295.
26 Bealey, F. & Pelling, H.: *Labour and Politics, 1900–1906*, pp. 3–4.
27 Inglis, K. S.: *Churches and the Working Classes in Victorian England* (London, 1963), pp. 11–16, 329–30.
28 *Gallup Political Index B.9.* (March, 1966); Alford, *op. cit.*, p. 154–5.
29 Budge, I. S. & Urwin, D. S.: *Scottish Political Behaviour. A Case Study in British Homogeneity* (London, 1966), pp. 63, 69–70.
30 Thayer, G.: *The British Political Fringe. A Profile* (London, 1965), p. 236.
31 Mark, Benney & Pear, *op. cit.*, p. 111; Campbell, P. W., Donnison, D. & Potter, A.: Voting Behaviour in Droylesden in October, 1951, *Manchester School of Economic and Social Studies* XX (January, 1952), pp. 62–3.
32 Birch, A. H.: *Small Town Politics* (Oxford, 1959), p. 112.
33 Vincent, J. R., *op. cit.*, p. 48.
34 Bealey, Blondel & McCann, *op. cit.*, pp. 182–3.
35 Nicholas, H. G.: *The British General Election of 1950* (London, 1951), p. 318.
36 Wallas, G.: *Human Nature in Politics* (London, 1908), pp. 83–4.
37 Bealey, Blondel & McCann, *op. cit.*, pp. 206–13; Milne & Mackenzie: *Straight Fight*, pp. 131–40; Milne & Mackenzie: *Marginal Seat*, p. 129.
38 Wallas, *op. cit.*, p. 86.
39 Milne & Mackenzie: *Marginal Seat*, p. 121; cf. Berelson, B. R., Lazarsfeld, P. F. & McPhee, W. N.: *Voting. A Study of Opinion Formation in a Presidential Campaign* (Chicago, 1954), p. 230; Trenaman, D. & McQail, J.: *Television and the Political Image*, pp. 166, 215.
40 Mark, Benney & Pear, *op. cit.*, pp. 145–6. Cf. Milne & Mackenzie: *Marginal Seat*, pp. 117–20; Birch, A. H., *op. cit.*, pp. 82–5; Donnison, D. & Plowman, D. E. G.: The Functions of Local Labour Parties: Experiments in Research Methods, *Political Studies* II (February, 1954), pp. 162–4; Fienburgh, W. & others: Put Party Policy on the Agenda, *Fabian Journal* 6 (February, 1952), pp. 29–31; Berelson, Lazarsfeld & McPhee: *Voting*, pp. 223–7.
41 *The Sunday Telegraph*, March 27, 1966.
42 Alford, R. R., *op cit.*, p. 110, n. 13.
43 *Daily Mail*, March 24, 1966.
44 American-Norwegian comparison: Campbell, A. & Valen, H.: Party Identification in Norway and the United States, *Public Opinion Quarterly* XXV (Winter, 1961), p. 510; reprinted in: Campbell, A. & others: *Elections and the Political Order* (New York, 1966), p. 251. American-German comparison: Zölnhofer, W. in: Scheuch & Wildenmann, *op. cit.*, p. 113.
45 Milne & Mackenzie: *Marginal Seat*, pp. 36–8; Campbell, Donnison & Potter: Voting Behaviour in Droylesden, p. 61; Mark, Benney & Pear, *op. cit.*, p. 175.
46 Milne & Mackenzie: *Straight Fight*, pp. 130–1; Milne & Mackenzie: *Marginal Seat*, pp. 41–2.

47 Milne & Mackenzie: *Straight Fight*, pp. 96–8; Milne & Mackenzie: *Marginal Seat*, pp. 85, 103–4, 123, 154; Mark, Benney & Pear, *op. cit.*, pp. 176–8; Berelson & others, *Voting*, pp. 306–313; Lazarsfeld, P. F., Berelson, D. & Gaudet, H.: *The People's Choice. How the Voter Makes up his Mind in a Presidential Campaign* (2nd edn., New York, 1948), p. 69.

48 Deakin, N. (ed.): *Colour and the British Electorate, 1964* (London, 1965), Chapters 2 and 7.

49 Butler & King: *British General Election of 1966*, pp. 279–80; Berrington: The General Election of 1964, pp. 23–9.

50 Butler & King, *op. cit.*, p. 285.

51 Berrington, *op. cit.*, pp. 40–48.

52 Butler & King: *British General Election of 1964*, pp. 349–50.

53 Butler, D. E.: *The British General Election of 1955*, p. 3.

54 Butler & King, *British General Election of 1964*, p. 353; *British General Election of 1966*, p. 287.

55 Williams, P. M.: Two Notes on the British Electoral System, *Parliamentary Affairs* XX (Winter 1966–7), pp. 24–30.

56 *The Sunday Times*, April 3, 1966.

57 NOP: *Daily Mail*, March 31, 1966; Research Services: *The Observer*, March 27, 1966; Gallup: *The Daily Telegraph Gallup Analysis of the Election '66* (London, 1966), p. 140.

9

The Civil Service

Aus: The Civil Service, Vol. 1. Report of the Committee 1966–68, Chairman: Lord Fulton.

Presented to Parliament by the Prime Minister and the Chancellor of the Exchequer by Command of Her Majesty, June 1968 (Cmnd. 3638). Her Majesty's Stationery Office, London, S. 9–14, 81–84, 104–106.

Der Ausschuß war von der britischen Regierung am 8. 2. 1966 eingesetzt worden, um die Struktur, die Rekrutierung, das Management sowie die Schulung der im Inland angestellten Beamtenschaft zu untersuchen und Reformvorschläge zu machen. Ein Teil der Empfehlungen des Ausschusses, u. a. die Errichtung eines besonderen Ministeriums für die Beamtenschaft, ist inzwischen verwirklicht worden.

The Civil Service today

1. The Home Civil Service today is still fundamentally the product of the nineteenth-century philosophy of the Northcote-Trevelyan Report.* The tasks it faces are those of the second half of the twentieth century. This is what we have found; it is what we seek to remedy. ...

7. The role of government has greatly changed. Its traditional regulatory functions have multiplied in size and greatly broadened in scope. It has taken on vast new responsibilities. It is expected to achieve such general economic aims as full employment, a satisfactory rate of growth, stable prices and a healthy balance of payments.

* Der hier erwähnte, 1854 veröffentlichte Bericht von Sir Stafford Northcote und Sir Charles Trevelyan trug wesentlich zur Reform des Systems der Rekrutierung der britischen Beamtenschaft bei.

Through these and other policies (e.g. public purchasing, investment grants, financial regulators) it profoundly influences the output, costs and profitability of industry generally in both the home and overseas markets. Through nationalisation it more directly controls a number of basic industries. It has responsibilities for the location of industry and for town and country planning. It engages in research and development both for civil and military purposes. It provides comprehensive social services and is now expected to promote the fullest possible development of individual human potential. All these changes have made for a massive growth in public expenditure. Public spending means public control. A century ago the tasks of government were mainly passive and regulatory. Now they amount to a much more active and positive engagement in our affairs.

8. Technological progress and the vast amount of new knowledge have made a major impact on these tasks and on the process of taking decisions; the change goes on. Siting a new airport, buying military supplies, striking the right balance between coal, gas, oil and nuclear-powered electrictiy in a new energy policy – all these problems compel civil servants to use new techniques of analysis, management and co-ordination which are beyond those not specially trained in them.

9. The increase in the positive activities of government has not been solely an extension of the powers and functions of the State in an era of technological change. There has also been a complex intermingling of the public and private sectors. This has led to a proliferation of para-state organisations: public corporations, nationalised industries, negotiating bodies with varying degrees of public and private participation, public participation in private enterprises, voluntary bodies financed from public funds. Between the operations of the public and the private sectors there is often no clear boundary. Central and local government stand in a similarly intricate relationship; central government is generally held responsible for services that it partly or mainly finances but local authorities actually provide. As the tasks of government have grown and become more complex, so the need to consult and co-ordinate has grown as well.

10. The time it takes to reach a decision and carry it out has often lengthened. This is partly because of technological advance and the resulting complexity e.g. of defence equipment. Another reason is that the public and Parliament demand greater foresight and order in, for example, the development of land, the transport system and other resources, than they did in the past.

11. Governments also work more and more in an international setting. The improvement in communications and the greater interdependence of nations enlarges the difficulties as well as the opportunities of government.
12. To meet these new tasks of government the modern Civil Service must be able to handle the social, economic, scientific and technical problems of our time, in an international setting. Because the solutions to complex problems need long preparation, the Service must be far-sighted; from its accumulated knowledge and experience, it must show initiative in working out what are the needs of the future and how they might be met. A special responsibility now rests upon the Civil Service because one Parliament or even one Government often cannot see the process through.
13. At the same time, the Civil Service works under political direction and under the obligation of political accountability. This is the setting in which the daily work of many civil servants is carried out; thus they need to have a lively awareness of the political implications of what they are doing or advising. The Civil Service has also to be flexible enough to serve governments of any political complexion – whether they are committed to extend or in certain respects to reduce the role of the State. Troughout, it has to remember that it exists to serve the whole community, and that imaginative humanity sometimes matters more than tidy efficiency and administrative uniformity.
14. In our view the structure and practices of the Service have not kept up with the changing tasks. The defects we have found can nearly all be attributed to this. We have found no instance where reform has run ahead too rapidly. So, today, the Service is in need of fundamental change. It is inadequate in six main respects for the most efficient discharge of the present and prospective responsibilities of government.
15. First, the Service is still essentially based on the philosophy of the amateur (or "generalist" or "all-rounder"). This is most evident in the Administrative Class which holds the dominant position in the Service. The ideal aministrator is still too often seen as the gifted layman who, moving frequently from job to job within the Service, can take a practical view of any problem, irrespective of its subject-matter, in the light of his knowledge and experience of the government machine. Today, ... this concept has most damaging consequences. It cannot make for the efficient despatch of public business when key men rarely stay in one job longer than two or three years

before being moved to some other post, often in a very different area of government activity. A similar cult of the generalist is found in that part of the Executive Class that works in support of the Administrative Class and also even in some of the specialist classes. The cult is obsolete at all levels and in all parts of the Service.

16. Secondly, the present system of classes in the Service seriously impedes its work. The Service is divided into classes both horizontally (between higher and lower in the same broad area of work) and vertically (between different skills, professions or disciplines). There are 47 general classes whose members work in most government departments and over 1,400 departmental classes. Each civil servant is recruited to a particular class; his membership of that class determines his prospects (most classes have their own career structures) and the range of jobs on which he may be employed. It is true that there is some subsequent movement between classes; but such rigid and prolific compartmentalism in the Service leads to the setting up of cumbersome organisational forms, seriously hampers the Service in adapting itself to new tasks, prevents the best use of individual talent, contributes to the inequality of promotion prospects, causes frustration and resentment, and impedes the entry into wider management of those well fitted for it.

17. Thirdly, many scientists, engineers and members of other specialist classes get neither the full responsibilities and corresponding authority, nor the opportunities they ought to have. Too often they are organised in a separate hierachy, while the policy and financial aspects of the work are reserved to a parallel group of "generalist" administrators; and their access to higher management and policy-making is restricted. Partly this is because many of them are equipped only to practise their own specialism; a body of men with the qualities of the French *polytechnicien* – skilled in his craft, but skilled, too, as an administrator – has so far not been developed in Britain. In the new Civil Service a wider and more important role must be opened up for specialists trained and equipped for it.

18. Fourthly, too few civil servants are skilled managers. Since the major managerial role in the Service is specifically allocated to members of the Administrative Class it follows that this criticism applies particularly to them. Few members of the class actually see themselves as managers, i.e. as responsible for organisation, directing staff, planning the progress of work, setting standards of attainment and measuring results, reviewing procedures and quantifying different courses of action. One reason for this is that they are not ade-

quately trained in management. Another is that much of their work is not managerial in this sense; so they tend to think of themselves as advisers on policy to people above them, rather than as managers of the administrative machine below them. Scientists and other specialists are also open to criticism here: not enough have been trained in management, particularly in personnel management, project management, accounting and control.

19. Fifthly, there is not enough contact between the Service and the rest of the community. There is not enough awareness of how the world outside Whitehall works, how government policies will affect it, and the new ideas and methods which are developing in the universities, in business and in other walks of life. Partly this is a consequence of a career service. Since we expect most civil servants to spend their entire working lives in the Service, we can hardly wonder if they have little direct and systematic experience of the daily life and thought of other people. Another element in this is the social and educational composition of the Civil Service; the Social Survey of the Service which we commissioned suggests that direct recruitment to the Administrative Class since the war has not produced the widening of its social and educational base that might have been expected. The public interest must suffer from any exclusiveness or isolation which hinders a full understanding of contemporary problems or unduly restricts the free flow of men, knowledge and ideas between the Service and the outside world.

20. Finally, we have serious criticisms of personnel management. Career planning covers too small a section of the Service – mainly the Administrative Class – and is not sufficiently purposive or properly conceived; civil servants are moved too frequently between unrelated jobs, often with scant regard to personal preference or aptitude. Nor is there enough encouragement and reward for individual initiative and objectively measured performance; for many civil servants, especially in the lower grades, promotion depends too much on seniority ...

24. One basic guiding principle should in our view govern the future development of the Civil Service. It applies to any organisation and is simple to the point of banality, but the root of much of our criticism is that it has not been observed. The principle is: look at the job first. The Civil Service must continuously review the tasks it is called upon to perform and the possible ways in which it might perform them; it should then think out what new skills and kinds of men are needed, and how these men can be found, trained and de-

ployed. The Service must avoid a static view of a new ideal man and structure which in its turn could become as much of an obstacle to change as the present inheritance.

25. We have sought to devise a form of management for the Civil Service that will ensure that it is better run and able to generate its own self-criticism and forward drive. One of the main troubles of the Service has been that, in achieving immunity from political intervention, a system was evolved which until recently was virtually immune from outside pressures for change. Since it was not immune from inside resistance to change, inertia was perhaps predictable.

The new Civil Service Department

249. For these tasks of central management to be discharged effectively in the Civil Service of the future, two major institutional changes are needed.

250. First... the responsibility for recruitment and selection at present carried by the Civil Service Commission should be brought together with the other functions of central management within a single organisation.

251. Secondly, the expanded and unified central management of the Service should be made the responsibility of a new department created specifically for that purpose. Our reasons for this are as follows.

252. The Treasury's concern for public expenditure led to its development as the central managerial authority for the Service as a whole. But the British Civil Service is now almost alone in continuing to combine these functions in a single department. In our view, the central management of the Service is not, under modern conditions, an appropriate function for the central finance department, for three reasons:

(a) The role of the central management of the Service needs to be enlarged. In particular, if it is to discharge its full responsibilities for senior appointments (which means ensuring that men and women from all disciplines are considered for these appointments on their basis of their individual qualifications and experience), it must follow that central management will need to have much greater knowledge than in the past of the most able civil servants of all disciplines, particularly those who are likely candidates for top posts, and influence over their appointments. If this enlarged responsibility for career development were added to the Treasury's responsibilities for financial and economic policy and for the control of public expenditure, there would be reason to fear too great a concentration of power in one department. The overall direction of the Service and the key to individual success within it should not both lie with the department that also uses the powerful weapon of central financial control.

(b) Each of the two sides of the Treasury needs to use an expertise separate and different from that required by the other; our proposals for increasing the professionalism of the Service will cause them to grow still further apart. We do not, therefore, think that central management should be predominantly staffed, as it is today at Assistant Secretary and Principal level, by those whose main training and experience have been in techniques of government finance and the control of expenditure. The present practice of manning both sides of the Treasury at this level by a constant interchange between them impedes the development of a full professionalism in each. A proportion of the staff of central management should come from other departments on loan, but the Treasury should not be the predominant source of this flow. It should come from all departments.

(c) Central management should be positively and creatively concerned with maintaining and improving the standards of the Civil Service. It should therefore be a separate institution with a single-minded devotion to its own professional purpose; and should be in a position to fight, and to be seen fighting, the Treasury on behalf of the Service.

253. In addition to these questions of principle, there is an important practical question of confidence. There is today among civil servants a lack of confidence in the Treasury as the centre of Civil Service management. In our judgment, the Treasury has contributed to this by employing too few staff on this work. A change is necessary for other sufficient reasons but also to demonstrate that a fresh start is being made. If our proposals are to have a fair chance of success, there must be no doubt about the effectiveness of the central direction. There will be no confidence that they will be implemented in the radical spirit we believe to be necessary, if central management is left where it is.

254. Accordingly we recommend as the first main step in the reform of the Service the setting up of a new Civil Service Department. This should absorb the functions of the Civil Service Commission....

255. The staffing of this new department will be of critical impor-

tance. The full development of the responsibilities we have described will call for men and women who have knowledge and experience of personnel management and organisation, both inside and outside the Service. This will require a mixture of long-term and short-term appointments. The new department should not in our view be predominantly staffed by officers who have spent most of their careers in the Treasury, and can thus have little experience of direct responsibility for management. Departments generally should be prepared to release some of their best man for a period of service in the Civil Service Department, especially from among those with departmental experience of personnel and organisation work. We believe that the work of the new department will include some of the most challenging and creative jobs that the Service of people with appropriate knowledge and experience of managing large organisations both at home and abroad.

256. The department should also include specialists (e.g. scientists and engineers) who will be able to bring an intimate knowledge and experience to bear on the recruitment, training and career management of members of their own disciplines. There should be an appropriate measure of central management for all the major occupational groups, and the members of each group should be able to feel that their interests are being looked after at the centre. In some cases, e.g. the lawyers, it seems appropriate for a senior practitioner of the specialism in question (not necessarily from the Civil Service Department itself) to be designated head of the profession or group, and to share with the Civil Service Department the responsibility for guiding the main lines of its management policy. Another helpful practice, already in use for some groups, is a management committee on which senior practitioners of a particular specialism and representatives of the Civil Service Department sit together. We see no reason why the pattern should not vary. But the Civil Service Department should itself command all the necessary information about the specialist groups and be so staffed as to be able to handle them with direct knowledge and professional management expertise.

257. The new department should include a Planning Unit.... Some members of the department should have the prime responsibility for considering new developments in personnel management, training and management techniques; through contacts with the world outside, both at home and aboard, they should keep the management of the Civil Service abreast of experience elsewhere; and through

their own expertise make it a model of progress in its field for others to follow.

258. We also recommend that the official head of the Civil Service Department should be designated Head of the Home Civil Service. We think that he should receive a sufficient lead in pay over the other official heads of departments in the Home Civil Service to mark his status. At present the lead of the Joint Permanent Secretary of the Treasury is £ 600 a year, and similar leads are held by three other top officials: the other Joint Permanent Secretary to the Treasury, the Secretary to the Cabinet and (outside the scope of our inquiry) the Head of the Diplomatic Service. As far as the Home Civil Service is concerned, the other leads are something of a historical accident: the three offices were at one time held by a single individual; he had a lead of £ 1,000 over other Permanent Secretaries; when the offices were separated, the lead was split. We doubt if these other leads should be perpetuated; in our view it is hard to substantiate that the posts concerned carry greater responsibility than those of many other Permanent Secretaries. At the same time, we are clear that the responsibilities we propose for the Head of the Civil Service are of a different kind. We propose therefore that the other leads should be abolished when the present incumbents leave their posts, and that all Permanent Secretaries should receive the same rate of pay, with the exception of the Head of the Home Civil Service whose lead should be of the order of £ 1,000.

259. The creation of a new Civil Service Department raises the important question of the relationship between the Head of the Civil Service and the Prime Minister. Today the Prime Minister has direct responsibility for senior appointments and for the machinery of government as well as for security in the Civil Service. On these subjects the present arrangement is that the Head of the Civil Service reports direct to the Prime Minister and not to the Chancellor of the Exchequer. It is our strong hope that similar arrangements will be maintained in the new department, with the Head of the Home Civil Service maintaining his present responsibility for these matters and reporting direct to the Prime Minister.

260. There should however be a change in the machinery for making top appointments. At present the Head of the Civil Service makes his recommendations to the Prime Minister after consultation with the Ministers and others directly concerned. We have no reason to doubt that all the relevant views are taken into account. We think however that this arrangement vests too much responsibilitiy in a

single individual and in a way that creates the impression that his recommendations to the Prime Minister are within his sole discretion. Many civil servants criticise this – we think rightly. In future, we consider that in putting forward names to the Prime Minister the Head of the Civil Service should be assisted by a committee. The committee should have a variable composition, depending on the appointments and candidates under consideration. It should be drawn from a panel. The panel should have a rotating membership, appointment to it being for a term of, say, two or three years. Normally the committee would consist of two or three Permanent Secretaries, an approximately equal number of scientists or other specialists and not more than two eminent people from outside the Service. The "outsiders" might have no personal knowledge of the candidates, but their wide experience of business or other outside activity could in our view help to avoid an inbred and purely Civil Service attitude to these appointments. The Head of the Civil Service, after consulting the Ministers concerned and this committee, should put forward recommendations to the Prime Minister. We recommend that this procedure should cover all appointments at the salary-level of Deputy Secretary and above.

261. Making the right arrangements for the ministerial control of the new department will be decisive for its success. We therefore feel bound to comment on this. We have already expressed the hope that the Prime Minister will continue to be directly responsible for senior appointments, as for the machinery of government and security. We are also, however, strongly of the opinion that it is in the interests of the Service for the Prime Minister to be seen to be ultimately responsible, not just for these specific questions, but also for the total task of managing the Service. No other Minister can assert the needs of the government service as a whole over the sectional needs of powerful departmental Ministers. At the same time, the Prime Minister cannot himself be expected even at present to handle all the day-to-day Civil Service problems that require ministerial attention. Still less will he be able to do so in the future if the central management of the Service becomes, as we propose, a much larger job than it is today. The Prime Minister will therefore need ministerial support. We do not believe that this responsibility should be allocated to a Minister who is also in charge of, and thus likely to be preoccupied by, the affairs of one of the other departments. We hope that we are not exceeding our terms of reference too much if we recommend that, outside the area for which he is directly responsible

already, the Prime Minister should delegate day-to-day responsibility to a non-departmental Minister of appropriate seniority who is also a member of the Cabinet. His part will be of vital importance, especially during the period of reorganisation...

Summary of main Findings

3. A new Civil Service Department should be set up with wider functions than those now performed by the "Pay and Management" group of the Treasury, which it should take over. The new department should also absorb the Civil Service Commission.*
4. The new department should be under the control of the Prime Minister. We hope that he will retain direct responsibility for senior appointments, machinery of government and questions of security. Outside this area, we suggest that the Prime Minister should delegate day-to-day responsibility to a non-departmental Minister of appropriate seniority who is also a member of the Cabinet.
5. The Permanent Secretary of the Civil Service Department should be designated Head of the Home Civil Service.
6. All classes should be abolished and replaced by a single, unified grading structure covering all civil servants from top to bottom in the non-industrial part of the Service. The correct grading of each post should be determined by job evaluation.
7. The Service should develop greater professionalism both among specialists (e.g. scientists and engineers) and administrators (i.e. the new counterparts of the present Administrative and Executive Classes). For the former this means more training in management, and opportunities for greater responsibility and wider careers. For the latter it means enabling them to specialise in particular areas of government. We identify two such areas and accordingly recommend the development of a group of economic and financial administrators, and a second group of social administrators.
8. Employing departments should have a larger role in recruitment and there should be a speeding up of procedures. A majority of us consider that in the recruitment of graduates for one or other of the groups of administrators more account should be taken of the relevance of their university courses to the job they are being recruited to do.

* Die Civil Service Commission ist die zentrale Institution für die Auswahl von Bewerbern für Beamtenstellen.

9. A Civil Service College should be set up. It should provide major training courses in administration and management and a wide range of shorter courses. It should also have important research functions. The courses provided by the College should not be restricted to civil servants; a proportion of places should be set aside for men and women from private industrial and commercial firms, local government and public corporations.
10. More resources should be devoted to the career management of all civil servants. All must have the opportunity to progress as far and as fast as their talents and appropriate training can take them. This involves major changes in promotion procedures.
11. While the Civil Service should remain predominantly a career Service, there should be greater mobility between it and other employments. We, therefore, recommend an expanded late entry, temporary appointments for fixed periods, short-term interchanges of staff and freer movement out of the Service. These proposals involve substantial changes in the pension scheme and the replacement of "established" status by new terms of employment.
12. In the interests of efficiency, the principles of accountable management should be applied to the organisation of the work of departments. This means the clear allocation of responsibility and authority to accountable units with defined objectives. It also means a corresponding addition to the system of government accounting.
13. Management services units with highly qualified and experienced staff should be set up in all major departments.
14. Departments should establish Planning Units.
15. In addition to the Permanent Secretary, there should also be in most departments a Senior Policy Adviser to assist the Minister. The Senior Policy Adviser would normally be head of the Planning Unit. His prime job would be to look to and prepare for the future and to ensure that present policy decisions are taken with as full a recognition as possible of likely future developments.
16. In some of the big technical departments, there may be a need for a further senior post: a chief scientist, engineer or other specialist.
17. We do not propose that the Senior Policy Adviser and chief specialist, together with the Permanent Secretary, should constitute a formal board. The working arrangements should be informal and variable from department to department and from time to time; different Ministers' individual ways of working will do much to determine the pattern.
18. There should be one man who has overall responsibility under

the Minister for all the affairs of the Department and he should continue to be the Permanent Secretary.

19. A Minister at the head of a department should be able to employ on a temporary basis such small numbers of experts as he personally considers he needs to help him.

20. We have suggested a number of further inquiries. Their subjects among others, should be:

(a) the desirability of "hiving off" activities to non-departmental organisations;

(b) ways and means of getting rid of unnecessary secrecy both in policy-making and in administration;

(c) the new pattern of joint consultation that will be appropriate for the Civil Service in the light of the Government's decisions on our report. This inquiry should be conducted jointly by the Civil Service Department and the staff associations;

(d) methods of making recruitment procedures as speedy and objective as possible.

21. If our proposals are accepted, we hope that the Government will take steps to see that the progress made in their implementation is reviewed. This could be by an annual report to parliament during the next five years. A small committee might be set up at the end of that period if needed.

22. We have seen that the Service has man and women with the ability, vision and enthusiasm needed to carry our proposals through to success. A Civil Service reconstructed on the basis of these proposals will, we believe, make possible the progressive and efficient conduct of our affairs.

Britain and the European Communities

Aus: Britain and the European Communities. An Economic Assessment.

Presented to Parliament by the Prime Minister by Command of Her Majesty. February 1970 (Cmnd. 4289). London, Her Majesty's Stationary Office, S. 3–37.

I. Introduction

Background

Her Majesty's Government decided on 2nd May, 1967 to make an application under Article 237 of the Treaty of Rome for membership of the European Economic Community (EEC), and parallel applications for membership of the European Coal and Steel Community (ECSC) and EURATOM. The Government's decision was debated by both Houses of parliament, and at the end of a three-day debate in the House of Commons the decision was approved by a majority of 426, one of the largest majorities in a vote in the House of Commons in peacetime. Her Majesty's Government thereupon applied for membership of the Communities on 10th May, 1967.

2. The Prime Minister's statement on the Government's decision was presented as a White Paper (Cmnd. 3269) which set out the reasons underlying the decision to apply for membership of the Communities, and the issues which it would be necessary to resolve during the negotiations for that purpose. On the economic side, the White Paper spoke of "the long-term potential for Europe, and therefore for Britain, of the creation of a single market of approaching 300 million people, with all the scope and incentive which this will provide for British industry, and of the enormous possibilities which an integrated strategy for technology, on a truly Continental scale, can create". On the other side of the account Parliament was also informed that, while all calculations were necessarily extremely speculative, the effect of adopting the EEC's common agricultural policy

as it stood might be to bring about a rise in the cost of living of $2^1/_2$–$3^1/_2$ per cent (reflecting a 10–14 per cent rise in the cost of food) and to create a cost to the balance of payments of between £ 175 million and £ 250 million a year. The overall cost to the balance of payments of entry, including the agricultural element, was estimated to require the redeployment of resources from present home use to exports, or to import substitution, of the order of about £ 100 million each year over a period of perhaps five years.

3. The political reasons for applying for membership of the European Communities were summarised in the White Paper as follows: "But whatever the economic arguments, the House will realise that ... the Government's purpose derives above all from our recognition that Europe is now faced with the opportunity of a great move forward in political unity and that we can – and indeed we must – play our full part in it. We do not see European unity as something narrow or inward-looking. Britain has her own vital links through the Commonwealth, and in other ways, with other continents. So have other European countries. Together we can ensure that Europe plays in world affairs the part which the Europe of today is not at present playing. For a Europe that fails to put forward its full economic strength will never have the political influence which I believe it could and should exert within the United Nations, within the Western Alliance, and as a means for effecting a lasting *détente* between East and West; and equally contributing in ever fuller measure to the solution of the world's North-South problem, to the needs of the developing world." Her Majesty's Government consider that events since the statement was made, and particularly the outcome of the Summit Conference of the Six on 1st and 2nd December, 1969, reaffirm the validity of the statement.

4. Following approval by Parliament of the Government's decision to apply for membership of the Communities, the then Foreign Secretary on 4th July, 1967, made a statement on behalf of Her Majesty's Government to the Council of the Western European Union (Cmnd. 3345), in which, after elaborating the political and economic and industrial reasons indicated above which underlay Britain's application to join the Communities, he set out the issues which Britain would seek to deal with in the course of negotiations for entry into the Communities. The major issues included the inequitable burden which the then existing financial arrangements for agriculture would place on Britain; the need for a transitional period or periods to permit a gradual adaptation to the circumstances of an enlarged Com-

munity; the need to make provision for the interests of the developing countries and territories whose economies are dependent on the Commonwealth Sugar Agreement; and the need to make provision for New Zealand's dairy products. On 4th December, 1969, the Prime Minister in the House of Commons confirmed that this statement by the Foreign Secretary remained the basis for our negotiations for membership.

5. In December 1967 the Council of Ministers of the European Communities failed to reach the unanimity necessary under the Community treaties to return a reply to Britain's application for membership. Her Majesty's Government decided nevertheless to maintain their application, and it was discussed at each meeting of the Council of Ministers of the European Communities in the ensuing two years. Finally, at the meeting of the member states of the European Communities on 1st–2nd December, 1969, it was agreed to open negotiations between the Community and the states which had applied for membership, and it was also agreed that the essential preparatory work by the Community would be undertaken with the least possible delay and in a most positive spirit. At the same time it was made clear that this preparatory work would be completed at the latest by the middle of 1970 and that negotiations with Britain and the other candidate countries could open immediately thereafter.

Developments since 1967 affecting the position of the United Kingdom

6. ... Since the Government's decision to apply for membership and the Parliamentary debates on it of May 1967, there have been important developments in the position of Britain and the Community. So far as Britain is concerned, the cost of entry into the Community has been somewhat increased by devaluation, but on the other hand there has been a very substantial improvement in our balance of payments and in the competitive strength of our economy. An external deficit of over £ 400 million in 1968 (£ 250 million after adjustment for Euro-currency borrowing to finance outward investment) has been converted into a surplus in 1969 likely to turn out around £ 300 million (and nearly £ 100 million more after the Euro-currency adjustment), with good prospects of continuing improvement. New developments in, *inter alia*, the control of public expenditure and the

money supply, and much modernisation of industry, have increased the stability and strength of the economy.

7. In the Community, apart from the substantial completion of the removal of internal tariff and other barriers to trade within the Community, there have been several major developments since 1967 which require a new assessment of the economic consequences for Britain of membership of the Community. First, the common agricultural policy has come under review because of its rising cost. In addition, temporary arrangements have had to be made to meet the situation following the changes in the parities of the French franc and the German mark. A fuller account of these developments will be found in this White Paper's chapter on agriculture and food.

8. The second major development is that at their meeting on 19th–22nd December, 1969, the Council of Ministers of the Communities reached agreement in principle on new financing arrangements for the Community budget, which are of great significance in three ways. First, after 1970 they would increasingly provide the Community for the first time with its "own resources", *i.e.*, the proceeds of the Community's agricultural levies, tariffs and taxes from which to finance expenditure on agriculture and certain non-agricultural items. Second, these arrangements when finally agreed would be changeable only by unanimous vote: as such their consequences would be one of the major items in the negotiations for enlargement of the Community. Third, the introduction of "Community resources" would be accompanied after 1974 by an extension of the budgetary powers of the European Parliament. These arrangements, which had not been finalised when this White Paper was printed and which are more fully described in Chapter II, are very complex, so that assessment of the effect of their implementation is bound to be precarious even for member countries, quite apart from the additional uncertainty of the changes which would have to be negotiated to provide for the United Kingdom and the other applicants to become members.

9. The third major development in the Community springs from the Summit meeting of the Six on 1st and 2nd December, 1969. In addition to the decisions in principle on agriculture and Community financing, the Six resolved to intensify, through harmonisation of economic policies, the Community's progress towards economic and monetary unfication; and also the development of common programmes of technological advance, and of a common social policy. They instructed their Ministers of Foreign Affairs to study the

best ways of achieving progress towards political unification, within the context of enlargement of the Community. The broad objectives towards which these policies are directed – in the economic, monetary, technological, social and political fields – are consistent with those indicated in the statement made on behalf of Her Majesty's Government in 1967 in support of their application for membership of the Communities.

Limitations on assessments of the economic effects of membership

10. The foregoing outline of some major developments since 1967 in our position and that of the Community provides the background necessary for an assessment of the economic effects of membership of the Community. It is clear from even so summary an account of these developments that a comprehensive, reliable and quantified assessment of the economic effects of membership, starting say in the early 1970s and building up during that decade, is quite impracticable. Not only are the areas of uncertainty already mentioned very large, but the technical problems of making comprehensive and realistic estimates of the effects of membership are equally formidable. It is equally impracticable to make reliable estimates of the situation in which we should find ourselves in the latter part of the 1970s if this country were not to join the Community. It should be emphasised that it is that future situation, some years ahead, and not our position today, which one has to try to compare with our position as a future member, if the effects are to be fairly assessed.

11. Any assessment of the economic effects of membership must therefore be in large measure qualitative. Nevertheless, in so large an issue, it is necessary to make such quantitative estimates as can be made, and to set these in the perspective of a general assessment of the likely effects of membership on the economy as a whole. The following chapters seek to do this in the sectors where significant economic effects may be expected, that is:

(i) agriculture and food;
(ii) trade and industry;
(iii) capital movements and invisible trade.

The effects of the removal of barriers to trade in coal and steel have been taken into account in the chapter on trade and industry, but otherwise this White Paper is not concerned with the ECSC or EURATOM. The basic assumptions made are constant throughout the estimates. It is assumed that in each case the effects of membership will not have their full impact until the second half of the seventies and *no allowance is made for the effect of negotiations on the terms of entry.* These estimates must be treated with caution for the general reasons given above and particularised in each chapter, but they do point to the direction and magnitude of certain effects, which in the concluding chapter are set in perspective in the overall assessment there attempted.

II. Agriculture and Food

Introduction

12. This chapter examines the ways in which adoption by the United Kingdom of the EEC's common agricultural policy would affect our agriculture, the cost of our food, and our balance of payments. For this purpose it is assumed that the Irish Republic, Denmark and Norway would also join the EEC and adopt the common agricultural policy at the same time as ourselves ...

Recent agricultural developments in the EEC

15. A number of regulations and directives have been adopted which elaborate and extend the operation of the common organisation of agricultural markets. Broadly speaking the main change since 1967 is that the single market stage has now been achieved for cereals, beef cattle, pigmeat, milk and milk products, eggs and poultry and rice. The EEC's target prices have remained at the same level over the last three years, except for some small increases for barley, maize and rice. The change in the United Kingdom exchange rate means, however, that EEC prices are now higher in sterling terms than they were before.

16. As the common organisation of markets for each product has been completed, the cost of supporting prices through market intervention and export subsidies has been transferred from national governments to the Community. Community expenditure on agriculture has increased very rapidly in recent years as can be seen from Table 1*,[1] because of the increased coverage of commodities under the common policy, the higher proportion of eligible expenditure being met by the Community's Agricultural Fund rather than na-

* Tabellen siehe Seite 262–271.

tional Exchequers, and the development of surpluses within the Community. Expenditure from the Guarantee Section of the Fund is estimated at £ 831 million for 1968–69, compared with £ 154 million for 1966–67. Expenditure from this section is now considerably higher than was anticipated; in January 1967, for example, the Commission estimated 1968–69 expenditure at £ 572 million. Roughly a third of the expenditure is on cereals, and another third on milk and milk products; a full breakdown by commodities is contained in Table 2. Expenditure from the Guidance Section of the Fund on the structural improvement of agriculture has been subject since July 1967 to a limit of £ 119 million. This makes a total estimated liability for expenditure from the Fund in 1968–69 of £ 950 million. A breakdown of receipts by member countries is given in Table 3.

17. The method of financing the Fund in 1969 was that member states paid in to the Guarantee Section 90 per cent of the proceeds of their levies on imports of agricultural products from non-Community countries. In addition, sugar producers in member countries contributed a special levy on the excess of their sugar production over their national quotas. The remainder of the Guarantee Section and the whole of the Guidance Section were paid for by budgetary contributions from the Governments of member countries according to an agreed percentage scale or "fixed key" roughly proportional to each country's gross national product; the scale used and the amounts contributed in 1968–69 are shown in Table 4.

18. In December 1969 the members of the Community agreed in principle on a new system of financial contributions for the future. For 1970 the whole cost of the Agricultural Fund would be met from national Exchequer contributions according to the following fixed key:

	per cent
Belgium	6·8
France	32·6
Germany	32·9
Italy	20·2
Luxembourg	0·2
Netherlands	7·3

From 1971 new arrangements would come into force for financing not only the Agricultural Fund, but also certain non-agricultural expenditure. It is not however yet clear precisely what non-agricultural items of Community expenditure would be covered by the arrangements. Under these arrangements, from 1971 to 1974 levies on agricultural imports would be handed over by member countries, together with an increasing proportion of customs duties on all goods. The amount of customs duties handed over would be equal to the difference between a "reference amount" and the amount of levies handed over. In 1971 this "reference amount" would be 50 per cent of the total levies and customs duties collected by each state and, in the following years $62^1/_2$ per cent, 75 per cent and $87^1/_2$ per cent successively. 10 per cent of the sums handed over would be refunded to member states to cover collection costs. The balance of expenditure would be met by members from national budgets according to the fixed key shown below:

	per cent
Belgium	8·25
France	28·0
Germany	31·7
Italy	21·5
Luxembourg	0·2
Netherlands	10·35

From 1975 onwards all levies and customs duties would be handed over (less 10 per cent to cover collection costs) and in the place of the budgetary contributions the balance would be met from contributions from member states corresponding at the most to a 1 per cent value added tax. All the above would be subject to the over-riding provision that in the years 1971 to 1974 no country's proportion of total contributions to this expenditure might rise by more than 1 per cent above or fall by more than $1^1/_2$ per cent below its previous year's proportion. For the years 1975 to 1977 these annual limits would be 2 per cent in either direction.[2]

19. Finally, during the past year certain changes in international exchange rates have had a significant effect on the operation of the common agricultural policy. The common prices for each member country are derived, according to the official exchange rate, from the prices expressed in Community units of account. When therefore the French franc was devalued in August 1969, the prices of products subject to the common agricultural policy would automatically have risen to the benefit of French farmers, and when the German Government revalued the mark in October 1969, their prices would automatically have fallen to the detriment of farmers there. These sudden changes in farm prices were not acceptable to the Governments concerned, and special measures were devised whereby the

French for a period of two years may impose a tax on agricultural exports to other member states and grant subsidies on imports from them; while the Germans for a period of four years may compensate their farmers by means of tax adjustments and direct subsidies. Thus the full application of the common agricultural policy is temporarily abated for these two members of the Community.

Future developments

20. The assessment of the effects of adopting the common agricultural policy depends on a forecast of how the common policy will develop within the present Community; what adjustments would be necessary to it on enlargement of the Community; and how United Kingdom food production and consumption would respond to the new conditions. All these matters are subject to much uncertainty.

21. Within the Community discussions are currently being held on the future shape of the common agricultural policy. The application of the policy at the relatively high prices for some products agreed by the members of the Community has contributed to a marked increase in agricultural production. As Table 5 shows, the Community now has in many cases a higher degree of self-sufficiency than before the common policy was introduced. For wheat, sugar, rice, cheese and butter, production within the Community has moved from a position in the early 1960s where it was at a lower level than consumption, to one of excess over consumption within the Community. This development of surpluses has caused expenditure from the Guarantee Section of the Agricultural Fund to rise very considerably, since the disposal or storage of excess supplies is carried out at the Fund's expense. If present production trends continue, the cost of dealing with surpluses will become still greater.

22. Various proposals have been put forward within the Community for dealing with these problems, in addition to arrangements agreed last year for encouraging the slaughter of surplus dairy cows. The Commission has submitted a Memorandum on the Reform of Agriculture in the European Economic Community (the "Mansholt Plan"), containing a set of economic and social measures intended to bring about major structural changes. Among other things, it suggests taking certain land out of agricultural use, easing the retirement of farmers, and helping those remaining in agriculture to improve their efficiency. These suggestions would involve considerable expenditure from the Guidance Section of the Fund as well as from na-

tional Exchequers. More recently the Commission has put forward proposals for reducing the prices of certain products under the common agricultural policy, with the aim of correcting the imbalance between supply and demand. If implemented, these proposals could be expected to lead to a reduction in expenditure from the Guarantee Section of the Fund. Table 6 gives the Commission's estimates for the cost until 1975 of each section of the Fund, with and without the application of the Mansholt Plan. It shows also a more recent reported estimate by the Commission, based on the application of part only of the Mansholt Plan together with certain proposals on commodity prices recently submitted to the Council. Other suggestions for reforms of various kinds have come from individual members of the Community. No decisions have yet been taken on these matters, but at their Summit Meeting at The Hague in December 1969 the Six affirmed their desire to press on with efforts to ensure a better control of agricultural production making it possible to limit budgetary charges.

23. The adoption by the United Kingdom of the EEC arrangements for agriculture would lead to large changes in prices for producers and consumers of food here. The magnitude of some of these changes would be so great compared with previous experience that it is difficult to make a reliable forecast of the response to them in terms of production and consumption.

24. Apart from these inherent uncertainties, there are also the possible consequences of adaptation of the common agricultural policy on enlargement of the Community. In the statement to the Western European Union in July 1967 (Cmnd. 3345) the Government set out the main questions in the field of agriculture which they wished to discuss with the Community before entry. This statement referred not only to considerations affecting British producers, consumers and the balance of payments, but also to our obligations to Commonwealth sugar producers and to the special problems of New Zealand. Unlike the uncertainties described above, however, these are essentially matters for negotiation with the Community, and no allowance for modifications to take account of these problems has been made in this assessment.

Method of assessing effects of adopting the common agricultural policy

25. It is clear that any assessment of the effects of adopting the common agricultural policy must depend upon a whole range of assumptions and be subject to a substantial range of possibilities. This is true of the likely effect on food prices discussed in paragraphs 27–30 below; it is even more true of the likely effects on agricultural production and trade which are discussed in pragraphs 31–37. The effects on production and consumption, together with higher import prices, will determine the effect on our import bill for food. This is one element in the direct balance of payments cost of adopting the common agricultural policy. The other element is the net contribution we must make to the Community's Agricultural Fund; this is discussed in paragraphs 38–43. The breakdown between these two effects is to some extent arbitrary, since the calculations in each sector cannot be considered in isolation. Outside the field of food and agriculture, there is also the effect on imports an exports resulting from the impact on industrial costs of the rise in food prices. This is dealt with in Chapter III.

26. Two points deserve emphasis. An attempt to assess the effects of adopting the common agricultural policy is an attempt to compare what might happen if we became a member of the Community with what might happen if we did not. Thus, although not related to a specific future year, the assessment allows for a period of time to elapse during which the necessary adjustments could take place. Secondly, the assessment assumes that, if we became a member, we should adopt the common agricultural policy essentially as it stands. This is a simplifying assumption which carries no implications whatever as to the changes which might be agreed upon in negotiations for our entry.

Effects on food prices, consumption and the cost of living

27. Food prices in the EEC are higher partly because of the different method of support for agriculture and partly because producer prices under the common agricultural policy for most farm products are set at higher levels than in the United Kingdom. Adoption of the common agricultural policy would involve a rise in food prices for most items through the imposition of levies on imports from non-Community sources and paying Community prices for imports from other members. The change in the system of support would

involve a substantial reduction of Government expenditure on agriculture, which in 1968–69 amounted to about £ 315 million of which about £ 125 million was in respect of direct price support to farmers. This reduction in Government expenditure would however be accompanied by a reduction in net Government revenue through payments to Community funds, for instance through the transfer of the proceeds of import duties.

28. The precise effect on food prices at the retail level is difficult to predict as it would depend on the extent to which distributive and retail margins changed as a result of the higher first-hand prices. United Kingdom retail food prices would not necessarily be the same as those in another Community country, since as can be seen from the examples in Table 7, there is within the Community at present quite a wide variation of prices. This is due to differences in the quality, composition and presentation of products and in the efficiency of the processing and distributive industries. On the basis of the present price differentials at the wholesale stage, and making certain assumptions about distributive and retail margins, the retail price index for food might be 18–26 per cent higher than it would otherwise have been and this would result in a 4–5 per cent increase in the cost-of-living index. The rise would of course be spread over a period of years with the full effect only being felt at the end of a transitional period and it would be associated with all the other various factors which normally influence the cost of living.

29. It is of course possible to vary the assumptions inherent in this calculation. The estimates published recently by the CBI[3] which rely upon different assumptions about the likely course of prices in the United Kingdom, whether or not we were members of the EEC, and about the effects of entry on distributive and retail margins, show generally somewhat smaller percentage increases in the cost of living. Given the surplus situation within the Community, it might well happen that the gap between present EEC prices and world prices would tend to narrow. If that came about, or if distributive and retail margins increased less than expected, then the increase in food prices attributable to the adoption of the common agricultural policy would be less. The estimate of the rise in food prices given in paragraph 28 therefore probably represents the most that is likely to occur.

30. What the effect of an 18–26 per cent rise in retail food prices taking place over a transitional period would be on the pattern of consumers' food purchases is diffcult to predict as the increases for some

products would differ markedly from those hitherto experienced. In the main the changes would consist of a switch from one food product to another, and spread over a period of years would result in food consumption going up more slowly than it otherwise would have done. It is estimated that the adoption of the common agricultural policy would cause overall expenditure on food (allowing for changes in the pattern of consumption) to be 15–22 per cent higher than it would otherwise have been. In 1967 the corresponding estimate was 10–14 per cent, and the difference is mainly attributable to the change in the relationship between United Kingdom and EEC prices cuased by the devaluation of sterling.

Agricultural prices and production

31. The prices at present received by producers in EEC countries for most farm products are higher than in the United Kingdom and it is expected that our producer price levels overall would rise significantly if the common agricultural policy were adopted as it stands.
32. In assessing the production response to the price changes, account has to be taken of a number of other factors. There is the uncertain future of some production grants under EEC regulations on state aids to agriculture and there is the increase in the cost of animal feedingstuffs resulting from the higher cereal prices, a factor of particular importance to pig and poultry producers. And, of course, the significance of particular price levels varies over time depending on farming costs and efficiency; on how farmers' responses are influenced by their assessment of future prospects; on the development of new techniques of production; and on the limits imposed by climate and the quality of land. Moreover, the amount of the response in terms of production naturally depends on what level production has reached at the time the price changes are introduced.
33. Taking all these factors into account, it is only possible to indicate a range – with a "lower" and "upper" estimate – of the possible response of production to these higher prices. But on the assumption that United Kingdom prices would be increased over a transitional period by the amount necessary to eliminate the present gap between them and the EEC prices, the overall effect might be to increase the volume of total agricultural production (net of feed and seeds used) by between 3 and 10 per cent above what it would otherwise have been. Although farmers' total revenue would also be increased appreciably, this would be partly offset by increases in production

costs, particularly for feedingstuffs as already described. Farmers' net income would nevertheless be higher than it would otherwise have been, although its distribution, and so the gains and losses, would differ greatly between commodities, types of farm and areas of the country.

34. These estimates assume that producer prices in the United Kingdom would rise from their current levels by the extent of the present difference between United Kingdom and EEC prices. But, in the event, the relationship between United Kingdom and EEC prices could be somewhat different by the time we had adopted Community prices. Given the pressure of surpluses in the EEC, it is possible that the gap between their prices and ours would narrow. It is also possible, although much less likely, that the price gap would widen. For illustrative purposes therefore an assessment has been made of the possible changes in production if the gap were 5 per cent wider than now when we adopted EEC prices; and also if the gap were to narrow by 10 per cent. With a wider price gap it is estimated that the volume of production might increase by between about 5 and 15 per cent depending, as before, upon whether the production responses were less or more favourable. With a smaller price gap, the overall level of production might be marginally higher or lower than it would be outside the Community depending upon whether the production response was greater or less.

Effects on trade in agricultural products

35. The changes in prices and in production and consumption of food would have consequences for the overall import bill for food and feedingstuffs. This is the first main element in the calculation of the balance of payments cost of adopting the common agricultural policy. Estimates of the changes in the United Kingdom import bill on various assumptions are given in Table 8. In view of the uncertainty surrounding the degree of response to higher retail prices, the calculations of the change in the import bill and of the levies collected on imports from third countries are based on an "upper" and "lower" estimate of changes in consumption. The estimates shown suggest that the change in the food import bill could range from a reduction of £ 85 million to an increase of £ 255 million, depending on the response of United Kingdom production and consumption, and the relationship between United Kingdom and EEC prices.

35. The estimates in paragraph 35 do not include the value of the import levies which would be imposed by the United Kingdom under the EEC agricultural system. Estimates of these are given separately in the table for each of the possible outcomes for the import bill. The amount of the levies is particularly difficult to forecast because they are charged only on imports from non-Community countries; certain assumptions therefore have to be made about the changes in the source of food imports. In effect, these levies represent an additional charge on the cost of importing food, since under the EEC system the levy proceeds would be paid over into Community funds; the implications of this are dealt with in the next section of this chapter.
37. The estimates given above of the changes in the import bill are intended to take account of the possibility of offsetting changes in exports of agricultural products. Compared with food imports, these exports are of course small, and half of their value is represented by exports of alcoholic and other drinks. If the United Kingdom becomes a member of the Community, other members would remove the tariffs and levies to which United Kingdom exports are at present subject, and the United Kingdom would do the same as regards imports from the Community. The effect on our exports of manufactured foods would depend on much the same considerations as apply to industrial exports generally and this has therefore been taken into account in the next chapter. Direct exports of certain agricultural commodities and of fish could be stimulated but a large net increase is not expected, since additional exports of products in which we are not self-sufficient would be likely to bring about a corresponding increase in imports.

Contribution to the Community Agricultural Fund

38. In addition to the effect on the import bill, which is considered in the immediately preceding section, the other agricultural element in the cost to the balance of payments is the amount of the net contribution by the United Kingdom to the Agricultural Fund.
39. The future cost of the Agricultural Fund depends not merely on the course of world and EEC prices, but on decisions which have yet to be taken on the Mansholt Plan and on market reforms, which in turn will affect the balance between agricultural production and consumption. These decisions will determine not only the future level of expenditure on market support and on schemes for structural reform, but also how far they will be financed out of Community

or national funds. The enlargement of the Community will itself increase the claims upon the Agricultural Fund, an additional cost which will be offset by reduced payments on market intervention or export subsidies to the extent that the enlarged Community can absorb commodities currently in surplus. The EEC Commission has estimated that expenditure on agriculture by the enlarged Community might in a few years' time amount to £ 1,560 million (3,750 million UA) if present policies continue and £ 1,750 million (4,200 million UA) if the reforms proposed in the Mansholt Plan are adopted. These estimates, the detailed basis of which has not been disclosed by the Commission, clearly depend upon certain assumptions about the extent to which the surplus problem is brought under control, and the extent to which any structural expenditure is borne by Community funds.

40. The amount we would be likely to get back out of this agricultural expenditure would probably be relatively small; perhaps of the order of £ 50 million to £ 100 million depending on the way the common agricultural policy developed.

41. The method of financing Community expenditure on agriculture and certain non-agricultural items which was agreed in principle by the Six in December 1969 is described in detail in paragraph 18 above. The essential features of this agreement are that the contribution to agricultural expenditure of each member state for 1970 was fixed as a percentage of the total sum required. For subsequent years, individual member states would be required to subscribe 90 per cent of the levies collected on agricultural imports; an annually increasing proportion of import duties up to a maximum of 90 per cent by 1975; and from 1975 any balance required would be provided by contributions corresponding at the most to a 1 per cent value added tax. There is, however, a further provision that, subject to unconditional payment of levies, the proportion of this expenditure paid for by each individual member state should not rise by more than 1 per cent or fall by more than 1·5 per cent as compared with the previous year from 1971–74; or rise or fall by more than 2 per cent annually from 1975–77.

42. Thus, the main determinant of the proportionate contribution of individual members would be likely to be the percentage share of agricultural expenditure which in December 1969 was agreed in principle for each of them for 1970. It is of course impossible to say at what level our share would have been fixed if we had then been a member. In the circumstances the best that can be done is to in-

dicate – as a form of ready reckoner – what our contribution might have been to the Agricultural Fund in 1970, and in subsequent years, if we had been a member and our share, within a Community of Ten instead3of Six, had been set at respectively 15 per cent or 20 per cent. This is done in the following table which relates these percentages to the Agricultural Fund which is assumed to rise from, say, £ 1,250 million in 1970 to £ 1,600 million in 1977. As explained in paragraph 18, it is not yet clear what non-agricultural expenditures would be covered by these arrangements but they would seem unlikely to increase our annual contribution by more than about £ 15 million. It is estimated that 90 per cent of United Kingdom agricultural levies might bring in about £ 150 to £ 200 million by the late 1970s; 90 per cent of United Kingdom customs duties might by then be about £ 240 million; and the yield corresponding to a 1 per cent value added tax could, depending on the coverage, range up to about £ 230 million. Since 90 per cent of a member country's levy income must be paid to the Community, it will be seen that, if the United Kingdom had been a party to the agreement reached in the Community in December 1969, our annual contribution to the Community's budget could not have been less than £ 150 million (equivalent to 90 per cent of our lower estimate of levy income). The above figures also show that on the same basis there would have been a theoretical upper limit to our contribution of about £ 670 million. In practice, our contribution would have been fixed within narrower limits by the percentage share agreed for us, and for other members of the Community, in the recent financial settlement.
43. For the purposes of illustration, an attempt has been made above to show on various assumptions what the cost of the common agricultural policy might have been for the United Kingdom if we had been a party to the recent agreement by the Community on agricultural financing. But of course we were not, and in the negotiations it will be necessary, not only to settle our starting contribution to the Fund, but also to settle the transitional arrangements under which we approach paying our full share of the recently agreed Community financing arrangements which will be changing from year to year.

Net effect on the balance of payments

44. Taken together, the trade effects and the financial charges described in the paragraphs above represent the net effect on the balance of payments of adopting the common agricultural policy. When this calculation was made in 1967, it was estimated that the net cost to the balance of payments would be £ 175–£ 250 million annually. The net cost is now likely to be greater than this, partly because of the effects of the devaluation of sterling and partly because of the greatly increased cost of the European Agricultural Fund. The preceding sections of this chapter have attempted to describe the elements which have to be taken into account in making an assessment of this kind and the reasons why a number of alternative assumptions can and must be made in relation to many of them; and to indicate some of the orders of magnitude which attach to them. It is clear that a very wide range of estimates is possible, although the extreme assumptions at either end of the spectrum could not be regarded as realistic since they would depend on all factors operating in the same direction. In practice it is much more likely that the outcome would result from a combination of factors some more favourable than others. But in the crucial area of our financial contribution to the Fund, there is just not a sufficient basis, in advance of negotiations, for making reliable assumptions either about its cost or our share of it. The present members of the Community have made it clear that they wish to bring the cost under control, but the implementing decisions have not yet been taken. They have reached agreement in principle on arrangements for meeting the cost, but their application in a reasonable and equitable way to our situation must be a matter for negotiation, as has always been recognised.

III Trade and Industry

Trade and industry in the Common Market

45. The Treaty of Rome provides for the progressive establishment of a Common Market with free movement of goods, persons, services and capital. It contemplates the evolution of common policies for agriculture, transport, foreign trade, regional development and for consultation and collaboration on economic and social matters. This chapter is concerned with Community policies directly affecting trade and industry.

46. A Customs Union was completed by the EEC on 1st July, 1968. It involved the complete abolition (other than in exceptional circumstances) of tariff and quota restrictions between the member states, and the replacement of the national external tariffs of the member states by a Common External Tariff (CET) which is applied aginst imports from all third countries except those having preferential arrangements with the Community.

47. The growth and pattern of the foreign trade of the EEC over the 10 years since the Community was formed is compared in Tables 10 and 11 below with the United Kingdom pattern.

48. Both the CET and the United Kingdom tariff will be progressively reduced as a result of the "Kennedy Round" tariff agreements reached in the GATT, and the comparison which follows relates to the situation as it will be after full implementation of these reductions which is due from 1st January, 1972. The duties on most raw materials are zero in the CET, as in the United Kingdom tariff; examples are raw wool and cotton, most metallic ores, unwrought copper and tin, natural rubber and most unprocessed hides and skins, many of which are important Commonwealth exports. A few materials of major importance such as aluminium, lead, zinc and newsprint, are dutiable under the CET[4] (currently at rates between 4·5 per cent and 9·0 per cent), but are subject to zero or very low duties in the United Kingdom: and certain materials are dutiable here but not under the CET. The bulk of the latter category are, however, materials of which most of our imports enter duty free from the Commonwealth Preference Area. Examples are asbestos and coir fibre. In the agriculture and food sectors, duty free imports from the Commonwealth Preference Area represent a considerable part of our total imports. In certain cases, Commonwealth supplies which are at present allowed into this country duty free would become subject to quite a high rate of duty under the CET for example mutton and lamb and bananas (CET currently 20 per cent).

49. In the range of semi-manufactures and finished manufactures, there are certain sectors where the general level of the duties is significantly different as between the United Kingdom tariff and the CET. Duties on machinery and most chemicals are higher in the United Kingdom, as well as those on clocks and watches, optical and photographic equipment, musical instruments and many kinds of precision instruments. But on the other hand the current United Kingdom tariff on plastics is lower, although this may be brought more in line with the CET as a result of the Kennedy Round agree-

ments. For the rest, the levels of the two tariffs are broadly similar.
50. In addition to establishing a Customs Union, the EEC has been developing a common approach to trade policy to govern its commercial relations with the rest of the world. The Six have negotiated as a unit in tariff negotiations, in relation to the GATT agreement on anti-dumping and in negotiating trade agreements with several countries. Further developments towards the establishment of a common commercial policy by the EEC are expected to follow after the end of the Treaty of Rome transitional period which expired at the end of 1969.
51. Progress in implementing other provisions of the Treaty affecting industry and trade has been less rapid. However, agreement has been reached on the introduction throughout the Community of a common system of value added taxation though not yet on uniform rates. Workers from member countries are free to take up employment in any member state and enjoy appropriate social security benefits wherever they are employed. Limited progress has been made in removing legal obstacles to the establishment and operations of companies across frontiers within the Community. Other developments are under consideration, including legal provision for the incorporation in any member state of "European companies" enabled to operate throughout the Community. The preparation of a common legal system for patents throughout the Community is being pursued at present, in parallel with international discussions (in which the United Kingdom and other European Free Trade Association (EFTA) countries are participating) on the establishment of a wider European Patent Convention. In the field of regional policies, there is broad similarity between the objectives of the member states and those of the United Kingdom although the emphasis on inducements and concessions accorded to industries in areas of above average unemployment varies from country to country. The formulation of a common transport policy for rail, road and inland waterway transport has proceeded slowly and is still far from completion, and no steps have been taken towards extending it to sea or air transport.

United Kingdom industry in an enlarged Community

52. For industry and trade, the main consequences of United Kingdom membership of an enlarged Community would be that we should then form part of a Customs Union of up to 300 million peo-

ple stretching from Scotland to Sicily and from the Irish Republic to the borders of eastern Europe. Within this vast area, industrial products would move freely – without tariff or quota restrictions – as soon as any transitional period had been completed. And over the years ahead it would be the intention to convert this Customs Union into a full economic union by the progressive alignment and harmonisation of commercial policy, *i.e.*, trading relations with third countries, of economic and fiscal policy; of company and patent law; of standards for industrial products, including specifications for public sector purchasing; and generally of the whole structure of law and practice within which industry would operate.

53. The creation of such an enlarged and integrated European market would provide in effect a much larger and a much faster growing "home market" for British industry. It would provide the stimuli of much greater opportunities – and competition – than exist at present or would otherwise exist in future. There would be substantial advantages for British industry from membership of this new enlarged Common Market, stemming primarily from the opportunities for greater economies of scale, increased specialisation, a sharper competitive climate and faster growth. These may be described as the "dynamic" effects of membership on British industry and trade. It has not been found possible to measure the likely response of British industry to these new opportunities nor, therefore, the effects on our economic growth and balance of payments. On the other hand we should have to make changes in our tariffs and food prices in order to join the Community and the net effect of these changes would be disadvantageous to British industry. These may be described as the "impact" effects of membership. It has been possible to make a rough estimate of the possible cost to the balance of payments of these impact effects.

54. It is noted in Chapter II that membership would lead to an increase in United Kingdom food prices to Community levels and accordingly to an increase in our cost of living. It has been estimated that the maximum increase which would be likely to occur if we joined the Community would involve the index of retail prices rising over a transitional period by about 4 to 5 per cent more than it otherwise would.[5] This additional increase in the cost of living spread over a transitional period of some years could raise the future level of wage settlements somewhat above what it otherwise would be and any consequent increases in industrial costs would of course adversely affect our competitive position.

55. It has also been argued that the requirement to harmonise the systems of indirect taxation of the member states would affect the cost of living here. It is not possible however to make any quantitative assessment of the effect in the United Kingdom, not least because the EEC have not settled on a common system of rates and coverage of value added tax.

56. At present we enjoy special preferential trading relationships with the Commonwealth Preference Area, EFTA and the Irish Republic. If we moved into a new enlarged Community, these existing trade relationships would be affected to our disadvantage. In the new circumstances, subject to any special arrangements made in the course of negotiations, we should generally apply the CET against imports from third countries, including the Commonwealth, and we could hardly expect that all our existing Commonwealth preferences would be maintained indefinitely. We stand to lose the tariff preference over the Six which we now enjoy in the Irish Republic and in EFTA countries. Finally, we should of course gain duty free entry for our exports to the Six and we should concede it on imports from them. Thus, in exchange for the new preferential position we should enjoy behind the CET in the enlarged Community, we should expect to lose most of our existing preferences. But in order to make a true comparison of our situation inside and outside the Community some years hence, it is necessary to take into account the probablility of continuing erosion of preferences in the Commonwealth and the possibility of new preferential trading arrangements between the Community and some of our trading partners. It is relevant in this connection that a number of Commonwealth countries in Africa have found it to their advantage in recent years to give tariff preferences, to our disadvantage, to the Six.

57. Finally, in considering the disadvantages of membership for industry and the economy, we must recognise that if the total burden on our balance of payments as a result of membership became excessive we might find that we were unable to pursue economic policies which enabled the full benefits of membership to be realised. Since such an outcome would be as contrary to the interests of the Community as of the United Kingdom, the Government would expect to find its avoidance a common aim of all concerned with the negotiations.

58. The effects of the tariff and cost changes would depend on the responses to these changed conditions of exporters and their customers throughout the world. Any attempt to measure what these responses might be and what effect they would have on our trade can only be based on past experience, including the recent experience of devaluation. The degree of the response in flows of trade to a given change, say a decline in tariffs or in relative cost levels, depends partly on the ability of supply industries to respond to the increased opportunities for profitable sales, and partly on the extent to which lower prices call forth increased demand. The elasticities used for the purpose of the estimates which follow allow for both kinds of response, and allowances are also made for some degree of absorption by United Kingdom and foreign suppliers of tariff and cost changes. Inevitably there must be great uncertainty about the degree of response. Higher and lower values have been taken for the response elasticities for both imports and exports. For imports it is assumed that, given a change of 1 per cent in prices arising from changes in tariffs or costs, the response in the quantity imported would be between $^1/_3$ per cent and $1^1/_2$ per cent. For exports the assumption is that the response to a 1 per cent change in prices would be a quantity change between $1^1/_2$ and $2^1/_2$ per cent. The assumption about the response of suppliers to tariff changes is that those faced with a tariff change to their advantage would absorb one-quarter of the change. This would increase their unit profits and it is assumed that a 1 per cent increase in unit profits would lead to a $^1/_2$ per cent increase in the volume exported on the lower assumption for elasticities and to a 1 per cent increase on the higher assumption. Suppliers faced with a tariff change to their disadvantage are assumed to react competitively by cutting their prices to the extent of one-quarter of the change. These assumptions imply a fairly modest degree of response by both buyers and sellers.

59. Using these elasticities it is possible on the basis of a number of other assumptions to make some very rough quantitative estimates of the effects of the cost and tariff changes described in paragraphs 54 and 56 an the value and pattern of United Kingdom visible trade in the mid-1970s. The Table 12 below sets out in summary form these rough estimates of the effects on United Kingdom exports and imports on the higher and lower assumptions about elasticities.

60. These estimates do not purport to evaluate the total net effect on our trade of joining the EEC. In order to arrive at them, it has been necessary to make a whole series of assumptions about the future course of world trade over the next five years or so and to adopt highly over-simplified assumptions about the effect and timing of a complex series of tariff and cost changes on the wide range of goods entering into our foreign trade. Each of these assumptions can be little more than an informed guess which may be very wide of the mark. The actual situation in the mid-1970s will be fundamentally affected by the relative development of the economies of the main industrial countries during the intervening years and this in turn depends on a wide range of factors which it is impossible to predict. It is particularly important to bear in mind that the estimates shown in Table 12 relate to a total flow of United Kingdom trade which by the middle of the decade is expected to be about 25 per cent greater than it is now and to be of the order of £ 18,000 million valued at 1968 prices. The significance of the figures showing the effect on the visible trade balance will therefore be relatively less than it would be today. Furthermore, these estimates only deal with the impact effects. For the reasons given in paragraphs 54 and 56 these effects are bound to be on balance adverse. No corresponding estimates can be made of the dynamic effects of membership but the next section of this chapter discusses these in qualitative terms and sets out the reasons for believing that providing United Kingdom industry responds vigorously to the opportunities there will be substantial benefits to set against the adverse impact effects.

The benefits for United Kingdom industry and trade of membership of an enlarged Community

61. The main consequence of membership for British industry is, as we have seen, that the "home market" will be serveral times larger than our existing home market, including EFTA. And the new home market will be a more rapidly growing one than the present home market. If wie join the Community, companies will be able to plan their sales and investment on the basis of a prosperous home market of approaching 300 million people.

62. The dismantling of tariffs within the present Community and the maintenance of a moderate common tariff against the rest of the world have resulted, as might be expected, in a particularly rapid increase in intra-Community trade. This trade multiplied four times

between 1958 and 1968, from £ 2,800 million to nearly £ 11,000 million. By comparison, United Kingdom exports to the Community over this period increased only $2^1/_2$ times, even though the Community was our biggest single export market during this period. The following table shows the rate of growth of exports by individual member countries to their Community partners in comparison with their exports to the world.

This pattern is reflected in the declining share of EEC imports obtained by third countries, which fell from 70·3 per cent in 1958 to 54·2 per cent in 1968. The United Kingdom share of EEC imports of manufactures in the same period fell from 10·6 per cent to 7·1 per cent.

63. The market we should be joining is not only larger but growing substantially more rapidly than ours. As shown by Table 14 below, from 1958–67 the annual rise in the gross national product (g.n.p.) per head averaged $2^1/_2$ per cent in the United Kingdom compared with 4 per cent in the Community.

Although a number of EFTA countries have also enjoyed a comparatively high growth rate, the preponderance of the United Kingdom in EFTA has meant that the EFTA market as a whole has grown much more slowly than the EEC.

64. The more rapid growth in the EEC compared with the United Kingdom is also indicated by the fact that between 1958 and 1967 industrial production in the Six rose by 68 per cent, in the United Kingdom by 37 per cent. Table 15 compares the development of output in certain industries in the United Kingdom and the EEC over this period.

65. There were and still are a number of factors at work encouraging faster now in the Community than in the United Kingdom. More workers now leaving agriculture for industry; the advantages of post-war rebuilding of major industries with new machinery and the latest technologies; and generally a significantly lower proportion of g.n.p. expended on defence, though the gap has been narrowing over the last few years. Nevertheless it seems highly probable that the creation of the Community itself generated a faster rate of growth through greater specialisation and greater competition than the economies of the Six member countries would have separately enjoyed and that, apart, from the likely beneficial effects on growth of the enlargement of the Community, an enlarged Community would

in any event continue to grow faster in future than the United Kingdom or EFTA on their own.

66. The creation of this very large and fast growing home market will provide greater opportunities and greater competition for British industry. The rapid development of intra-Community trade is a reflection of growing international specialisation, and the need for United Kingdom industry to participate fully in this was a theme which found a considerable amount of support in the recent industrial assessments made by the Economic Development Committees of the National Economic Development Council in analysing medium-term prospects. It is of course true that the widening of the field of competition will stimulate the industries of other member countries as well as those of the United Kingdom, but for the EEC countries this would be a further phase in a process to which they have been subjected for a number of years, and the future rate of growth of the enlarged Community may not be exceptionally high by EEC standards. On the other hand, for the United Kingdom the new market would be a stimulus and an opportunity on a quite different scale from that provided by EFTA and with a rate of growth which could also be expected to be substantially higher than in EFTA. In this connection, it is of interest to note that, when the prospect of British membership was before industry in the early 1960s, there were indications of a much more significant increase in interest and activity on the part of British than of Community industry. A study of the trade trends in 1960–63 shows that the proportion of United Kingdom exports going to the EEC increased perceptibly.

67. Moreover, a faster growing market will provide British industry with opportunities, which it has not shared with the rest of western Europe since the war, for a *sustained* high level of investment in new plant and equipment. Such investment would serve to improve our competitive position, not only in relation to the Six, but also to the rest of the world. The economic position of Belgium in the 1950s had features in common with that of the United Kingdom. Over the period 1953–60 the annual average rate of growth of g.n.p. was 2·9 per cent in Belgium and in the United Kingdom. But over the period 1960–67 the rate of growth in Belgium had more or less caught up with the faster growth rates of her fellow members in the European Community: Belgium's average over this period was 4·6 per cent compared with 3·0 per cent for the United Kingdom, and this higher growth rate was achieved with a net surplus on the current Belgian

balance of payments over the period as a whole. This experience will not be directly applicable to the United Kingdom. Only time would show the response of British industries to the new opportunities and greater competition which in turn would determine the extent of the long-term benefits to the United Kingdom growth rate and balance of payments. But an increase of 1 per cent in our g.n.p. would be equivalent in the mid-1970s to something approaching £ 500 million a year at present prices.

68. *Inward investment into the United Kingdom.* Linked with the question of growth is the degree to which the United Kingdom will in future attract overseas investment – particularly from the United States. In addition to its benefits to the reserves, this has been of considerable benefit to the United Kingdom economy in several ways; in providing jobs (particularly in development areas), in its contribution to exports and in the dissemination of technology and management techniques. If the United Kingdom remained outside the Community, it is likely that American investment in the Six would be stimulated at the expense of the much smaller and less rapidly growing United Kingdom market. If on the other hand the United Kingdom entered, it is likely that we would attract substantially more American investment to this country than if the United Kingdom remained outside. The fact that net additional American investment in this country in 1968 totalled £ 246 million shows that the stakes are high.

69. *Protecting United Kingdom trade interests.* Apart from these factors of growth and investment, there remains the question of the United Kingdom's ability to protect its economic interests if it remained outside the Community. Since the formation of the European Economic Community, the United Kingdom's position in international trade negotiations has been weakened because a country's bargaining power depends largely on the size of its market, and ours is now relatively small compared with the Community and the United States. We might find ourselves in the position of seeing arrangements governing international trade negotiated in the main by others – in particular the European Economic Community and the United States. On the other hand, as a member of an enlarged Community, we should share in the bargaining strength of the biggest trading *bloc* in the world and have an important voice in determining how that strength was used.

70. *High technology industries.* So far, the effects of membership on British industry have been considered as a whole. But the future of

the so-called high technology industries – in the rest of western Europe just as much as in the United Kingdom – depends decisively on whether or not it proves possible to create an enlarged Community.

71. Approaching one half of manufacturing output of the United States and western Europe is in industries which rely heavily on advanced technologies – such as engineering, electrical and electronics, chemicals. These have been and still are fast growing sectors in most developed countries. Their growth depends on a number of factors – marketing and rate of innovation for example – besides research and development (R and D) which nevertheless play a most important role. The very high expenditure on research and development in these industries is illustrated in Table 16. This expenditure on R and D is accompanied by high risks and rapid outdating of products.

72. In this very important matter, European industry suffers from three relative disadvantages:

(a) the support that is given in the United States, both directly and indirectly, by the large scale of Government expenditure on R and D is far more massive than is practicable in Europe;

(b) national markets in Europe – even the Community as it is at present – are too small to generate the financial and other resources needed for the adequate growth of such industries, particularly in competition with the United States. Even the enlarged Community's gross national product would fall short of that of the United States;

(c) the larger the company and its financial resources, the greater its capacity to incur substantial expenditure on R and D; in this sense, there is a certain threshold linked with the size of the company. The threshold may be quite small for some highly specialised producers but, in general, western Europe suffers seriously from lack of companies of a sufficient size to be able to command R and D resources on the scale required to compete effectively with the United States. In an enlarged Community there would be the opportunity, because of the larger market, for European firms, British and Continental, to grow to the point where adequate R and D expenditure became profitable and practicable in fields where today it is not.

73. This does not of course mean that technological co-operation in Europe as it exists is impossible. In the defence field there have been some successes and the recent agreement on the gas centrifuge is an indication of what can be achieved on civil projects when the economic viability can clearly be established. But on the whole the record has been disappointing. More generally, a beginning has been

made on studies of possible future technological co-operation in Europe, through the Working Group of the Community's Medium-Term Economic Policy Committee, under the chairmanship of Professor Aigrain. Proposals have been made by this Group for new co-operative European studies and research in the fields of computers, communications, surface transport, metallurgy, meteorology, oceanography and pollution. As a result of this initiative, leading manufacturers of computers in the United Kingdom and other European countries have already begun discussions amongst themselves about concerting their ideas for the development of advanced computers. The United Kingdom amongst other European nations has been invited to be associated with the further development of the proposals by the Working Group and we have gladly accepted.

74. But such co-operation can only be fully productive within an enlarged economic union, for the goal is not co-operation for its own sake, but the opportunity over a period to build European enterprises on a continental scale and thus for Europe to hold its own in future industrial development with the United States and the Soviet Union. And in all this the record of the United Kingdom in technological development entitles us to hope and the rest of Europe to expect that our role will be a prominent one.

75. *Company size and monopoly.* The benefits of membership of an enlarged Community will by no means go only to large companies in Europe. The opportunities for successful specialisation by the small entrepreneur should be greater in a larger and more competitive market. Technological innovation in the United States, particularly in the new and more speculative fields, has often been supported by very small industrial enterprises. But successful competition with the United States in the high technology industries of the future will increasingly depend on the existence of at least some west European companies of comparable size to their United States counterparts. At present, most of the largest companies in the United Kingdom and in the rest of western Europe are much smaller than their United States competitors (see Table 17). The existence of an enlarged Community can be expected not only to provide the environment in which European companies would be able to grow in size and in command of resources, but also an environment in which companies of such size would be acceptable. Within the United Kingdom, for example, it is necessary for the Government to weigh the advantages of the economies of scale and concentration

of resources offered by a prospective merger against the possible dangers of a monopoly or near monopoly situation which might result. Within an enlarged Community, the position with regard to monopolies would be different. What would be a monopoly situation within the United Kingdom would not necessarily remain one when the United Kingdom formed part of a larger market to which French and German companies would have duty-free access.

Conclusion

76. The probable effects on industry and trade of entry into the EEC may be summarised as follows. On the one hand, there are the impact effects. The increase in wage-levels following the rise in food prices would tend to reduce the competitiveness of our industrial producers and this, combined with the tariff changes involved in membership, would affect both exports and imports in directions damaging to the balance of payments. A very rough estimate of the adverse effect of these two factors on trade in the mid 1970s is that it could be of the order of £ 125–£ 275 million. If to this was added an excessive balance of payments burden arising from the acceptance of the EEC's agricultural arrangements, defensive policies might be enforced on the United Kingdom Government which would restore the balance of payments position at the cost of damaging the growth of industry's market in the United Kingdom.
77. On the other hand, there are the dynamic effects resulting from membership of a much larger and faster growing market. This would open up to our industrial producers substantial opportunities for increasing export sales, while at the same time exposing them more fully to the competition of European industries. No way has been found of quantifying these dynamic effects but, if British industry responded vigorously to these stimuli, they would be considerable and highly advantageous. The acceleration in the rate of growth of industrial exports could then outpace any increase in the rate of growth of imports, with corresponding benefits to the balance of payments. Moreover, with such a response, the growth of industrial productivity would be accelerated as a result of increased competition and the advantages derived from specialisation and larger scale production. This faster rate of growth of productivity would, in turn, accelerate the rate of growth of national production and real income.

78. Finally, it must be remembered that the comparison which has to be attempted is between our position as members of an enlarged Community and our position if we remained outside it in the mid-1970s. During that period the preferences which we at present enjoy might well have been further eroded and our general trading interests prejudiced by developments over which we should not have been able – as non-members – to exercise so much influence.

Anmerkungen

1 Community agricultural prices and expenditure are officially defined in terms of the Community "unit of account" (UA) which at present is equivalent in value to the United States dollar. All figures in the text and tables of this chapter have been converted at the exchange rate of 2·40 UA per £ Sterling.

2 For the purposes of calculating the German share after 1970, their agriculture percentage in 1970 would be deemed to be 31·5 per cent.

3 "Britain in Europe: A Second Industrial Appraisal", Confederation of British Industry, December 1969.

4 Under certain circumstances, member states may be authorised to import specified quantities of a product at a duty lower than prescribed in the Common External Tariff. These tariff quotas, which are reviewed periodically, cover only a small proportion of Community imports.

5 The index of retail prices has risen by 34 per cent between January 1962 and December 1969.

Table 1 Expenditure from European Agricultural Guidance and Guarantee Fund (Fonds Europeen d'Orientation et de Garantie Agricole) 1966–67 to 1968–69

£ million

	1966–67	*1967–68*	*1968–69*
1. *Guarantee Section*(1)			
Export restitutions	94	302	441
Market intervention	59	244	389
Other expenditure	—	1	1
Total	154	547	831
2. *Guidance Section*	51	119	119
3. *Total*	205	666	950

(1) In 1966–67 the Guarantee Section was contributing towards eligible expenditure by member Governments to the extent of seven-tenths, but in later years to the full extent.
Source: EEC Official Journals Nos. I. 109 of 10th May, 1968, and L 36 of 12th February, 1969.

Table 2 Expenditure from Guarantee Section by Commodity, 1968–69

£ million

Commodity	Export restitutions	Market intervention	Total
Cereals	193	88	281
Milk and dairy products	133	127	260
Oils and fats (includes olive oil)	3	95	98
Fruit and vegetables	1	19	20
Rice	8	—	8
Pigmeat	18	—	18
Beef and veal	4	5	9
Sugar	71	55	126
Eggs	1	—	1
Poultry	2	—	2
Processed products	8	—	8
Total	442	389	831

Source: EEC Official Journal No. L 36 of 12th February, 1969.

Table 3 Receipts from Agricultural Fund by Country, 1966–67 to 1968–69

£ million (figures in brackets show percentages of total)

	1966–67			1967–68	1968–69
	Guarantee Section	Guidance Section	Total	Guarantee Section	Guarantee Section
Germany	8·5	0·8	9·3 (7·8)	40·0 (12·4)	90·2 (18·5)
France	48·2	0·8	49·0 (41·0)	125·8 (38·9)	197·6 (40·6)
Italy	30·0	1·3	31·3 (26·2)	60·1 (18·6)	73·2 (15·0)
Netherlands . . .	23·4	0·3	23·7 (19·8)	68·6 (21·2)	90·7 (18·6)
Belgium	5·6	0·3	5·9 (4·9)	28·6 (8·9)	35·0 (7·2)
Luxembourg . . .	0·3	—	0·3 (0·3)	0·1 (—)	0·6 (0·1)
Total	116·0	3·5	119·5 (100·0)	323·2 (100·0)	487·3 (100·0)

Note: The large differences between the totals in Tables 1 and 3 are because the former refer to amounts budgeted for each year, while the latter refer to amounts actually paid following claims by member countries. The accounts for 1966–67, 1967–68 and 1968–69 are only partially complete.

Sources:

1966–67–"Statistisches Jahrbuch über Ernährung, Landwirtschaft und Forsten 1969". Verlag Paul Parey, Hamburg.

1967–68–EEC Official Journals Nos. L 204 of 14th August, 1968 and L 103 of 30 April, 1969.

1968–69–EEC Official Journals Nos. L 173 of 15th July, 1969 and L 13 of 19 January, 1970.

Table 4 Contributions to Agricultural Fund by Country, 1968–69

	£ million (figures in brackets show percentages of total)					
	Guarantee Section					
	Import levies(1)	Budetary contribution		Guidance Section	Total	
Belgium and Luxembourg . .	37	38	(8·3)	10	83	(9·0)
Germany	102	143	(31·2)	37	282	(29·7)
France	47	147	(32·0)	38	232	(24·4)
Italy	124	93	(20·3)	24	241	(25·4)
Netherlands . .	62	37	(8·2)	10	109	(11·5)
Total	372	458	(100·0)	119	950	(100·0)

(1) Includes special levy on sugar production.
Source: EEC Official Journal No. L 36 of 12th February, 1969.

Table 5 Self-sufficiency of the Six in principal farm products

Commodity	*1962–63 and 1963–64 (average)* (per cent)	*1967–68* (per cent)
Wheat	99·5	112·5
Feed grain	77·1	78·6
Total cereals (excluding rice)	86·3	91·1
Rice (husked)	79·0	100·8
White sugar	98·7	104·6
Vegetables	102·4	102·5
Fresh fruit (excluding citrus fruit)	91·3	89·9
Citrus fruit	43·9	not available
Beef and veal	90·3	88·8
Pigmeat (including bacon)	99·2	100·0
Poultry meat	91·4	97·8
Mutton, lamb and goat meat	92·3	84·2
Eggs	94·4	97·1
Cheese	98·0	102·7(1)
Butter	99·5	111·1(1)
Oils and fats	38·5	41·8

(1) Provisional figures.
Source: Economic Union and Enlargement: the European Commission's revised opinion on the applications for membership from the United Kingdom, Ireland, Denmark and Norway, October 1969.

Table 6 Estimates of expenditure from Agricultural Fund by the Six, 1970–75

A Without Application of Mansholt Plan

				£ million
	1971	*1972*	*1973*	*1975*
Guarantee Section	1,125	1,185	1,250	1,355
Guidance Section	120	120	120	125
Total	1,245	1,305	1,370	1,480

Source: EEC Document COM (69) 700, July 1969.

B With Application of Mansholt Plan

				£ million
	1971	*1972*	*1973*	*1975*
Guarantee Section	1,000	960	875	665
Guidance Section	415	500	625	585
Total	1,415	1,460	1,500	1,250

C With Modified Application of Mansholt Plan and Commission's Proposed Commodity Measures

						£ million
	1970	*1971*	*1972*	*1973*	*1974*	*1975*
Guarantee Section	1,045	1,030	1,025	945	965	985
Guidance Section .	185	260	325	475	525	575
Total	1,230	1,290	1,350	1,420	1,490	1,560

Source: EEC Document COM (69) 1200, November 1969.

Table 7 Retail prices of main foodstuffs in the EEC and the United Kingdom, October 1969

Shillings and pence per lb.

	Beef			Pork			Chickens (oven ready, for roasting)		Milk (per pint)		Butter	
	s.	d.		s.	d.		s.	d.	s.	d.	s.	d.
Belgium	15	4	(steak)	9	9	(rib chop)	4	10		10	7	11
France	12	8	(steak)	6	0	(chine, with bone)	4	3		9	7	5
Germany	9	4	(hind, boneless)	7	10	(chop)	3	10		11	7	4
Italy	12	0	(first quality)	10	6	(first quality)	n.a.		1	0	9	7
Netherlands	11	11	(roasting)	8	8	(rib chop)	4	6		10	7	6
United Kingdom	8	7	(sirloin, without bone)	6	3	(loin, with bone)	3	9		11	3	4

	Cheese	Sugar	Bread
	s. d.	s. d	s. d.
Belgium	5 10 (various types)	1 5	11
France	7 2 (Gruyere)	1 1	1 4 (average of Baguette Parisien)
Germany	7 11 (Emmenthal with rind)	1 2	1 2 (dark, mixed)
Italy	12 7 (Parmesan)	1 6	1 3
Netherlands	5 11 (Gouda, matured)	1 2	11 (brown)
United Kingdom	3 7 (Cheddar type)	9	11 (white)

Notes:

(1) Prices relate to October 1969, except for Italy for which they relate to July 1969.

(2) As far as possible the quotations given are for the most representative type or quality consumed in each country. Because of the differences between countries of the types, presentation and quality of foodstuffs, the prices can provide a broad indication only of price relativities.

(3) n.a. = not available.

Source: Collation by Ministry of Agriculture, Fisheries and Food of latest available data from various official national statistics.

Table 8 Estimated change in United Kingdom food imports and estimated levy receipts

				£ million
	Larger change in consumption		Smaller change in consumption	
	Food imports(1)	Levies	Food imports(1)	Levies
Present difference in prices				
1. Upper production response .	− 85	185	+ 105	210
2. Lower production response .	+ 60	195	+ 250	220
Middle production response				
3. Present difference in prices .	− 15	190	+ 175	220
4. Smaller difference in prices .	+ 80	165	+ 255	185
5. Larger difference in prices . .	− 75	195	+ 120	230

(1) Estimated change in food and feed import bill (net of exports) at c.i.f. prices.

Table 12 Summary of Impact Effects on the Balance of Trade in Items other than Food

		£ million at 1968 prices
	Lower Elasticities	*Higher Elasticities*
Exports	− 75	− 175
Imports (1) . . .	− 50	− 100
Balance of Trade	− 125	− 275

(1) Increase in imports shown as −.

Table 14 Growth of gross national product per head at 1963 market prices 1958–67

Average annual percentage increase

EEC countries		EFTA countries	
Germany	3·7	United Kingdom	2·5
France	3·9	Sweden	3·8
Italy	4·8	Norway	4·0
Belgium	3·8	Denmark	4·2
Luxembourg	n.a.	Austria	3·7
Netherlands	3·7	Switzerland	3·1
Average all EEC countries (1)	4·0	Portugal	5·2
		Average all EFTA countries(1)	3·0

Source: OECD National Accounts of OECD Countries, 1958–67.
(1) At 1963 exchange rates.

Table 15 United Kingdom and EEC output, 1958–67. Index numbers (1958 = 100)

	Categories(1)	*Output United Kingdom*	*EEC*
Division 71 of which	Machinery other than electric(2)	178	209
715·1	Machine tools for working metals(2)	183	213
Division 72	Electrical machinery, apparatus and appliances(2)	183	202
Division 73 of which	Transport equipment(3)	137	215
ex 732	Passenger cars(1)	148	217
	Commercial vehicles(3)	123	140
Division 5	Chemicals(4)(5)	183	244

Source: Based on various sources, including figures published in "The Motor Industry of Great Britain" series by The Society of Motor Manufacturers and Traders.
(1) Categories are defined in terms of the United Nations Standard International Trade Classification (SITC).
(2) Values of deliveries at current prices (expressed in United States dollars,
(3) Based on figures relating to numbers of vehicles.
(4) Including synthetic rubber and photographic chemical materials.
(5) Volume of output.

Table 16 1964 expenditure on research and development

	United States		United Kingdom		Fjance		Germany	
	£ million	Per cent	£ million	Per cent	£ million	Per cent	£ million	Per cent
Total expenditure	4,781	100·0	489	100·0	262	100·0	318	100·0
of which —								
	1,825	38·2	139	28·4	59	22·5	—	—
Electrical	943	19·7	97	19·8	68	26·2	90(1)	28·2
Chemicals	580	12·1	65	13·3	47	17·8	102	32·0
Machinery	368	7·7	31	6·4	13(2)	5·0	58(4)	18·1
Motor vehicles	426(2)	8·9	32	6·6	14	5·4	58(4)	18·1

Source: Based on OECD study of R and D in member countries.
Notes: The above figures, which have been converted at the 1964 official exchange rates, cover R and D expenditure by private industry, public corporations and research associations, including Government expenditure in private industry, but not Government expenditure in Government establishments.
(1) Includes instruments. (3) Includes shipbuilding and other transport.
(2) Inludes metal products and instruments. (4) Includes metal products.

Table 17 Company Turnover

Gross sales: £ million

Country	Chemical		Electrical engineering, electronics, computers, etc.		Motor vehicle		Aircraft and aerospace		Machine tool	
United States	Du Pont	1,500	General Electric	3,500	General Motors	9,500	McDonnell Douglas	1,500	Pratt & Whitney Machine Tool Division of Colt Industries	280
	Union Carbide	1,100	IBM	2,900	Ford	5,900	Boeing	1,400		
	Monsanto	750	Western Electric	1,600	Chrysler	3,100	General Dynamics	1,100		
	W. R. Grace	720	Westinghouse Elec.	1,400			United Aircraft	1,000		
	Dow Chemicals	690	RCA	1,300			Lockheed Aircraft	920	Norton Co.	140

	Allied Chemicals	530	General Telephone and Electronics	1,200			Grumman Aircraft	480	Cincinnati Milling Machines	120
United Kingdom	ICI	1,200	GE and EEC Ltd.	900	British Leyland Motor Corp. Ltd.	910	Hawker Siddeley Group	380	John Brown (Wickmann)	78
	Shell Chemical	470	Thorn Electrical Industries	270	Ford Motor Co.	490	Rolls-Royce	320	Staveley Industries	47
	British Oxygen	140	Plessey	170	Vauxhall Motors	220	BAC	190	Alfred Herbert & Co.	40
	British Petroleum	130	International Computers (Holdings)	90	Rootes Motors	180				
Italy	Montecatini Edison	960	Olivetti	250	Fiat Sp. A	890				
					Alfa Romeo	90				
Germany	Hoechst	790	Siemens	870	Volkswagenwerk	1,200	Messerschmidt	76		
	Bayer	720	AEG/Telefunken	570	Daimler-Benz	610	Bolkow Blohm			
			Bosch	390	Opel	400	VFW	41		
					BMW	110				
France	Rhone Poulenc	500	Thomson Brandt (includes CSF)	380	Renault	720	Sud-Aviation	140		
					Citroen	530	SNECMA	120		
					Peugeot	410	Avion Marcel	150		
					Simca	230	Dassault			
							Nord Aviation	64		
Netherlands	AKU	380	Philips	1,100	DAF	60				
	KZO	230								
Japan	Idemitsu-Kosan	290	Hitachi	950	Toyota Motors	700				
			Matsushita Electric Industry	700	Nissan	690				

Notes: Sales are given to two significant figures. They have been assembled from a variety of sources for the calendar year 1968 or the nearest convenient financial year. Because of the variety of sources complete comparability is not possible, but the figures represent orders of magnetude for broad comparative purposes. The sales figures given for individual firms in some cases include sales for products other than the broad industrial sectors under which firms are listed.

Abdruckgenehmigungen

Für die Abdruckgenehmigungen sind die Herausgeber folgenden Verlagen und Lizenzträgern zu Dank verpflichtet:

Fontana Paperbacks, London SW 1 für R. H. S. CROSSMAN: Introduction to BAGEHOT: *The English Constitution.*

Anthony Sheil Associates Limited, London WC 2, für L. S. AMERY: *Thought's on the Constitution.*

Dem Verfasser und Sweet & Maxwell Ltd., London EC 4, für A. H. BROWN: "Prime Ministerial Power" in *Public Law* (1968).

The Hansard Society for Parliamentary Government, London SW 1 für D. N. CHESTER: "The British Parliament 1939–1966", in *Parliamentary Affairs* 1966 (vol. XIX).

Heinemann Educational Books Ltd., Academic and General Publishers, London W 1 für R. T. MCKENZIE: *British Political Parties.*

Hutchinson Publishing Group Ltd., London W 1 für G. MARSHALL & G. C. MOODIE *Some Problems of the Constitution.*

John Allen & Unwin Ltd., London WC 1 für P. G. J. PULZER: *Voting Behaviour.*

The Controller of Her Majesty's Stationery Office für die Erlaubnis des Abdrucks von Auszügen aus den Parlamentspapieren "The Civil Service" und "Britain and the European Communities".